The Messianic Church Arising!

*Restoring the Church
to Our Covenant Roots*

By Dr. Robert D. Heidler

Cover Art: The menorah, or seven-branched candlestick, is the only religious symbol on earth designed by God Himself. The pattern for the menorah was given to Moses by God on Mt. Sinai (Ex 25:31-40). It symbolizes God's Holy Spirit (Zech 4:2-6, Rev. 4:5), and the Spirit's manifestation in the earth through His church (Rev. 1:20, 2:1).

A Note to Messianic Jewish Friends

This book was written to Gentiles. For that reason, I am using terms and expressions easily understandable to Gentile Christians. This includes using terminology common in the Gentile church, rather than that used in Messianic Jewish writings. In most cases I refer to *Yeshua* as "Jesus." I include the vowels in the word "God" (not G-d) and I call the Hebrew Scriptures the "Old Testament" rather than the *Tanach*. I am not being insensitive in doing this, but feel it is necessitated by the need to clearly communicate these vital truths to a Gentile Christian audience.

© 2006, Robert D. Heidler, Glory of Zion International Ministries

ISBN: 0-9791678-2-5

Robert D. Heidler
624 W. University Drive PMB 137,
Denton, TX 76201
Email: Rheidler7@AOL.com

Printed in Canada

TABLE OF CONTENTS

DEDICATION

I am writing this dedication page in the Cenacle, the "Upper Room" on Mount Zion in Jerusalem. This is the place where the Holy Spirit fell on Pentecost almost 2000 years ago. Archaeologists tell us that this room was also a Messianic Synagogue in first century times. In this place the Messianic Church once met, prayed, preached, experienced God's Presence and saw healing and miracles. From this place they went out to change a world!

I chose to write this here – after finishing the manuscript of the *Messianic Church Arising* – because this is where it all began. May the power of the Holy Spirit that once filled this room soon fill the church again! I dedicate this book to those early Messianic believers who experienced God's Presence and power in this place.

I also dedicate this book to the Messianic Jewish movement today: men and women who are laying down their lives for the truth that *Yeshua* is the Messiah of Israel, and of the world.

I dedicate this book to my friends in Jerusalem who pray for the peace of this city and the restoration of the church. Especially to Rick and Patty, Martin and Norma, John and Una, Nick and Maggie, Steve and Tonya, Hilda, Kish, Ruben, and Lindy.

I dedicate this book to my wonderful wife, Linda, who has stood with me and prayed for me, offering many helpful suggestions, in the long process of preparing this manuscript.

I dedicate this book to my parents, Robert and Gloria Heidler, who instilled in me a love for God's Word at a very early age.

I dedicate this book to my children, Lindy, Mike, and Josh, who will live to see the things we can only dream of.

I dedicate this book to Dr. Chuck Pierce, who first directed me to study the feasts of God and seek the restoration of the apostolic church.

And finally, I dedicate this book to you, the reader, and many others like you, who will press the church forward to experience the full recovery of our covenant roots!

Dr. Robert Heidler
The Cenacle, Jerusalem, Israel
June 26, 2006

Foreword
By Dr. Chuck D. Pierce

When the Lord sovereignly visited me when I was in my latter teens, He imparted two key dynamics that have my molded life. In a hospital bed in East Texas, where I was recovering from double pneumonia, the Lord spoke to me and said, *"I can restore all that you have lost."* That was a major, faith-stretching statement because of the loss my family had experienced.

The other major, life-changing revelation occurred when I turned on the television from that hospital bed to watch the Olympics and witnessed the horrible massacre of the Israeli athletes in Munich. The terrorists' actions overwhelmed me. The Spirit of God then revealed to me Satan's hatred of God's covenant people and land.

As I began to devour the Word, God brought to life how I was aligned with the Jewish people and their land. From Genesis 12, I saw that "their war was my war...and their blessings were my blessings."

We are living in times where this covenant understanding is the most important revelation we can have in the earth! Robert Heidler has written *The Messianic Church Arising: Restoring the Church to Our Covenant Roots,* one of the best and timeliest books written to date that will help you understand this concept. This book will change your life and help prepare you for the days ahead.

When we talk about the days ahead my prayer is, "Lord, let the hope of the Kingdom of God begin to dawn on all mankind. Let a worldwide knowledge of God begin to sweep the earth. Establish Your love on the earth, and may the order of everything that is not aligned with Kingdom purposes change." For this prayer to come to fulfillment, we have to understand the resisting forces that would stop this from manifesting.

The Church is building so that God's Kingdom rule can be seen in the earth realm. There are other forces, motivated from Satan's rule and reign, also building. These forces are working against the plan of God. We cannot avoid confrontation with these forces in days ahead. This confrontation will occur spiritually as well as physically.

God is shaking the Church into a level of reality. One key for the church in days ahead will be understanding the concept of "One New Man." The Church must understand and remain faithful to the purposes of a sovereign God whose fiirstfruit land and people is still in the forefront of His heart.

We are called to reach the entire world and co-labor with the Lord for the fullness of the Gentiles. However, our demonstration of Kingdom life should also accelerate what the Lord is doing through His covenant people, the Jews.

There is no question that the Jews are God's covenant people. They are His firstfruit people. It is easy for those of us who are Gentiles to forget that *we* are the ones who have been grafted in.

In Romans 11, Paul, speaking to the Gentiles, says, *"For if the firstfruit is holy, the lump is also holy; and if the root is holy, so are the branches. And if some of the branches were broken off, and you, being a wild olive tree, were grafted in among them, and with them became a partaker of the root and fatness of the olive tree, do not boast against the branches. But if you do boast, remember that you do not support the root, but the root supports you...For I do not desire, brethren, that you should be ignorant of this mystery, lest you should be wise in your own opinion, that blindness in part has happened to Israel until the fullness of the Gentiles has come in. And so all Israel will be saved, as it is written: 'The Deliverer will come out of Zion, and He will turn away ungodliness from Jacob; for this is My covenant with them, when I take away their sins '"* (vv. 16-18, 25-27).

God loves His covenant people, the Jews, and He has not forgotten them. We would be wise to remember that, no matter where our forefathers came from, if we are part of God's covenant plan through Jesus Christ, our spiritual roots are tied in with His covenant people, the Israelites.

Dan Juster, author and Messianic leader in the Body of Christ, shared the following message for the present Church on what we have to repent of in order to move forward in days ahead:

We must ***repent*** for sharing a partial Gospel message. We have preached a partial, and therefore a false, gospel.

Salvation through the sacrifice of Jesus is only part of the gospel, and serves as our entrance into the Kingdom. The true gospel is the Good News of the Kingdom. This releases the power of God within us to resist the power of the enemy. The power of God is manifested in healing, deliverance, and relationships. The Kingdom has to do with our behavior and discipling people to live by the law of the Kingdom (Mt. 5).

We must *repent* of the American mindset of tolerating personal peace and affluence, with Jesus being presented as the means to make us comfortable.

We must *repent* for our failure to perceive and pursue the fullness of the Church. Church is often perceived as a social club, or a place to go and "get some of God" once a week. That mentality is wrong. God does not want us to "go to church" in the traditional sense. The question should not be, "Where do you go to church?" but "Where are you submitted for training for the work of ministry?"

We must *repent* for abandoning Jewish responsibilities. God has called us to make Israel jealous. Her re-ingrafting will mean "life from the dead" for the Gentiles. We need deeds of love and kindness, intercession and giving to promote her salvation. (From a message given at Glory of Zion Outreach Center in Denton, Texas, October 8, 2000.)

Repentance changes our mind so we have the mind of Christ. We must change our thinking processes to demonstrate the next dimension of grace that God wants demonstrated on the earth.

Israel and the Jews are of utmost central importance to our Christian heritage. All of the early church leaders were Jews. In the book of Acts we find that the first century Church was completely Jewish.

Then Peter took salvation to the Gentiles. Even though the Jews didn't understand why Peter had done this, Peter convinced them there was a new work going on beyond the household of Israel. Paul continued this new work and multiplied it. The early Church related closely to its Jewish roots and even blessed the Jewish community in Israel (Roman 15:25-27). Paul, the apostle, clearly taught that global redemption and restoration of the world depended upon God's original plan to rightly relate Jews and Gentiles in the Body of Messiah.

Ephesians 2:14-16 says, *"He Himself is our peace, who made both groups (Jews and Gentiles) into one and broke down the barrier of the dividing wall ... that in Himself, He might make the two into* **one new man**, *thus establishing peace, and might reconcile them both in one new body."*

Satan hates this one new man concept. He hates Israel because she brought forth the Redeemer of the human race. He also hates those who operate in an overcoming remnant mentality to continue God's redemptive purposes on earth (Rev. 12:17). As we mentioned above, Paul warned us in Romans 11:18 to *"not be arrogant to the natural branches."* Therefore, if the Church does not stay rightly related to God's ultimate purpose of the human race with all nations reconciling around Israel, we will fall into anti-Semitic thinking.

The anti-Christ system hates everyone who has aligned with the Spirit of God in the earth, but is especially determined to annihilate God's covenant for the nation of Israel. We have seen this spirit rise up through history. Martin Luther brought great reform to the Church concerning faith. However, he didn't fully understand how Jews fit into God's covenant plan. Consequently, anti-Semitic religious theology invaded society. The enemy was able to use this to bring the holocaust about.

God's call on the Church was to make the Jewish people jealous (Rom 11:11). But we find that very often, the actions of Christians have actually kept them away from their Messiah.

Marty Waldman's article "Historic Issues: Jewish Roots of Christianity" helps us understand this issue more fully. He says:

> The Church has also propagated a more subtle form of anti-Semitism through particular doctrines such as replacement theology and dual-covenant theology. Replacement theology disregards Israel's chosenness as well as its irrevocable calling by God (Rom 11:28-29). 'The Church is Israel' has been the theological position of the Roman Catholic Church and was further adopted by John Calvin as well as other Reformers.
>
> Dual-covenant theology disregards the need for Jewish people to receive Yeshua as their Messiah, stating that they

are saved through their father Abraham. Many Christian Zionists and other well-meaning Christians who want to build a bridge of communication with the Jewish community have adopted dual-covenant theology. This insidious doctrine robs the Jewish people of salvation in their own Messiah. It also magnetically draws the Jewish and Christian communities back to the original stronghold of agreement that a Jew cannot remain Jewish and believe in Jesus. That stronghold rejects the validity of the Messianic Jewish community.

Many Christians hold this theology today even through it is a ploy of the enemy to divert attention away from the fact that God is faithfully grafting the Jewish branches of Romans 11 back into their own olive tree. The Spirit of God is moving through the hearts of many believers today, and the Church is beginning to recognize the hand of God in the Jewish community, particularly as He draws the remnant of Israel back to Himself. (Pray For the Peace of Jerusalem newsletter, Volume 2, Number 2, p. 4)

The Amalekites present the best example in the Word of the link between anti-Semitism and lawlessness. In his book *In That Day*, Rabbi David Levine states, "The spirit of Amalek typifies all those who oppose the Jews and God's plan to use the Jews. This spirit has motivated many people under widely different circumstances, but always toward the same goal, the destruction of the Jewish people. (See Exodus 17:8-15; Numbers 24:20.)

Sometimes the battle has been waged politically, sometimes militarily. Other times it is fought on the cultural front, or philosophically, or religiously. Pharaoh was motivated by the spirit of Amalek, as was Haman, and of course, Hitler too, was so motivated that he destroyed six million Jews" (p. 83).

Exodus 17:8-16 chronicles the first time the Israelites went to war as a group after they had left Egypt. The Amalekites tried to prevent them from progressing in the path that God had ordained for them. Notice how the pattern the Israelites had to operate in to defeat the enemy is still important to us today. The apostolic-type of leadership (Moses) had to take his stand. The priest-pastor types (Aaron and Hur) had to hold up their hands. And the prophetic-warrior type (Joshua) had to go forth and war. This proper alignment was necessary for God's people to see victory.

In Exodus 17:13-15 we find: *"So Joshua overcame the Amalekite army with the sword. Then the LORD said to Moses, 'Write this on a scroll as something to be remembered and make sure that Joshua hears it, because I will completely blot out the memory of Amalek from under heaven.' Moses built an altar and called it The LORD is my Banner."*

When we see the Messianic Church arising and coming into proper apostolic/prophetic/intercessory alignment, we will see a sweeping move of God across the earth. This should be one of our key prayer points as we pray for God's covenant people.

Israel is still the apple of God's eye and His inheritance. She remains close to His heart (Deut. 32:9-11; Ps. 33:11-12; Ps. 148:14; Zech. 2:8; Rom. 11:29). We should pray with compassion over Israel's condition (Ps. 102:13-14). We should give the Lord God no rest until He establishes Jerusalem and makes her the praise of the earth (Is. 62:1, 6-7). We should seek the spiritual and physical good of the Israeli people and to pray for the peace of Jerusalem (Ps. 122:4, 6-7, 9; Rom. 1:16; Rom. 2:9-11; Rom. 15:25-27) .

If ever there is a book that reveals your Christian alignment, *The Messianic Church Arising* is that book! You will read and be revived. You will read and be refreshed. You will read and be challenged to live a holy life. You will read and cry, "Lord, let me return to my roots and receive Your blessing!" You will read and be determined to go forth, provoking a world around you to change and see its covenant alignment!

I challenge you to "drink" this book and be poured out into a world thirsty for change!

Introduction

"Israel was God's firstborn and if we ever lose sight of that we will not understand His covenant purposes in the world today." – Chuck Pierce

In the fall of 1997, an incident occurred that changed my life. I was invited to teach a course at the Messianic Jewish Bible Institute in Odessa, Ukraine, on *Church History from a Messianic Perspective.*

I've been involved in the Messianic movement for many years. I understand the prophetic significance of the Messianic movement and strongly support it. I also love church history. Since this course dealt with two subjects that are close to my heart, I looked forward to teaching it. But I wasn't prepared for what I would find as I began the research for the course.

Like most Christians, I knew the church began under the wing of Judaism, but assumed that, at an early stage in its growth, the apostles began to divorce it from its Jewish heritage and establish it as a Gentile organization. As I began the work of preparation, the first question I wanted to answer was, "Exactly *when* did the church stop being Jewish?"

When the Church Lost Its Jewishness

I began with a study of the book of Acts, fully expecting that by about Acts 15 there would be evidence that the church had made a clean break with Judaism. The more I studied, however, the more it became evident that the apostles had *no intention* of separating from Judaism.

Acts 15:5, for example, speaks of members of the church who were still actively involved in the party of the Pharisees. In Acts 21:20, James boasts that in Jerusalem there were many "tens of thousands" of Jews who had believed in Jesus and remained zealous for *Torah*. Repeatedly we see Paul and other members of the church still taking Nazarite vows, still practicing Jewish ritual, still observing Sabbaths and feasts, and still bringing offerings to the Jerusalem Temple (21:23-26, 24:14-17, etc.).

In Acts 23, when Paul was before the Sanhedrin, the leaders of the Pharisee party *stood up in Paul's defense,* saying, "We find nothing wrong with this man!" (Acts 23:9)   Paul never speaks of his Judaism in the past tense.   He proudly proclaims, "I am a Jew!" (Acts 22:3) and "I am a Pharisee!" (Acts 23:6).   In the very last chapter of Acts Paul meets with Jewish leaders in Rome and assures them that he still identifies himself with Judaism and has done nothing to violate Jewish customs.

Throughout the book of Acts, members of the church continued as active members of the Jewish community.   Even more surprising, some members of the Jewish community seemed to hold the church in high esteem.

I arrived at the end of Acts without ever finding the expected break with Judaism.   As I continued my research, I was startled to discover that, as late as the second century, it was still common for Christians to attend synagogue on Sabbath and church on Sunday *(See Appendix Two)*!

While some Gentile writers in the second and third centuries were clearly anti-Semitic, there is strong evidence that much of the church remained pretty Jewish.   It was not until the fourth century, under the influence of Constantine, that the church finally broke from its Jewish roots.   Even then, however, it took centuries of persecution to completely remove the Jewish influences.

This left me with an unexpected question, "Was it really God's will for the church to break with its Jewish roots?"   If the apostles established and maintained the church in Jewishness, have we lost something God intended us to have?

This raised even more questions, "What have we *lost* through the destruction of our Jewish heritage?" "Does God desire the church to *reconnect* to those roots?" And finally, "In practical terms, what does it mean to be connected to our Jewish roots?"   This book is the result of my attempt to answer those questions.

At the outset, I want to stress that there are no easy answers to these questions.   When we speak of our Jewish roots, there are two extremes to be avoided.   At one extreme are Gentiles who become so enamored with Judaism they reject God's New Covenant and take up the yoke of the Mosaic Law.   That is not biblical.   God does not demand that Gentile believers live as Jews.   That issue was settled in Acts 15.

At the other extreme, we find that in much of the church today our Jewish heritage is largely ignored or deliberately avoided. Those who seek their Jewish roots are sometimes accused of rejecting the work of Jesus. That *also* is not biblical. Remember that *Jesus was Jewish.* The early church saw no conflict in embracing *both* a Jewish heritage and a Jewish Messiah. What many Christians have failed to see is that, in reality, the New Testament is just as Jewish as the Old. Our problem is that we have grown up with a set of church *traditions* inherited from the Middle Ages from which the Jewish elements have been deliberately removed.

Between those two extremes lies the opportunity to see the church recover a valued inheritance. In my quest to resolve these issues, I have gained a growing conviction that God *is* in the process of restoring this heritage to His church, and that this restoration will bring the greatest revival in history.

A Unique Time in History

The work of God on earth frequently follows the pattern of Romans 1:16… "to the Jew first, *then* to the Gentile." If we sense God is about to do a new work in the Gentile church, it's good to look and see what He is doing *now* among the Jews!

And God *is* doing something incredible among the Jewish people! Down through the ages, those who have tried to talk to Jews about *Yeshua* (Jesus) have seen little response. As Paul said, there has been a *veil* over their eyes, and most Jews have not been able receive the truth of Jesus' identity as their Messiah.

As recently as 1967, there were no known Messianic Jewish congregations anywhere in the world. While many Jews had come to know Jesus as Messiah, most of these had, in some measure, forfeited their Jewish identity and become part of the "Gentile" church.

In that year, however, a startling change took place. In 1967, during the Six-day War, Israel retook the city of Jerusalem. For the first time in nearly 2000 years, Jerusalem was no longer "trampled under foot by the Gentiles" (Lk. 21:24). That event marked a major turning point in God's prophetic program. The veil that had been over the eyes of the Jewish people began to lift.

Since that day, more Jews have come to know their Messiah than in all the generations since the first century. It is a miraculous change, and it is increasing. Some have estimated that more Jews have come to know their Messiah in the past *five years* than in the previous 2000.

I'm not talking about Jews losing their Jewish identity and joining a Gentile church. Most Jews who turn to *Yeshua* today claim a greater appreciation for their "Jewishness" than they had before! They attend Synagogue on Sabbath, they celebrate the feasts, they observe the ceremonies and rituals that are part of Judaism, but they now find a new depth and meaning in those observances.

Today there are hundreds of Messianic synagogues all over America, and hundreds more in nations around the world. These are Jewish congregations that are faithful to observe the Hebrew traditions. Yet they honor and worship "Yeshua" as the promised Savior and Messiah of Israel.

God is doing a miraculous work. It is the restoration of something that has been lost for fifteen hundred years, and it's about to turn the "religious" world upside down! The rise of Messianic Judaism will have far-reaching implications for the church and for the evangelization of the world.

In the midst of Israel's return, however, God is calling to the Gentile church. He is calling us, first of all, to feel His heartbeat. He is calling us to understand and share His love for the Jewish people *(See Appendix One)*. He wants us to share His joy at the rebirth of Messianic Judaism.

But God is saying more to us than that. As Paul states in Romans 11:15, the return of Israel to their Messiah will not only mean new life for Israel, it means "**life from the dead**" for the Gentile church. Paul says that the restoration of Messianic Israel will reawaken something long dead in the church. It will release the LIFE of God to His church in a whole new dimension. I believe Paul's promise of "life from the dead" is a reference to the great "last-days revival" millions of Christians around the world are praying for. And it's all tied to our relationship to Israel.

The purpose of this book is *not* to make you Jewish. The purpose of this book is to help you experience the *fullness* of your Christianity. To know Christianity as God intended it. New Testament Christianity. Messianic Christianity. The purpose of this book is to help any Christian begin to regain the blessings of our lost inheritance.

Chapter One
The Church God Planted

"That day there were added about three thousand souls... Everyone kept feeling a sense of awe and many wonders and signs were taking place... [They were] continuing with one mind in the temple, and breaking bread from house to house... praising God and having favor with all the people, and the Lord was adding to their number daily." –Acts 2:46-47

Once upon a time... there was a church that *worked*. Its members loved each other, took care of widows and orphans, fed the hungry, and transformed cities. It taught the Bible, built believers to maturity, and satisfied the longing in their hearts to touch God. This church didn't just *talk* about the power of God: it healed the sick, raised the dead, and cast out demons. It won the lost with incredible effectiveness, discipled its converts, and equipped them to minister. Its effectiveness was not limited to one culture or ethnic group. It grew with explosive power wherever it was planted.

It's the church we have all been looking for, but never found... a church you and I have never seen, but I fervently believe we soon will. This church has often been called the *early* church, the *New Testament* Church, or the *first-century* church. For reasons we will soon see, I like to call it the *Messianic Church.* It's a church that would work in any generation. It's the Church as GOD designed it!

This incredible church was not a myth or a fairy tale. It was real. It is documented in historical records. It was a church made up of real people with real problems, but was characterized by a life and power the world could not resist.

The early church was the most powerful institution the world had ever seen. It exploded onto the world stage in Acts chapter two, and nothing had the power to stand against it. Pagan religions could not compete with it. Greek philosophy could not comprehend it. Persecution only purified it and made it grow more rapidly!

On the day of Pentecost, the Holy Spirit fell on 120 people in the city of Jerusalem. By the end of that day, the infant church had grown to about 3000 men and women (Acts 2).

Within about a year, the church more than *tripled* in size, numbering more than ten thousand people.[1] Some historians estimate that by the time of Stephen's martyrdom (as early as two years later) the church in Jerusalem had grown to about 20,000 members.

In their alarm, the religious leaders in Jerusalem tried to slow the growth of the church through persecution. They were unsuccessful. Despite severe persecution at times, the Messianic Jewish congregation in Jerusalem continued to grow. It is possible that at its peak, half of the population of the city of Jerusalem was in the church.

The pattern of rapid growth seen in the Jerusalem church was followed wherever the church went. Many of the early churches had grown to over fifty thousand members by the end of the first century.

A good example of this growth is seen in the church at Ephesus. Acts 19 indicates that Paul went to Ephesus, started a church, and remained there for two years teaching his converts. During those two years, not only was the entire city of Ephesus evangelized (a city of around 200,000 people), but all of the cities in the surrounding province were also reached. The church in Colossae, as well as the seven churches mentioned in Revelation 2 and 3, were all probably planted during that two-year period.

The church in Ephesus grew so rapidly it disrupted the city's economy. Local idol makers were losing business because many of their customers were converting to Christianity. One of the idol makers, a silversmith named Demetrius, called together others of his trade and complained, "This fellow Paul has convinced and led astray *large numbers* of people here in Ephesus and in practically the whole province of Asia. He says that man-made gods are no gods at all!"

The idol makers were so angered by the decline in their business they fomented a riot. Acts 19:29 tells us, "Soon the whole city was in an uproar!"

Can you imagine the church today making that kind of an impact on a city by the power of its evangelism? Can you imagine *your* church having that level of impact on your community? Picture what it would be like if so many people were coming to the Lord through your church that the drug dealers and porno shop owners in your city rioted in the streets to protest their loss of business!

By the time Paul wrote his first letter to Timothy around A.D. 63, the church in Ephesus had probably grown to around sixty thousand members. No wonder Timothy felt intimidated when Paul installed him as the leader of that congregation! At its height, the church in Ephesus may have had as many as 100,000 members. The early Christians literally "took the city" for Jesus!

In the year A.D. 112, about eighty years after Pentecost, the Roman author Pliny wrote a letter to Emperor Trajan. In this letter, he complained that in the province of Asia Minor, where Ephesus was, "...temples to the [pagan] gods are almost totally forsaken and *Christians are everywhere a multitude.*"[2]

This pattern was repeated throughout the empire. Tertullian writes to the pagans in his *Apologia*, "We have *filled* every place belonging to you—cities, islands, castles, towns, assemblies, your very camp, your tribes, companies, palace, senate, forum! We leave you your temples only. We can count your armies; our numbers in a single province will be greater."[3]

According to Chrysostom, the Christian population of Antioch in his day was about 100,000, or one-half of the whole city.[4]

Living in Perpetual Revival

All over the world today, Christians are fasting and praying for revival. There is a sense that God is about to "break through" to His church in a wonderful way. Some places are experiencing a measure of revival even now.

If you have studied the great revivals of history, you know that revival is a time of heady excitement. The church comes *alive*. There is a tangible sense of the Presence of God. Miracles take place, lives are changed, and thousands of unbelievers are saved. If the revival lasts long enough, whole nations can be transformed.

But revival rarely lasts long. Usually, after a few months, the Presence of God departs. Things get "back to normal." Even the greatest revivals of modern history only lasted a year or two. Those who experience a revival sometimes spend the rest of their lives looking back and telling stories of how great things were "in the revival."

The New Testament church, however, lived in *continual* revival! The Presence of God came upon the church at Pentecost and *did not depart!* The early church experienced what no other brand of Christianity has ever been able to reproduce: a *perpetual* revival lasting hundreds of years. *A sustained multigenerational revival!* It spread *everywhere*, and the world could not stand against it.

By the end of the first century, the early church had spread throughout the known world. It extended from India on the East to England on the West, and from Germany on the North to Ethiopia on the South. Its expansion amazed the world. In one city, when Paul and Silas came to town, the pagans cried out in horror, "These men who have *turned the world upside down* have come here also!" *(Acts 17:6 KJV).*

It was not unusual for a church to be planted in a city and rapidly grow to 20 or 30,000 members. Some historians estimate that by the end of the third century, *half of the population of the Roman Empire* had converted to Christianity.[5] This growth took place within a totally pagan, immoral culture, during times of severe persecution.

Justin Martyr, about the middle of the second century, writes, "There is no people, Greek or barbarian, or of any other race, by whatsoever appellation or manners they may be distinguished… whether they dwell in tents or wander about in covered wagons— among whom prayers and thanksgivings are not offered in the name of the crucified Christ."[6]

The historian **Philip Schaff** writes, "It may be fairly asserted, that about the end of the third century the name of Christ was known, revered, and persecuted in every province and every city of the empire," and, "In all probability at the close of the third century the church numbered ten millions of souls."[7]

A Visit to the Early Church

We've seen the power of the church, how it grew and "took over" the world in the short span of 70 years. We've sensed the anointing that was upon it. But what was the early church like? What gave it such life and power?

In the remainder of this chapter, I would like to give you a picture of a church you have never seen. It's a church most of us have never imagined. I want you to see what the early church was before it died. I pray God would paint this picture in your mind so vividly you will never forget it.

A lot of Christians assume that, on the day after Pentecost, Peter went out, rented a big building, put a steeple on top, hung up a sign that read, "First Baptist Church of Jerusalem," and started holding services the next Sunday. Most of us have not stopped to even grasp what the New Testament church really was.

I would like to take you with me to visit a gathering of the early church. Everything I describe will be based on historical descriptions of the first century church, either in the New Testament or in other early Christian literature.

As we prepare to visit this church, I want you to get ready for some surprises, because you are not going to see much that looks familiar. Most of the things Christians today associate with church simply did not exist at that time.

No one in the first few centuries had ever seen a church building, a steeple, a stained glass window, a pulpit or pew, a hymnal or church bulletin. No one wore a coat and tie, and there was no written liturgy to follow. Most of those things would not become a part of church tradition until more than a thousand years later! (I am not saying that any of those things are *wrong*. We do need to see that the "essence" of what a church is does not involve these things. The early church lacked all of those things, yet had a power far beyond anything the church today can comprehend.)

What was the worship of the early church like, then? Let's imagine we are walking down a street in the city of Rome. It is A.D. 95... more than 60 years have passed since the day of Pentecost. We are about to "drop in" on a typical church service in that city.

The church we are going to visit is a house church. The early church operated on two levels: the house church and the congregation. Even if the church grew to 20 or 30,000 members, its primary unit would still be the house church. From time to time the house churches would also *congregate* in a larger group (the *congregation*). This often took place outdoors or in a rented auditorium. In Jerusalem, they met in the temple courts.

The time is Saturday evening. By Jewish reckoning, the first day of the week began at sundown on Saturday. The church meets in the evening because many of the people have to work during the day. We arrive at the door of a typical Roman house and are warmly welcomed by the host.

Let me warn you before you go in to be prepared for a serious case of "culture shock." What you are about to witness is *not* church life as you have known it.

As we walk through the door, you look across the entrance into the large open courtyard of the home. There appears to be some kind of party going on. Some of the people are playing flutes, lyres, and tambourines, while others are singing, dancing, and clapping their hands.

You immediately look around to make sure you came into the right house! As you listen to the words, however, you realize that this is the right place, for the words of the songs are words of praise to Jesus! These people are overflowing with joy because they have come to know the living God.

What you are witnessing is the way the early church praised God. This type of worship is foreign to much of the church today, but from the biblical and historical records, this is what the worship in the early church was like. It was a free and joyful celebration, with a great deal of singing and dancing.

Most church services would begin with the people getting in a ring (or several concentric rings) and dancing Jewish-style ring dances (like the *Hora*).

Here's how some early Christian writers described their worship:

Clement of Alexandria (writing in the third century), describes the "daughters of God" leading the church in a ring dance: "The righteous are the dancers; the music is a song of the King of the universe. The maidens strike the lyre, the angels praise, the prophets speak; the sound of music issues forth, they run and pursue the jubilant band; those that are called make haste, eagerly desiring to receive the Father!" [8]

Ambrose of Milan, the man who led Augustine to the Lord, writing in A.D. 390 exhorted his people to worship with these words: "Let us dance as David did. Let us not be ashamed to show adoration of God. Dance uplifts the body above the earth into the heavenlies. Dance bound up with faith is a testimony to the living grace of God. He who dances as David danced, dances in grace." [9]

St. Basil (4th Century) wrote, "Could there be anything more blessed than to imitate on earth the ring dance of the angels!" [10]

This picture of the church rejoicing before the Lord in dance comes as a surprise to many people. Many people have thought of the early church's worship as somber, quiet, and almost mournful. That concept of church worship, however, did not become prevalent in the church until after the fourth century when the church was overrun by the asceticism of pagan philosophy.

In Augustine's day (A.D. 400), opposition to dancing was rising, but he urged his people to "keep the sacred dances."[11]

So, here we are in a large courtyard. There is a great deal of singing, dancing, and rejoicing in the Lord. As the songs slow down a little, many people get down on their knees before the Lord. Most are lifting up hands to Him. A tremendous sense of the Lord's presence fills the courtyard.

During the church's praise and worship, there are spontaneous shouts of praise. Some shout, "Amen!" to voice their agreement with what others have said. As we enter into the worship, we are overwhelmed by the love and acceptance of the people.

After much singing and dancing, food is brought out. People find their seats and prepare for the meal. We are surprised to see people eating a meal in the middle of a church service, but this is described by Paul in I Corinthians, as well as by Jude and Peter. This shared weekly meal is called the "love feast," or *Agape*.

To begin the meal, the woman of the house lights the candles, saying a special prayer of thanksgiving. Then one of the leaders stands with a cup, blesses the Lord, and passes it around so each one can drink from it. He then picks up a loaf of bread and offers thanks. It also is passed from person to person. This is the Lord's Supper in its original context.

The meal is a joyful time centered on devotion to the Lord. As they eat, the believers talk about the things of God, share testimonies, recite and discuss Scripture, and sing praises to the Lord. You are impressed that, while very few have personal copies of any biblical books, *most* of those present appear to have large portions of the Bible memorized.

During the meal, one of the leaders stands and reads a letter they received that week from an apostle named Junia. Junia was not one of the original twelve apostles, but by this time there were *many* apostles in the church.[12]

As you hear the letter read, you are surprised to learn that Junia is a woman! (In Romans 16 Paul describes a woman named Junia as "outstanding among the apostles."[13])

The leaders of this house church had written to Junia several weeks earlier to seek advice on some issues, and in her letter, Junia carefully addressed each of their questions. It is clear that all present hold Junia in high regard, for they all pay careful attention as her letter is read.

After the meal ends, worship continues until, at some point, a change begins to take place. There is a subtle shift in the atmosphere. The air seems to thicken. A tangible sense of the Presence of God comes and rests in the place. First Corinthians chapter five describes it this way: "When you are assembled in the name of the Lord Jesus... and the *power* of our Lord Jesus is present..."

Those who have studied revival literature recall that a *tangible sense of God's Presence* has frequently accompanied the great revivals of history. The manifest Presence of God is, in fact, the *hallmark* of true revival. In the *presence* of a holy God, sinners find salvation, backsliders find repentance, and the miraculous becomes commonplace.

In the early church, this was a weekly occurrence. When the members of the body assembled, they came as "living stones" forming the temple of God. As the presence of the Lord had once filled Moses' tabernacle (Ex. 40:34) and the temple of Solomon (II Chr. 7:1-2), so the Presence of God filled His *new* temple, the church. This is what Jesus promised, "Where two or three come together in my name, there am I with them" (Mt. 18:20).

As those assembled sense the Presence of God, some fall to the ground in worship. Others stop and are silent, welcoming the Lord's Presence.

As the Presence of God rests in their midst, ministry begins to take place. I Cor. 14 describes the Holy Spirit sovereignly manifesting His gifts as His people assemble. A woman on the far side of the courtyard stands and gives a word of knowledge for healing. A man raises his hand and people cluster around to pray for him. He is instantly healed.

Someone else stands up and reads a passage of Scripture. Another man, a teacher, gives an explanation of the passage. A woman stands and gives a beautiful prophetic song. Many are so touched by its beauty and anointing they begin to weep.

Prophetic words are given. There are tongues and interpretation. Through it all, they continue to move in and out of worship. This scenario is clearly described in I Corinthians 14:23-32.

This is how the early church met and ministered. At one point a man introduces a family who have been sitting quietly near the back of the crowd. They are his neighbors. You can tell by the look on their faces that this is their first time here, and they are not sure they are in the right place.

The man says they have come tonight because their 12-year-old daughter has contracted an illness that has left her totally blind. They have come for the church to pray for her. Those with the gift of healing come and stand with the elders as they anoint the little girl with oil and pray. Suddenly the little girl begins to cry. With tears running down her cheeks, she cries out, "I can see! I can see!"

The mother crouches down and hugs her daughter, and within four or five minutes the entire family is saved, giving their hearts to Jesus.

A prophetic word is given revealing the secrets of someone's heart. That person comes forward and says, "I don't know Jesus but I know God is here. I want to know Him."

Ministry continues. This is where much of the evangelism in the church took place… through the miraculous power of God working in the midst of His people. Most of us don't even have a concept of that happening, but it was the norm in the early church.

Irenaeus (writing around A.D. 195) tells us that in his day, prophetic words, tongues, and miracles of healing were common in the church. He adds that the church *frequently* saw people *raised from the dead* through the prayers of the saints![14]

Early in his walk with the Lord, **Augustine** had expressed doubts about the miraculous. After witnessing many examples of miraculous healing in his own church, however, he publicly retracted his earlier statements and devoted much of his life to a ministry of healing. He commented, "Miracles have no purpose but to help men believe that Christ is Lord."[15]

In *The Decline and Fall of the Roman Empire*, **Gibbon** described the life of the early church this way, "The primitive

Christians perpetually trod on mystic ground... They felt that on every side they were incessantly assaulted by demons, comforted by visions, instructed by prophecy, and surprisingly delivered from danger, sickness, and from death itself, by the supplications of the church."[16]

Our meeting of the church has now run late into the night, but no one seems to notice. Finally the meeting begins to break up. The sense of the Spirit's presence begins to lift, but there are still several small groups gathered in prayer.

As people prepare to leave, there is a great deal of hugging and kissing. It seems like a family reunion, and it is! It is the weekly reunion of the family of God.

How would you like to be part of a church like that? That's what the early church was. It was a temple where the glory of God dwelt. On any given Saturday evening there would have been hundreds of such meetings all over the city of Rome.

That's also the kind of church they had at Antioch, Corinth, Ephesus, Colossae, and Jerusalem. That's the kind of church that took the known world in one generation.

An apostle like Paul would go into a city, start a church... and the Presence of God would come. Within a few years *tens of thousands* of people would be saved and the entire region affected. By the end of the first Century the church had spread *everywhere* because the pagans didn't have anything that could stand against the power of God and His church.

Incredibly, that's how the church met for over 300 years!

The Nature of the Early Church

If the average Christian today could step into a time machine and visit that church at the end of the first century, they would be surprised by many things. But I believe their greatest surprise would *not* be the dancing, eating, or even the miracles.

The *most* surprising thing to most Christians would be the JEWISHNESS of that church! **What we have just seen is a picture of the church BEFORE it broke from Judaism!**

Even though most of those present at our "house church" meeting were *Gentiles*, it was a very *Messianic* church! This church, like most of the early churches, was founded by a Messianic Jewish missionary like the Apostle Paul. They quoted a Jewish Bible, followed the Jewish Messiah, and worshipped the God of Israel. Most of their leaders were Messianic Jews. Their values, lifestyle, and worldview were heavily influenced by Judaism. In the first few centuries, Gentiles who joined the church knew they were "linking in" to something Jewish!

For the first four hundred years of the church's existence, most Gentile Christians celebrated the biblical feasts. They observed Saturday as a Sabbath (a day of rest), then worshipped together on the first day of the week to celebrate Jesus' resurrection.

Evidence indicates that it remained common practice for Christians to be closely linked with the Jewish community. In fact, it is likely that a number of those who attended our "house church" meeting *also* regularly attended a synagogue!

Mark Nanos, in his book, *The Mystery of Romans*, writes, "Evidence indicates that in Rome Christianity and Judaism were inseparable... perhaps until the middle of the second century..." In another place he adds, "Christians in Rome continued to be part of the Jewish communities and synagogues for a long time." [17]

Eric Meyers, Professor of Religion and Archaeology at Duke University, writes that the tensions most people associate between Jews and Christians did not really occur before the fourth century, when Christianity became the official religion of the Empire under Constantine. During the first few centuries, the tension between Christians and Jews was "an internal *family* conflict, between cousins and brothers and sisters." [18]

Dr. Wayne Meeks, Professor of Biblical Studies at Yale University, comments, "As late as the 4th and 5th century, we have evidence of Christians still existing within Jewish communities, and we have evidence of members of Christian communities participating in Jewish festivals." [19]

*(PLEASE NOTE: For more documentation on the JEWISHNESS of the early church. I would encourage you to read **Appendix Two** at the end of this book.)*

All of this comes as a surprise to most Christians! Most of us have assumed that the apostles *rejected* Judaism! But the truth is...
THAT NEVER HAPPENED!

As we saw in the introduction, it was a common thing for first-century Christians to observe Sabbaths and feasts, take part in Jewish rituals, and worship in the temple and synagogues. Even the apostle Paul – the apostle to the *Gentiles* – never spoke of his Judaism in the past tense! As we will see in chapter eight, Paul planned the itinerary of his missionary journeys around the biblical feasts! He proudly declared that he was both a Jew and a Pharisee (Acts 22:3 & 23:6)! In the last chapter of Acts, Paul met with the Jewish leaders in Rome and assured them that he was an observant Jew!

Many assume that the early Christians were anti-Semitic. That is not accurate! Clement, Bishop of Rome at the end of the first century, describes the Jewish people as *"the portion of the Lord,* and... *the measurement of His inheritance."* He writes, "Out of Jacob [Israel] are all the priests and Levites... of him is the Lord Jesus according to the flesh and the kings of the line of Judah; and *the rest of his tribes are held in no small honor!"* [20] I don't know about you, but that does *not* sound like an anti-Semitic statement to me! Clement, Bishop of Rome, clearly honored and respected the Jews.

To the early church, Judaism was the root through which its life was nourished. Through that God-given heritage, the church received vital keys to its power and growth. Christians were grieved that many Jews rejected their Messiah, but they rejoiced in the lavish inheritance God had provided through their Jewish roots.

For three hundred years, the church followed the pattern established by the apostles and experienced a life and a power the world could not comprehend!

Then in the fourth century, through a compromise instigated by a pagan Roman emperor, the church allowed its Jewish heritage to be removed. Cut off from its life-giving roots, the early church died! For a thousand years, the church was dead!

By the year 500, almost nothing of the early church remained. During the dark ages, the church became a corrupt political organization with vast wealth and military power but little spiritual reality.

Then, starting with the Protestant Reformation, God began a process of restoration. Since that time, many of the church's lost treasures have been regained! God has restored the Word of God and the truth of salvation by faith! More recently He restored the gifts and empowering of the Holy Spirit! We rejoice in all that the Lord has accomplished, but the restoration is not yet complete! The church today still lacks the power and life of the early church! As never before in history, Christians are calling out to God to restore ALL that was lost! I believe a vital part of that restoration is a *restoration* of the church to its Jewish roots!

I believe we live at one of the most significant moments in history. God is up to something! Dr. C. Peter Wagner has commented that the church today is undergoing a greater transformation than it did in the days of the Protestant Reformation. God is effecting *change* in every part of His church. I believe this is a *kairos* time, an **appointed time**, chosen by God for the ***restoration*** of His church.

We are witnessing things for which men and women of God have prayed for hundreds of years. The gifts, ministries, and power of the early church are being revived. God is pouring out His Spirit! Our sons and daughters are prophesying, our young men are seeing visions, and our old men are dreaming dreams. The face of the church is changing.

I believe God is in the process of restoring the church's lost inheritance. The life the church once enjoyed, it will have again. In this book, we will see how *any* Christian in *any* church can begin to see our lost inheritance restored!

Chapter Two
The Root and the Branches

*"At that time you [Gentiles] were separate from Messiah, excluded
from citizenship in Israel and foreigners to the covenants of the promise,
without hope and without God in the world. But now in Messiah Jesus
you who once were far away have been brought near through the
blood of Messiah." –Eph. 2:12-13*

As we look at the life and power of the early church, it's
important to see that the early church did not just "happen!" It
wasn't an accident of history. It did not naturally evolve. It was
PLANNED!

The church had been part of God's plan for humankind since
creation. For two thousand years, God worked to set the stage for its
appearance. As the time for the church's birth drew near, Jesus
announced to His followers, *"I will build My church!"* (Matthew
16:18).

Ephesians chapter three describes the church as a MYSTERY
that had been hidden since the foundation of the world! The mystery
of the church was this: God had a plan to make *Gentiles* FELLOW-
HEIRS, together with the Jews, enabling them to experience all of
the blessings of Israel's Messiah!

Throughout the Old Testament era, God had worked through
His chosen people, the Jews. If you were a Gentile and wanted to
know the true God, you had to first become a Jew! God had bound
Himself to the Jews by eternal covenant, and His covenant blessings
were the rightful inheritance of every believing Jew.

But all along, God had a secret plan! His plan was, through
the church, to graft believing Gentiles into His covenant so they *also*
could receive His blessings!

Ephesians 2:11-19 describes it this way:

> "Remember that you Gentiles... were *separate* from
> Messiah, *excluded* from citizenship in Israel and *foreigners*
> to the covenants of the promise, *without hope* and *without
> God* in the world..."

"BUT NOW in Messiah Jesus you [Gentiles] who were far away have been brought *near*…"

"His purpose was to create ONE NEW MAN out of the two [Jews and Gentiles].   Consequently, you [believing Gentiles] are *no longer* foreigners and aliens, but *fellow citizens* with God's people [believing Jews] and members of God's household!"

That's how God views the church! The church is God's way of including the Gentiles in the blessings of Israel's covenant!

To help us see the church as He sees it, God gives us a wonderful illustration: **the fruitful olive tree!**

The apostle Paul describes this tree in Romans chapter eleven: *"if the **root** is holy, so are the **branches**. If **some branches** have been **broken off** and you, though **a wild olive shoot** have been grafted in among the others and now share in the nourishing sap from the olive root…" (Rom 11:16-17).*

GOD'S VIEW OF THE CHURCH
Romans 11:15-24

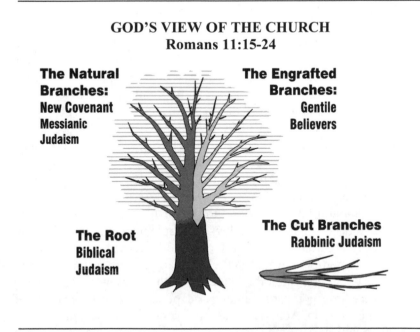

The Natural Branches:
New Covenant Messianic Judaism

The Engrafted Branches:
Gentile Believers

The Root
Biblical Judaism

The Cut Branches
Rabbinic Judaism

This passage describes the church as a tree with four distinct parts: (1) a holy **root**, (2) **natural branches**, (3) **branches that are broken off**, and (4) a **wild branch grafted in**. Notice what these four elements represent:

THE OLIVE ROOT – It's interesting that God chose an olive tree for this illustration. If you have traveled to the Middle East and seen living olive trees, the first thing you probably noticed was the root! An olive root is often huge, all out of proportion to the rest of the tree! An olive root can also be ancient. Several years ago on the island of Cyprus, Linda and I saw some olive trees that may have been growing when Jesus walked the earth! Out of the massive ancient root flows the rich sap that allows the branches to bear abundant fruit!

In Paul's illustration, the *church's* root is **Biblical Judaism**. Biblical Judaism was the religion of Abraham, Moses, and David. It is the religion revealed in the Hebrew Scriptures. If you open your Bible to Matthew, everything on the left-hand side is the root. It's the 2,000 years of preparatory revelation God poured into Israel to create a people through whom He could send His Son.

THE LIVING BRANCHES – The living branches are the natural outgrowth of the root. These branches represent *New Covenant Messianic Judaism*. That's what the Apostle Paul was. That's what Matthew, Mark, Luke, John, James, and Peter were. They were not Baptists, Methodists, or Catholics. They were Messianic Jews. They went to Synagogue. They worshipped in the temple. They celebrated the feasts. They were Jews who knew Israel's Messiah. They were more Jewish than any Messianic Jew today. Historical records indicate they were accepted by the Jewish community as part of Judaism!

The natural branches were not an insignificant part of Israel. Many have been taught that the Jewish people rejected their Messiah. That is only a partial truth. Many of Israel's *leaders* rejected Jesus, but the common people received Him gladly. The primary reason Jewish leaders persecuted the church was that they were *threatened* by its incredible popularity among the people. *Large numbers* of Jews believed. In Acts 21:20, James reports on the situation in Jerusalem with the triumphant boast, "Behold, how many *thousands* of Jews have believed!" In the Greek, that boast is even more impressive. The Greek word here is *muriades (myriad)*, which usually means *"tens of thousands."* Large numbers of the priests believed (Acts 6:7). Even Pharisees believed (Acts 15:5). Judging by the rapid growth of the early Jerusalem church, first century Jews were initially *much more responsive* to the Gospel than the pagan Gentiles Paul preached to.

THE "CUT OFF" BRANCHES – This passage tells us that some of the natural branches were cut off because of unbelief. These **"cut off" branches** represent *Rabbinic Judaism*. As natural branches, the whole tree is their rightful inheritance. In a real sense, it's *their* tree! God promised it to them! Like Israel at Kadish Barnea, however, they are forfeiting their blessing through unbelief.

These natural branches are like the little boy who misbehaved at his birthday party and was sent to his room! All of the guests [Gentiles] continue to play the games and eat the treats, but he can't enjoy it!

It's *his* party. It was *planned* for him! He was supposed to be the *guest of honor!* But he has excluded himself!

Romans 11 goes on to assure us, however, that this situation is temporary! God will one day engraft these branches back into the tree to enjoy every blessing God has promised!

THE WILD OLIVE BRANCH – Finally, God took a branch from a wild olive tree—the Gentiles *(Goyim)*—and grafted it in among the natural branches. That **wild olive branch** represents the *Gentile church*.

Paul tells us that this "wild Gentile branch" had formerly been *"excluded* from citizenship in Israel, foreigners to the covenants of promise, without hope and without God" (Eph. 2:12).

When Gentiles place their faith in the *Messiah* of Israel, however, God engrafts them into the *root* of Israel, to share all of the rich blessings of God's covenant. Those "who once were far away" are "brought near by the blood of Messiah" (Eph. 2:13). They become "fellow citizens with God's people and members of God's household" (Eph. 2:19).

As "grafted in" branches, every blessing we enjoy comes through that root! Jesus said, "Salvation is of the Jews!" (Jn. 4:22).

Did you know that every good thing you receive from God is a result of being grafted into a *Jewish* root? Through the Jews we have received the Scriptures, the covenants, and the promises. From the Jews we even received our Messiah, Jesus (Rom. 9:4-5). From that Jewish root, the church draws its LIFE!

In light of this, Paul gives a warning to Gentile Christians: Recognize that "you don't support the root; the root supports you" (Rom. 11:18). Biblical Judaism is the *root* from which you grow. Being engrafted into that root, you share in its nourishing sap. It feeds you. It nourishes your life in Christ. God wants you to draw from that root all the life He implanted there for 2,000 years.

The nourishing sap from the roots in not limited to "spiritual" blessings! It includes the wisdom of God to bring success in every area of life!

It involves keys to a life of joy and contentment!

...keys to cause your family to flourish!

...keys to a life of health and wellbeing.

It even involves keys to *financial* prosperity!

When you study Jewish history, you find that Jews have generally experienced a lifestyle of blessing and prosperity that the church has not been able to comprehend!

In his book *The Jewish Phenomenon*, author Steven Silbiger describes the incredible prosperity of Jews in America. He points out that most American Jews arrived here within the last two generations. They were driven out of Europe by persecution and arrived on our shores as poor immigrants. Yet, within two generations, the Jews have achieved a level of success unknown by any other ethnic group!

Silbiger points out that the proportion of Jews in America is very small. In fact, Jews make up only 2% of the U.S. population. Yet...

- 20% of professors at leading universities in this country are Jewish.
- 25% of American Nobel Prize winners are Jewish.
- One third of American multimillionaires are Jewish.
- 40% of the top 40 of the Forbes 400 richest Americans are Jewish.

* 40% of the partners at leading New York and Washington D.C. law firms are Jewish.[1]

While not every Jew is wealthy, Jews do have much higher average incomes than non-Jews. Dr. Thomas Sowell, in his book *Ethnic America*, writes, "Even when neither education nor age is a factor, Jews earn more." [2] Silbiger comments, "Among families headed by males with four or more years of college and aged 35 to 45, *Jews still earn 75 percent higher incomes.*" [3]

The success of Jews in America is not unique. Silbiger shows that in any society where their upward mobility has not been deliberately blocked, Jews have tended to rise into positions of wealth and influence in numbers far exceeding their percentage of the population.

How do we account for the incredible success of the Jewish people? Silbiger attributes the economic and social success of the Jews to "a combination of factors related to the Jewish religion and culture." [4]

In his book, Silbiger describes how various elements of Judaism have helped bring the Jews financial success. The point of his book is that Gentiles could experience the *same success* if they would do the *same things!* Interestingly, the things Silbiger describes are things God *wanted* His church to have! That incredible level of financial success was part of our God-given inheritance!

The causes of the Jews' success are found in the things God instilled in the Jewish people thousands of years ago. God promised that those who observe the instructions He gave to the Jews WILL experience success!

"Do not let this Book of the Law [*Torah*] depart from your mouth; meditate on it day and night, so that you may be careful to do everything written in it. *Then you will be prosperous and successful*" (Joshua 1:8. See also Deut. 28:1-14 and Ps. 1:1-3). The Jews' commitment to honor these precepts has given them the success God promised!

Many prophets today are talking about a coming "transfer of wealth," when God will transfer the "wealth of the world" into His kingdom. I believe part of that transfer involves reclaiming the lost inheritance of our Jewish roots!

The things God gave the Jews have set them apart from all other peoples. But those same "success principles" were *also* part of the *Church's* heritage! Biblical Judaism was not only the religion of Abraham, Isaac, and Jacob; but also of Jesus and the apostles. The apostle Paul wrote that Biblical Judaism was the *root* from which the church drew its strength (Rom 11:16-17).

To understand why God poured such blessing upon the Jewish people, we need to understand WHY God chose the Jews...

God's Choice of the Jews!

British journalist William Ewer wrote a famous little two-line rhyme:

> **How odd of God**
> **To choose the Jews!** [5]

Someone answered that couplet this way...

> **But odder still are those who choose**
> **The Jewish God, but hate the Jews!**

There are many down through history who have puzzled over God's choice of the Jews. But if you understand WHY God chose the Jews, you will be very thankful that he did!

To understand why God chose the Jews we need to see that through embracing paganism, mankind had lost any understanding of spiritual reality. Romans chapter one describes the human race this way: "their thinking became futile and their foolish hearts were darkened" (Rom. 1:21).

Men and women had become so perverted in their thinking they no longer knew Who the true God was or how to relate to Him. In the ancient world, the vilest sins were turned into acts of pagan worship! Men had so embraced idolatry they had lost even the ability to comprehend the truth of God when they heard it!

That is true today in many places. Many Christians assume you can walk up to any pagan and say, "Jesus loves you!" ...then lead them in a prayer, and they're saved! Those who have served on the mission field will assure you that it's not quite that easy!

Pagans have lost the ability to understand the things of God. When you mention "God" to a pagan, his first response will probably be, "*Which* god?" His picture of deity is not an almighty, all-powerful God. His picture of "god" is probably some local deity with limited power and depraved morality. The pagan concept of "god" is much closer to our concept of "demon."

Even when you are able to communicate the gospel to a pagan and see them saved, there will be a long process of learning before they understand the foundational truths of Christianity. That's exactly the problem the earliest missionaries faced as they tried to communicate God's truth into a pagan world.

The early apostles discovered that it was *difficult* for pagans to understand the gospel. When God's revelation was communicated to people with a pagan mindset, the result was often confusion. They didn't have any categories to understand what God was saying.

On Paul's first missionary journey, he went to Lystra and performed some miracles. When the apostles had performed miracles in Jerusalem, the people saw it as a sign from *Yahweh*. In Lystra, however, their response was quite different. They shouted, "gods have come down to us in human form!" They called Barnabas "Zeus" and Paul "Hermes," and wanted to offer sacrifices in their honor!

The same thing happened in Malta. In Acts 28:6, when Paul was bitten by a serpent, the people expected him to fall down dead. When he didn't die as they expected, their next assumption was, "He must be a god!"

When Paul taught in Athens (Acts 17), the Greek philosophers concluded, "He seems to be advocating foreign gods!" They heard Paul speaking about Jesus and the resurrection and assumed he was promoting a *god* named Jesus and a *goddess* named Resurrection! Because of their pagan mindset, they could not grasp Paul's message.

As you read the New Covenant Scriptures, you find whenever the gospel penetrated into the pagan world, such misunderstandings of the message were common.

Even *converted* pagans had a hard time understanding the truth of God! The church in Corinth had no concept of *righteousness*. In the temples of Corinth, prostitution and drunken orgies were acts of worship. The new converts at Corinth had *no idea* such things would be abhorrent to God! Paul had to write a letter of correction to the Corinthian church because some of these converts were living in immorality and getting drunk at the Lord's Supper!

Converts from paganism didn't understand that it was wrong for a Christian to participate in idolatrous feasts. In the first century, pagan temples also served as restaurants and butcher shops. Animals were sacrificed to the pagan gods, then butchered and the meat sold or served at a pagan feast. Such feasts had been a standard part of their culture. Gentile Christians didn't think anything of it. So Paul has to deal repeatedly with the issue of eating meat sacrificed to idols.

Holiness was one of the hardest concepts for Gentiles to grasp. The Gentile world didn't have a concept of holiness. The closest thing pagans had to the concept of holiness was *asceticism*. Greek asceticism taught that everything *physical* is evil and everything *spiritual* is good. To be "good" meant to divorce yourself from the physical world and its pleasures. This affected the Gentile church in many ways.

By the middle ages, if you wanted to be holy, you took a vow of poverty, moved into a monastery, and literally *tortured* yourself!

Asceticism affected *worship*! Biblical worship was very Jewish. It involved much dancing and celebration. There was a great deal of physical expression: lifting hands, clapping hands, bowing down, etc. The human body was viewed as an instrument to express praise to God.

As Christianity penetrated the Greek world, there was an increasing tension with these expressions of worship. If the physical world is evil, how can *physical* expressions of praise be acceptable to God?

These attitudes still affect much of the church today. Have you ever wondered why many Christians can *read* passages exhorting us to dance to the Lord, clap our hands to the Lord, raise our hands in praise, etc... and yet never feel comfortable to actually *do* what these passages instruct? It's because we still filter God's instructions on praise through a pagan mindset.

Most Christians would be shocked to learn how much of our accepted thinking is really a paganized distortion of biblical truth. Many Christians have been taught that when you die, your spirit goes to an ethereal place called Heaven where you will live as a disembodied spirit for all eternity. That's why, on television, when they want to show someone in heaven, they set out dry ice and have people walking around ankle deep in clouds. Did you know that is a *pagan* concept of the afterlife? It comes from the pagan belief that everything physical is evil. Pagan philosophers taught that when we are freed from this wicked physical universe, we enter a wonderful *non-physical realm* where we will exist forever as a spirit being.

You will not find that taught anywhere in the Bible. The Bible teaches that the time you spend out of your body will be temporary. God will one day raise you up with a new physical body, a *glorified* physical body that will never die. God will also destroy the present heaven and earth and create a new heaven and earth where righteousness dwells. The holy city, the New Jerusalem, will come down out of heaven to earth and Jesus will reign on the throne of David over the entire universe. That's the biblical teaching on eternity. You will spend the endless ages of eternity in a sinless *physical* body, in a recreated *physical* universe! If this surprises you, read the book of Revelation! It's there!

Why have we accepted ideas that are contrary to the Bible? It's because God's revelation has been filtered through a pagan mindset. I'm convinced that our walk with God is hindered in ways we cannot even imagine because our pagan Gentile mindset blinds us to much of God's revelation.

A Nation of Priests

If the pagan mind has such a difficult time understanding the truth of God, how can the world come to know Him? God's solution to this problem was to raise up a priestly nation, specially trained to understand and communicate the truth of God. His plan was to choose a people and prepare them, like an athlete in training, putting them through difficult situations and placing on them stringent requirements to instill in them the ways of God. They would be equipped to serve as lights to the nations, to communicate the things of God to the rest of mankind.

That's why God created the Jewish people. He took the offspring of Abraham and for 2000 years He shaped their culture and understanding to bring them into line with His truth. He gave them a revelation of His nature… that there is only one God, that He is a jealous God, and that He will not share His glory with pagan idols. He revealed that He is a holy God, a loving God, and a righteous God.

He gave them a prophetic view of history. They learned where history started, where it's headed, and what Messiah would come to do.

Through His *Torah,* He shaped the daily lives of the people. He taught them about holiness: holy days, holy people, and holy places. He taught them about righteousness and repentance. He divided their world into clean and unclean to teach them the defilement of sin and what it means to be set apart to God. He taught them about sacrifice and about blood covenant. Many ancient peoples knew something about blood covenant, but they didn't know it like the Jews did!

God instilled in them a biblical cycle of life. The Sabbaths and the feasts formed a rich tapestry against which life was played out, teaching and reminding them each year of the central principles of life with God.

God gave them practical wisdom for success. He taught them how to prosper, to demonstrate to the world the blessing of being God's people.

Through repeated chastening and correction, He hammered into their minds what is required of those who would walk with God.

Then after two thousand years of preparation, Messiah came. Because of the foundation God had built into the Jewish people, they knew who He was and what He would accomplish.

When John the Baptist introduced Jesus, he did not have to spend three hours describing who Jesus was and what He came to do. He just said, "Behold the Lamb of God who takes away the sin of the world!" They knew what he meant! They knew what a sacrificial lamb was, and what Messiah would do. (Interestingly, most of the Jews who rejected Jesus were those who had turned from their own Jewish roots and become enamored with pagan Greek philosophy!)

Throughout their history God revealed that He had chosen the Jews to be a nation of priests, a people specially prepared to communicate His truth to the Gentile nations. When God first brought the Israelites out of Egypt, He told them, "You will be for me a kingdom of priests" (Ex. 19:6). As the *Levitical priests* ministered the things of God to Israel, so the *nation of Israel* would minister the truth of God to the Gentiles.

God promised the Jews that, "Nations *(Gentiles)* will come to your light, and kings to the brightness of your dawn" (Isa. 60:3), and

"You will be called priests of the Lord, you will be named ministers of our God" (Isa. 61:6).

In Zechariah, God spoke of a future time when "ten men from all languages and nations will take firm hold of one Jew by the hem of his robe and say, 'Let us go with you, because we have heard that God is with you'" (Zech. 8:23).

God called the Jewish people to be a light to the Gentile nations. God placed in them the truths we need to know if we are to walk with God. **That's the rich sap from the olive root!**

Many have assumed when Paul announced, "I am going to the Gentiles!" that it was a rejection of his Judaism. Far from it! It was the *fulfillment* of his Judaism! He was saying, "I'm pressing on to fulfill the call of our people, to be a light to the Gentiles."

Wherever he went, he ministered first to the Jews. Those were the ones prepared by God to receive his message. The first Gentiles saved were usually those already attending Synagogue, who had already gained some understanding of God. Wherever possible, Paul started each church with a *core* of Messianic Jews. They were to be the leadership of the early church. Their duty as members of God's priestly nation was to communicate the ways of God to the Gentile converts.

For the first three centuries of its existence, the church was a pretty Jewish place. Its worship followed Jewish patterns. Its organizational structure was loosely patterned after the synagogue. It observed the feasts of Israel and many other elements of biblical Judaism. It held fast to the root and was richly nourished.

Beginning with Constantine, however, and through the dark ages, most of the Jewish elements of our faith were destroyed through persistent and brutal persecution by an anti-Semitic church leadership. The church today suffers because those things have been lost.

I believe we live in a day when God is restoring what Satan has stolen. God is placing in the hearts of His people a hunger to recover our lost inheritance. The more we understand our roots, the more we will understand and be able to walk in the things of God.

God is doing an incredible work in our day. We don't yet know what the final outcome will look like, but I wait with eager anticipation to see it unfold. The promises of Isaiah 60 and 61 *will be* fulfilled. The Messianic Church is rising!

Chapter Three
The Death of the Early Church

*"And he said, 'Son of man, do you see what they are doing—things that
will drive me far from My sanctuary?' ...He then brought me into the
inner court of the house of the LORD, and there at the entrance to the
temple... men were bowing down to the rising sun." -Ezekiel 8:6,16*

The early church was the most powerful institution the world
had ever seen. Pagan religions could not compete with it. Greek
philosophy could not comprehend it. Persecution only purified it and
caused it to grow more rapidly. Yet, by the sixth century, it was
largely destroyed. By the year 600, almost nothing that had
characterized the early church remained. The church became a
corrupt political power, hated and feared by the common people,
with little evidence of the life and power it had once known.

How did the Messianic Church die?

The event that eventually brought an end to the early church
took place early in the fourth century. It was an insidious event
engineered, I believe, by Satan himself. Surprisingly, it was an event
that came disguised in the form of a great blessing. The "death
knell" for the early church was the "conversion" of the Roman
emperor Constantine.

The year was A.D. 312. It was a time of turmoil in the
Empire. The Imperial throne was empty and several rivals fought to
seize control. Two of the rivals were Constantine and Maxentius.
During this struggle, Maxentius challenged Constantine to battle.

Constantine, alarmed by rumors that Maxentius was a master
of magical arts, prayed to the "supreme god" for help. To
Constantine, the supreme god was *Mithras*, the Persian sun god.

In response to his prayer, he reportedly saw a vision of a
flaming cross in the sky next to the sun, along with the words,
"Conquer by this!" He then confronted Maxentius and won the
battle.

The result was that Constantine came to the throne with the
announcement that he was now a follower of Jesus. The Christians
could hardly believe it. The church had gone through centuries of

scattered local persecution. Then, during the reign of Diocletian (A.D. 287 to 305), they endured one of the most severe persecutions the church had known. Diocletian's persecution was a brutal, empire-wide attack on the church. Many thousands were tortured and killed. During that eighteen-year period, the church lost almost all its leadership. Since the leaders were the most visible members of the church, they were the first ones killed. Bibles were confiscated.

It was a time of great distress. Almost everyone in the church saw friends or relatives martyred. But now a new Roman Emperor had come to the throne claiming to be a follower of Jesus.

To most of the church, this seemed an answer to prayer. Christianity suddenly changed from being an *illegal* religion to a *favored* religion. The days of persecution and ridicule had ended. Christian leaders, who had once been looked down upon, were now given great honor. It became an *advantage*, both politically and socially, to be a Christian. Here are just a few examples of the way Constantine showered the church with favor…

… Eusebius wrote that **Constantine was generous with money and honors for prominent converts**. This resulted in a large number of upper-class conversions.

…He proclaimed Sunday as an official Roman holiday so Christians could worship freely. He gave his Christian soldiers the day off on Sundays. Later, **he made rest on Sunday obligatory for all**.

…**Constantine spent large sums of money building new churches**. Many were erected in Rome itself and magnificent buildings were put up on famous sites in Jerusalem. Numerous churches were built in the new capital and throughout the empire.

…Constantine donated a great deal of property to create endowments for churches. One writer commented that in Italy, "he despoiled the Imperial patrimony for the benefit of the new God." As a result, **the Church soon became the single most important landowner in Italy.**[1]

In A.D. 356, Constantine's son Constantius took Constantine's actions one step further. He prohibited all pagan sacrifices on pain of death. He closed all pagan temples, destroyed many of them, and converted others to churches.

For Christians, used to centuries of persecution, these changes were wonderful. With the new freedoms and privileges that resulted from Constantine's conversion, the church joyfully hailed him as a new apostle Paul.

The results of these changes in the long run, however, were disastrous. The problem was that Constantine not only legalized Christianity, he tried to improve on it.

Changes in the Church

In return for his favor, Constantine demanded control. One of the titles given to a Roman emperor was *"pontifex maximus"* (high priest). By Roman law, the emperor was in charge of all religious affairs in the empire. The emperor, for centuries, had been head of the pagan religious system.

Now that Christianity was a legal religion, Christians warmly accepted Constantine as *Pontifex Maximus* of the church. They hailed him as a new apostle. He evidently viewed *himself* as an apostle. In his "Church of the Holy Apostles," Constantine set up monuments for 13 people: the 12 apostles *and himself!* And *his* monument was bigger than the others. [2]

As Constantine looked at his new religion, there were many things that perplexed him. The Christians seemed primitive and unsophisticated in many respects. They lacked the organizational skill of the Romans. It particularly bothered him that Christianity seemed to have such a strong Jewish element. So he began to make changes.

In the year 325, Constantine called and presided over the first general council of the church, the *Council of Nicea*. While its announced purpose was to settle doctrinal disputes, Constantine used it as an opportunity to reorganize the church and give it a new image. The church was so *grateful* to him for his blessings; they let him do it.

Let's look at some of the changes Constantine made:

1. The Death of the House Church

As we have seen, the focus of early church life was the house church. Each local church was divided into units small enough to meet weekly in homes where fellowship and ministry could take place on a personal basis. Although the church regularly met together in larger meetings also, the house churches provided the *foundation* of church activity.

Shortly after he legalized Christianity, Constantine built a church called *St. John Lateran* in Rome. The style of this building is called a *basilica*. Its interior design was patterned after the throne room of the imperial palace.

At the front of the basilica was a section called the *apse*, which was reserved for the clergy. It had a throne in the center where the bishop could sit, surrounded by a semi-circle of his advisors. The throne was designed to reflect the bishop's new position as a trusted servant of the Emperor.

Facing the apse was a large open area, the *nave*, where the Bishop's subjects (the members of the church) could come and listen. The setting was rigid and formal.

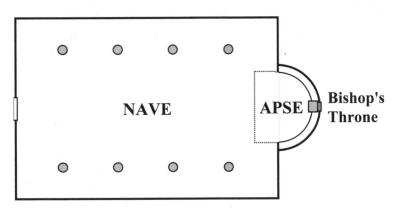

Floor Plan of a Typical *Basilica*

Encouraged and financed by the imperial government, this pattern for church construction spread rapidly. Basilica-type churches were built all over the empire.[3]

Constantine then enacted a law that "houses of prayer" must be abolished, and forbidding Christians from holding church in private homes. This decree was harshly worded and designed "to strike terror into the minds of his subjects." It went on to prohibit "holding church *any* place but the Catholic Church."[4]

The change from the informal house church to the formal basilica changed the whole concept of church. Before Constantine, a church was a family of believers. After Constantine, the church became a building.

2. A Change in Worship

Not only did Constantine give the church new buildings to meet in, he decided to improve the *way* the church worshipped. Less than one year after his "conversion" Constantine made the following decree: "I am going to make plain to them what kind of worship is to be offered to God... What higher duty have I as emperor than to... cause all to offer to Almighty God true religion and due worship."[5]

Worship in the house church had been Spirit-led and intimate, with little in the way of set forms or liturgies. With Constantine as high priest, this changed drastically. To Constantine's Roman mind, the highest expression of worship was found in the solemn rituals of the Roman Imperial court.

Under Constantine, these rituals, originally developed for pagan emperor worship, were imported into the church. Worship services became solemn public ceremonies. Fixed written forms of worship developed. The burning of incense and the carrying of candles became widespread expressions of worship.[6]

A few years ago, the Learning Channel televised a six-part series on the Roman Empire called *Rome: Power and Glory.* The last few minutes of that series contained a profound statement. The narrator said, "It's interesting that imperial Rome is probably best preserved in the church it once persecuted. Look at a church and what you see in its architecture is the architecture of the imperial throne room. Sit in a church and what you hear is imperial court ceremony: the solemnity, the choir, and the hymns are all derived from the ceremonies of the Roman imperial court."[7] That's Constantine's legacy.

But Constantine not only changed *where* the church worshipped and *how* the church worshipped, he struck at the very heart of what the church was. He cut the church off from its Jewish roots and grafted it into the root of Greek paganism.

3. The Rejection of the Church's Jewish Roots

By the beginning of the fourth century, the church had developed a great deal of diversity. In Syria, for example, groups of Ebionites still survived. The Ebionites were heretical Judaizers who rejected the writings of Paul and taught that Gentiles must be circumcised to be saved.

At the other extreme, in the large metropolitan cities of Rome and Alexandria, the church had been strongly influenced by paganism and Greek philosophy. These churches rejected much of their Jewish heritage, mingling pagan practices and ideas with those of the Bible.

Across most of the empire, however, the church still held fast to the Jewish heritage received from the apostles. As I demonstrate in Appendix Two, most of the church continued to celebrate Sabbaths and feasts, stress the learning of Torah, and in many places, maintained close fellowship with the Jewish people.

From a twenty-first century perspective, we would probably identify many of these churches as Messianic Jewish congregations. Gentile members walked in the liberty of the New Covenant, while benefiting from the rich heritage of their Messianic roots. When Constantine came to power, however, all of this began to change.

Like many Romans, Constantine hated the Jewish people. The Romans had long considered the Jews *peculiar* for their "strange" ways, but after Israel's rebellion against Rome and brutal defeats in A.D. 70 and A.D 130, Romans openly despised anything Jewish. Officially, the Jews were labeled a "conquered people hostile to Rome."

Because of his hatred of the Jews, Constantine determined to establish the paganized Christianity of Rome and Alexandria as the *standard* for the entire church. Every church in the empire was commanded to conform to this non-Messianic standard. Those who would not conform were severely persecuted.

Constantine's attempt to purge the church of its Jewish elements began with the Council of Nicea (A.D. 325). In the letter of Constantine to the bishops following the council, he declared that it was *improper* for the church to follow the customs of the Jews. Speaking of the church's observance of Passover, he wrote, "Let us, then, have nothing in common with the Jews, who are our adversaries... this irregularity [observing Passover] must be corrected, in order that we may no more have *anything* in common with the parricides and murderers of our Lord."[8]

Eusebius, a contemporary and supporter of Constantine, summed up the decision made at Nicea this way:

"It appeared an unworthy thing that we should follow the practices of the Jews... Let us have nothing in common with the detestable Jewish crowd; let us withdraw ourselves from all participation in their baseness.... Pray continually that your soul may not be sullied by fellowship with their customs... All should unite in avoiding all participation in the conduct of the Jews."[9]

Bernard Lazare describes the changes resulting from Nicea this way, "[Before Nicea] Christians attended the synagogues, [and] celebrated the Jewish holidays... It required the action of the Nicaean Council to free Christianity of this last bond by which it had still been tied to its cradle."[10]

Those who followed Jewish practice were marked *anathema* (*cut off* or *accursed*), which eventually evolved into a crime against the state, punishable by death.

We should not assume that acceptance of Nicea's decree was immediate and universal. For hundreds of years additional church councils found it necessary to repeat the ban on Messianic Christianity, often threatening severe punishments for those who continued to celebrate their Jewish heritage.

The Church's Attempt to Stamp Out Jewish Influences

THE COUNCIL OF ANTIOCH (A.D. 345) – "If any bishop, presbyter or deacon will dare, after this decree, to celebrate Passover with the Jews, the council judges them to be anathema from the church. This council not only deposes them from ministry, but also any others who dare to communicate with them." [11]

THE COUNCIL OF LAODICEA (A.D. 365) - "It is not permitted to receive festivals which are by Jews, nor to hold a festival together with them (Canon 37). Christians must not Judaize by resting on the Sabbath, but must work on that day... but if any be found to be JUDAIZERS let them be ANATHEMA from Christ."[12]

THE COUNCIL OF AGDE, FRANCE (506) – "Clerics must not take part in Jewish festivals."[13]

THE COUNCIL OF TOLEDO X (seventh century) – "Easter must be celebrated uniformly" [at the time set by the decree of Nicea rather than at the time of Passover.][14]

THE COUNCIL OF NICEA II (787) – "[Those who] openly or secretly keep the Sabbath and follow other practices in the manner of the Jews are not to be received into communion, nor into prayer, nor into the church."[15]

In the light of these statements, one must ask an obvious question: If the Jewish elements of Christianity died out before the end of the first century, as many have been taught, why were church councils still fighting to stamp out these influences seven hundred years later!

History records that in spite of brutal persecution, groups retaining Jewish influences persisted for hundreds of years around the fringes of the old empire. Beyond the borders of the empire, in places like India, Persia, China, and Ethiopia, these influences persisted even longer.

4. The Influx of Paganism
Constantine not only *divorced* the church from Judaism, he *married* the church to paganism.

Constantine claimed to be a Christian but did not seem to understand who Jesus was. Constantine was a devoted follower of *Mithras*, the Persian Sun God--the "Unconquerable Sun." When Constantine saw the vision of a cross in the sky next to the sun, he apparently assumed that Jesus was a manifestation of Mithras. Because of this, while Constantine professed to follow Christ, he also continued to openly worship pagan deities.

Constantine's triumphal arch, built after his "conversion," bears the image of Mithras, the "unconquered sun." Constantine kept the sun god on his coins. In his new city of Constantinople, he set up a statue of the sun god, bearing his own features.[16]

In 321, when Constantine made the Christian day of worship a Roman holiday, he didn't call it, "Christ Day." He called it "the venerable day of the Sun." (That's where we get the name *Sunday*.[17] It's interesting that the *Christian* emperor Constantine named the *Christian* day of worship in honor of the *pagan* sun god!)

Constantine's confusion over the identity of Jesus seems to have infected many of the unconverted pagans now crowding into the church. A fourth Century mosaic found in the city of Rome portrays Jesus as the sun god, driving his chariot across the sky! By the 5th century it had become common practice for worshippers entering St Peter's Basilica in Rome **to turn at the door and bow down to worship the rising sun!**[18] *(Ezekiel 8:6-16 specifically says this is a practice that will cause God's Presence to depart from His people!)*

This influx of pagan thinking affected the church in a number of ways.

The early church celebrated the biblical feasts established by God in the *Torah*. The paganization of Christianity under Constantine replaced these with a new set of holidays. The pagan holidays of Rome were now "baptized" into the church as Christian holidays.

Before the time of Constantine, Christians never celebrated Christ's birthday. But the pagan Romans had long celebrated December 25 as the birthday of Mithras. In the year 274, the Emperor Aurelian had actually designated Mithras' birthday as an official Roman holiday.[19]

Also known as *Saturalia*, Mithras' birthday was one of the Romans' favorite festivals, a time for good cheer and gift giving. On that one day of the year, masters would serve their slaves. Romans would give food to the children of the poor. Now that Jesus was viewed as a manifestation of the Sun god, *Saturnalia* was declared a *Christian* holiday… "Christmas," the birthday of Jesus![20]

Another new feast for the church was the celebration of the spring fertility festival. Each year the Pagans held a feast to honor the goddess of fertility. The Canaanites called this goddess Asherah. Persians called her Aestarte. Babylonians called her Ishtar. The ancient Britons called her Eastre (from which we get the word *Estrogen*).

It bothered Constantine that Christians celebrated Christ's death and resurrection on *Passover*, a Jewish holiday. At Nicea, he outlawed this celebration and directed that Christ's death and resurrection be celebrated on the Sunday following the first full moon after the vernal equinox, a time associated with the spring fertility festival.

This was also a festive holiday for the Romans. Being a fertility goddess, the symbol of Ishtar (or Eastre) was the egg. The ancient pagans would decorate eggs and give them as gifts in celebration of this festival.[21]

The result of Nicea was that Christ's resurrection was taken out of its biblical context and celebrated in the context of a pagan feast. Perhaps the strangest part of this celebration is that, in the English-speaking world, we did not even change the name. When Christians all over the English-speaking world celebrate the resurrection of Christ, they don't say, "We are celebrating *Resurrection* Sunday." They say, "We are celebrating **Easter***!" (Eastre).* We actually call the celebration of Christ's resurrection by the name of a pagan goddess!

While some pagan influences were evident in the church before Constantine, his decrees made "paganized" Christianity the official standard for the church. By the end of the fourth century, the empire was officially "Christianized." Pagan temples became Christian churches. Pagan shrines became Christian shrines. In some cases, pagan priests even became Christian priests. Only the names were changed. Pagans were told that they lived in a Christian empire and it was their responsibility to live as Christians!

The trouble is, even though they were now officially part of the church, they didn't know Jesus. They were still pagans. Their beliefs had not changed. They responded to the official decrees by giving "Christian" names to their pagan deities and continuing to worship as they had before.[22]

One common cult was the cult of Isis. Isis, an Egyptian goddess, was called the "Great Virgin" and "The Mother of God." She is commonly shown holding the child Horus, in a pose very similar to early Christian pictures of Mary and Jesus.

Worshippers of Isis began calling Isis by the name "Mary." In this way, they could continue to worship her. Worshippers of Artemis (Diana) also used this ploy.[23] Through this, the honor and reverence justly due to Mary was frequently perverted into a form of idolatry that would have horrified the mother of Jesus!

In the same way, worshippers of other pagan gods used the names of Christian saints and martyrs. If you were a pagan farmer and were told you could no longer go to your temple and pray to the *god of harvest,* what would you do? You would go to the church building that *used to be* your temple and pray to the *patron saint of harvest!* Your worship hasn't changed. You are simply calling your god by a new name. This practice was widespread. The pagans changed the names of their gods to acceptable "Christian" names and were able to legally continue their pagan worship. In this way, old paganism became more and more blended with Christianity.[24]

By the year 600, paganism had inundated the church. Many of the church's leaders were unbelievers. Those who held fast to the truth were persecuted as enemies of the empire. Superstition and idolatry were rampant. Bibles were written in a language people couldn't understand and chained to the pulpit where they couldn't be read.

The church became a powerful and wealthy political organization with little evidence of true spiritual life. When the political system of Rome crumbled, the church stepped in to fill the vacuum. The church became a respected military power but lost the supernatural power of God it had once known.

Legend has it that when Francis of Assisi was given an audience with Pope Innocent III, the Pope brought Francis into his throne room and proudly displayed his gold and jewels. "Do you see, Francis," he boasted, "the church can no longer say as Peter once did, 'silver and gold have I none.'" Francis replied, "Yes, your Holiness, but neither can the church say 'In the name of Jesus, rise up and walk!'"

By the year 800, church councils had *outlawed* the Jewish lifestyle once embraced by Jesus and the apostles. For a Christian to observe the Sabbath or celebrate Passover became a crime punishable by death. Obedience to these decrees was enforced through torture and execution.

(NOTE: This is not an indictment against the many godly Christians in the Catholic Church today. Many contemporary Roman Catholic leaders would be the first to renounce the horrors perpetrated in the name of Jesus through these dark centuries.)

The ultimate result of Constantine's "conversion" was that the Messianic Church died. Most of the things that characterized the early church were gone by the sixth century.

Cut off from the rich sap of the olive root, the disconnected Gentile branches could not sustain life. For a thousand years the church sank lower and lower. By the time of Luther, the church was a political organization "selling" forgiveness in the form of "indulgences" to finance its great building projects.

The rich heritage God had prepared for the church through 2000 years of Israel's history was lost, and we have not yet fully recovered it.

But God was not finished with His church. Beginning with the reformation, He began the process of restoration. In the 16th century, He restored the Bible and the doctrine of salvation. In the 18th century, He began to restore a desire for holiness. In the 20th century, He restored the gifts.

Much that the church had lost has been restored, but we have not yet seen the branches re-engrafted to the root. As we move into the 21st century, I believe that restoration is beginning.

Jesus said, "Unless a kernel of wheat falls to the ground and dies, it remains alone. But if it dies it produces many seeds." Through His life, death and resurrection, life was released to the world.

The history of the church is also one of life, death, and resurrection. I believe the end product of the church's resurrection will be the greatest harvest of souls the world has ever seen.

Chapter Four
What the Church Lost
(When We Lost Our Jewish Roots)

What really happened when Constantine cut the church off from its Jewish roots? The loss of our Jewish roots involved much more than celebrating a different set of holidays. It meant the loss of the biblical worldview and value-system God had built into the people of Israel. It brought to the church a completely different way of looking at God, at the Bible, and the Christian life. The beginnings of this process can be traced to the early second century.

From Jerusalem to Athens

As Gentile converts came into the church, they carried with them much baggage from their pagan backgrounds. By the early second century, we find men rising into positions of church leadership who did not appreciate the significance of our Jewish heritage. These early Gentile leaders, often called the "church fathers," were highly significant men. A few of them had actually known and been taught by the apostle John. For most of them, however, their primary training was not in the Scriptures, but in the pagan Greek philosophers.

One of my biggest disappointments in seminary was reading the writings of these men. When I took my first course in church history, I eagerly anticipated reading what these men had to say. Surely men living so close to the times of the apostles would have incredible insights into the Christian life!

What I found when I read the "fathers" was baffling. These men had very little insight into anything! They quoted the New Covenant Scriptures frequently and were obviously committed to the Lord, but they understood almost nothing. Even basic truths, such as salvation, were very poorly grasped.

One of the earliest of these Gentile writings is called the *Didache*, supposedly a record of the teaching of the apostles. Rather than a trove of rich insights into the Christian life, however, the *Didache* is almost laughable for its lack of understanding. Concerning effective fasting, for example, the *Didache* instructs:

"Do not let your fasting be as the hypocrites, for the hypocrites fast on the second and fifth day of the week, therefore let your fasting be on the fourth and sixth day!"[1]

Concerning baptism, the *Didache* gives instructions on how to best baptize new converts to Christianity. Its main emphasis is that baptism should be done in cold running water! If running water is not available, still water may be used, but it should be the coldest water available.[2]

This is a far cry from the level of spiritual insight expressed by the writers of the New Testament! The historian Phillip Schaff comments that going from the writings of the (Jewish) apostles to the (Gentile) fathers is like going from a city in a beautiful, well-watered oasis, into a dry and barren wilderness![3]

Part of the problem with many of these Gentile writers was that they wanted to embrace the message of Jesus without rejecting pagan philosophy. Several of these men had been students of Greek philosophy before their conversion and accepted the works of the Greek philosophers as wisdom given by God. Because of this, there was a deliberate attempt to blend the teachings of the New Covenant Scriptures with the teachings of pagan philosophers.

To accomplish this, they had to reinterpret Scripture to fit a pagan worldview.

Origin (185-254) has been called "The most influential theologian of the early church." In constructing his theology, he sought to synthesize the principles of Neoplatonism and Stoicism with those of Christianity.[4] To do this, he developed a system of allegorical interpretation that allowed him to "spiritualize" the Word of God, reading ideas into the text that were foreign to the Bible. Using this method, Origin was the first to promote the idea that the church had replaced Israel as God's chosen people.

Augustine is considered the "founder of theology" by both Roman Catholic and Protestant theologians. The Concise Columbia Encyclopedia comments that Augustine "firmly joined" Neoplatonism with Christianity[5] and "incorporated Plato's doctrines and Neoplatonism into Christian theology."[6]

Perhaps the most distressing change made by the church fathers, as they filtered biblical truth through their pagan mindset, was that they redefined the way of salvation. According to the Bible, salvation comes by "believing in" Jesus.

When this was reinterpreted through the intellectual Greek mindset, the wording changed from "believing in" to "believing that." According to many of these writers, salvation comes by "believing that" certain doctrines are true. This small change in wording had enormous implications. Salvation was redefined as an intellectual agreement with a set of doctrines. Heaven was reserved for those who were "doctrinally correct." Instead of, "WHO do I trust to be saved?" (Answer: Jesus) ...the issue became, "WHAT doctrines must I affirm to be saved?" This launched the church into 2000 years of intense doctrinal speculation, trying to precisely define every point of doctrine, and doubting the salvation of anyone who disagreed.

While these changes were at work in the church from the second century, they remained limited in acceptance until the days of Constantine. Once Constantine had divorced the church from its Jewish roots, however, the effects of the pagan Greek influences accelerated rapidly.

How These Changes Affected the Church

What did the church lose when biblical faith was mixed with Greek paganism? There is much that could be written concerning this, but I would like to point to four areas where this change had a profound effect on the life of the church.

1. The Loss of the Hebraic Attitude Toward God

As a result of God's dealings with Israel, the Jewish people had developed a profound AWE of God. They considered His name too holy to pronounce. Instead of saying the name Yahweh, the Jews would simply say, "The Lord." They viewed His name as so holy that when a scribe was copying a manuscript and came across the name of God, the scribe would put down his pen and take up a special pen to write the divine name. God's name was considered too holy to be written with a common pen.

The Greeks and Romans never had that kind of awe of their gods. Their gods had many of the same weaknesses and failings as mortal men. There might have been a fear of a thunderbolt from Zeus, but not true awe.

To the Jew, the person of God was treated with great respect. God was not a subject for analysis; He was the object of loving worship. The Jews knew that the puny human mind would never be capable of understanding God. The only appropriate response to Him is to love, serve, and obey Him. To put it another way, the Hebrews approached Scripture, not to *understand* God, but to learn how to please Him.

The Greek mentality, on the other hand, deified human intellect above God. They assumed the human mind *could* ultimately understand God, and believed if you could understand something, you could control it. Their goal was to "figure out" God logically... to define, describe, and understand Him. They saw the God of the universe as a subject they could scientifically examine, placing Him on a spiritual microscope slide and dissecting Him with the scalpel of human intellect.

As the church lost its Hebrew roots, it embraced this intellectual Greek preoccupation to analyze God. This launched the church into many centuries of unproductive theological debate.

A good example of this is the council of Chalcedon. Chalcedon was a church council held in 451 to settle a controversy concerning the deity and humanity of Jesus. All sides in this controversy believed in Jesus and agreed that He was both God and man. Their issue was to accurately define how His humanity and divinity related to each other. The Eastern Church (Nestoreans) taught that Christ's human and divine natures existed side by side within him. The Roman church taught that Christ's two natures joined in complete unity, yet did not become one. A third party, led by Eutyches, taught that Christ's two natures coalesced into one new nature.[7]

The council of Chalcedon, after weighing the arguments on all sides, gave the following definition: "One Christ in two natures united in one person, yet remaining 'without confusion, without conversion, without division, without separation.'"[8] On the basis of this decision, the Roman church condemned the Nestorians and Eutychians as heretics and broke off fellowship. The divisions in the church caused by this issue remain to this day!

It is amazing to me that anyone in this debate would presume that our human minds could understand how the deity and humanity of Christ interrelated, or that it was somehow beneficial to debate this issue. One of my seminary professors described this kind of theology as trying to "unscrew the inscrutable!"

I don't believe it would have ever occurred to a Jewish mind to even ask such a question.   In the words of biblical scholar Rabbi Joseph Soloveitchik, "We [Jews] are more interested in discovering *what God wants man to do* than in describing God's essence."[9]   That was also the attitude of the Messianic early church. The Messianic leaders in the first few centuries were so occupied in worshipping, serving, and obeying the Lord that they found no time to dissect Him.

2. The Loss of the Hebraic Attitude Toward Scripture

The Jewish people not only have an awe of God, they have an incredible reverence for the Scriptures. The Jews, because of their devotion to the Scriptures, have often been called "the people of the Book." Jews are taught that it is the duty of everyone who walks with God to read and study *Torah* (Scripture) for themselves. Historically, every synagogue was a teaching and training center where individuals were trained in the things of God.

Although many secular Jews today do not know the Scriptures, this attitude has not been the norm for most of Jewish history.

A good picture of the traditional Jewish attitude toward the Bible can be seen in the movie *Fiddler on the Roof.* This movie presents the story of Tevye, a simple Jewish farmer in turn-of-the-century Ukraine.

In his song, "If I Were a Rich Man," Tevye fantasizes about what his life could be like if he were a wealthy man. He dreams of a life of ease and comfort, of providing a fine house for his wife, and of being a respected man in the community. As he visualizes this life of wealth, he ends by revealing the deepest desire of his heart. If he were a wealthy man, he confides, the "sweetest thing of all" would be that he could sit in the synagogue every day and study the sacred books with the learned men. For Tevye, the highest goal in life was to study *Torah.*

That is a common Jewish attitude toward Scripture. Even today, many Jews have a reverence for the Bible most Christians cannot relate to. Each week in most synagogues, when the sacred *Torah* scroll is taken out of the ark to be read, it is walked up and down the aisles of the synagogue. Those near the ends of the aisles reach out and reverently touch the *Torah*, then put their fingers to their lips, symbolically "tasting" its sweetness!

Once a year the Jews have a celebration called **Simhat Torah** (Rejoicing in the *Torah*). At this celebration, the *Torah* scrolls are taken out of the ark, and the men of the congregation dance with them in the aisles! This sounds strange to most Christians. (When was the last time you danced with your Bible!) But this is not idolatry... its love! God has instilled in the Jewish people a love for His Word.

In the Hebrew world of the first century, this love of the Bible was demonstrated in an incredible way. Jewish parents began teaching their children to read Hebrew at the age of three. If the parents were not able to teach the children themselves, they would hire someone else to do it. By age six, Jewish children were expected to know how to read and write in Hebrew. At age six, children began daily study in the synagogue schools. They studied *Torah* in the original Hebrew and were required to memorize it. This study began, not with Genesis, but with Leviticus, which was considered to be the most important book. By the time of their *bar mitzvah*, at about 13 years, most observant Jews were expected *to understand* and *to have memorized* the *entire Torah*, plus large sections of the Psalms and the prophets! This education in *Torah* was common for both men and women.[10] (Timothy received his instruction in *Torah* from his mother and grandmother.) By the time of his *bar mitzvah*, the *average* Jewish man in the first century had a better knowledge of the Scripture than many seminary graduates today!

As the church lost touch with its Hebrew heritage, this reverence for the Word was lost. In its place, the church developed an attitude toward Scripture more in keeping with a pagan Greek worldview. The Greek mentality was that the average Christian does not need to know the Bible. Serious study of the Word was reserved for professionals, the clergy. Those who desired to read the Bible must be trained first, so they don't come to any unacceptable conclusions. In this they followed the model of the pagan temples, where the leaders were initiated into the sacred mysteries, while the common people worshipped in relative ignorance.

Dan Juster writes, "A primary Jewish truth was that all men are responsible before God and should be able to read the Synagogue scrolls for themselves and teach the Word to their children. Every

Jew… was expected to know how to read, how to write, and how to understand the scrolls…   In the church, because of the Gentile hierarchical perspectives, the laity could become illiterate.   People were not personally responsible to know the Word, they were to believe what they were told without questioning authority."[11]

By the Middle Ages, not only the common people, but even many kings and priests, were illiterate.   Even those few who were able to read were often denied access to the Bible. Knowledge of the Bible was viewed as a dangerous, even subversive thing, and strongly discouraged by the church.   Biblical knowledge was reserved for the clergy. In 1517 in Coventry, England, five men and two women were burned at the stake for teaching their children the Lord's prayer and the Ten Commandments in English!"[12]

The ideal of the masses knowing the Word was lost and has still not been fully recovered.   While the reformation made it possible for every Christian to read the Word, many Christians still have the attitude that biblical knowledge is only necessary for professional ministers.

In many Evangelical and Charismatic churches, the average Christian knows little more than some Bible stories and a few proof texts. If someone is curious about anything more than that, they are not expected to study their Bible; they are expected to ask their pastor.   Christians are not taught *how* to study the Bible for themselves. "Time in the Word" for most believers is limited to a quick daily devotional reading, "a chapter a day keeps the devil away."

Because of this, Christians are robbed of the benefits of "transforming their minds" (Rom.12:1-2) through the Word of God. They don't receive the wisdom of God to handle the daily decisions of life. As a pastor, I can say that many of the people who come to me for counsel over problems in their lives are "in a mess" because they do not know what the Word of God says!

Christians do not walk in the level of blessing that comes from daily studying and meditating on the Word.   In Psalm 1, God promises that those who delight and meditate on the Word will be greatly blessed and will prosper in all they do. As we saw in chapter two, although Jews are not walking with Messiah, their devotion to God's Word has given them incredible creativity and success, just as God promised it would!

3. The Loss of the Judaic Emphasis on the Home

Spiritual life in 20th century American Christianity is primarily a church activity. It takes place in a church building and is led by paid professionals. Most of the activities require little more of the individual than to show up.[13]

This is quite different from the Jewish mentality of the early church. In the Jewish mentality, the primary place for spiritual development was the home.

Dowgeiwicz writes:

"Judaism survived persecution in every generation because the real structure and function of religious life was home centered.

Although so many synagogues were destroyed over the course of centuries, Judaism survived because every Jew was expected to be knowledgeable about the faith of his ancestors. Therefore Judaism could always survive in the home. The home was a little sanctuary, a *miqdash meyat*, to be set aside for the worship of God, the study of His Word, and a place of hospitality."[14]

Many Christians today don't realize that through most of the Bible, God's people had no "church" to go to! They had no place to meet for regular public worship! Our view of worship is so tied to a church building we cannot even relate to that!

As you study the Bible, you find that the tabernacle and Temple were not places for weekly public worship. Until the Babylonian captivity, the synagogue probably did not exist. For most of Jewish history, and continuing even today, the primary focus of Jewish worship is the home. The same is true of the "Messianic" early church. That's why, before the days of Constantine, you don't find Christians constructing many church buildings. They had a different model for worship: a home-centered model.

Biblically, most of the major feasts and celebrations were not corporate gatherings at the synagogue or temple, but family gatherings, presided over by the father, who functioned as the elder and priest of his family. As you read the book of Exodus, you find that Passover is designed to be celebrated in the home around the dinner table.   In *Sukkot*, or Tabernacles, the parents build a temporary shelter (*sukkah*) in the back yard and the whole family "camps out" with God for a week.

The most important worship celebration is the weekly welcoming of the Sabbath, which again takes place in the home. Each Friday evening, the father of the household—a man trained in the Scriptures from the age of six—would lead his extended family in the Sabbath celebration. This was a household worship service for the entire extended family, which would include children, grandchildren, servants, etc. A first-century extended family would have been a multi-generational household sometimes numbering twenty to thirty people. Part of the responsibility of every Jewish father was to lead this group in praise to God, to offer thanks for God's blessings, and to pray blessing over his wife, his children, and everyone else present.

The meal would begin with the mother lighting the Sabbath candles and blessing God for the gift of Sabbath. The family would often sing together joyful songs of praise. At the start of the meal, the father would lift a glass of wine and pray a traditional prayer, blessing God for his gracious provision. He would then hold up a loaf of bread and pray a similar blessing. He would break the loaf of bread and pass it around for all to partake.

The Sabbath meal was a joyful time centered on devotion to the Lord. As they ate, the members of the family would talk about the things of God, recite and discuss Scripture, pray, and sing praises to the Lord. Often friends and neighbors would be invited to join in the celebration. Dowgiewicz writes, "Conversation is enjoyed long after the Sabbath candles have burned down. There is time to share, to listen, to plan and to laugh." [15]

As we read the New Testament, we need to remember that this family Sabbath celebration had been the central element in the spiritual life of every member of the early church from their earliest childhood. I believe it had a profound impact on the formation, structure, and success of the church.

In our church, when we started cell groups, one of the main problems was finding leaders. Where do we find enough men and women who are mature in their knowledge of the Word, apt to teach, and who feel comfortable leading a group in prayer and worship? In traditional Christianity, most men and women have *never* done these things in *any* setting. They have grown up in a church where ordained ministers perform all leadership functions and where the average Christian is not expected to know the Bible. Consequentially, when we try to have any form of house church, finding qualified leaders is a major problem that limits church growth.

This was not the case in the early church. Because of the Jewish tradition of family worship, it was *normal* for almost any believer to feel comfortable leading in prayer, worship, and the discussion of God's word. This provided the early church with a large pool of potential leaders. When 3000 people were added to the church in Acts 2, most of these men and women came into the church *already* accustomed to taking spiritual leadership in a "home group" setting.

The early church could grow rapidly because it was made up of *thousands* of men and women whose level of experience and biblical knowledge would surpass many seminary graduates today. That's why in Acts 8, they could *all* go out and preach the Word (Acts 8:1,4). These Messianic believers were well equipped to function as leaders in the new congregations planted all over the world.

The Jewish Sabbath celebration provided a pattern for the development of early Christian house churches. On Friday evening each Jewish extended family *gathered in a home for a meal* to celebrate God's creation and welcome His provision of rest. On the following evening the Messianic *spiritual* family (the house church) *gathered weekly for a meal* to celebrate God's redemption and welcome His Holy Spirit!

The home worship celebrations, held every Sabbath, served as a training ground for early church leaders. Paul said the prerequisite for leading the church is to do a good job leading your own family (I Tim. 3:4-5). As men and women learned to lead their *family* in worship on the Sabbath, they were gaining the spiritual skills necessary to lead a *house church* into the Presence of God.

As long as the church retained this Jewish heritage, it continued to grow and prosper throughout the world with incredible speed. When it allowed this legacy to be removed, it lost the power to fulfill its mission.

4. The loss of the Hebraic Attitude to Life

One of the primary things that keeps non-believers from coming to Jesus today is the world's perception of the church as a joyless, judgmental, legalistic group of people. Unfortunately, through much of our history, this has not been a totally inaccurate perception.

When stoic philosophy and Greek asceticism were merged with biblical teaching, the result was a joyless Christianity where poverty and suffering were seen as virtues. In the Middle Ages, those who wanted to be close to God would take vows of poverty and celibacy, separate themselves from friends and family, and literally torture themselves, in the hope that a life of physical suffering would somehow make them holy.

This attitude, while not biblical, is still with us today, though in less extreme forms. For many today, the Christian life is not intended to be enjoyed, but endured. It's like taking medicine: "I don't like it but I know it's good for me."

This attitude has caused the world to view Christians as people who don't enjoy life, and who don't want anyone else to. I recently saw a bumper sticker that read, "Puritanism is the fear that someone, somewhere, is having fun." That's how the world views Christians!

Several years ago, we called our church to 21 days of prayer. The first two weeks were declared to be weeks of prayer and fasting. We had a daily prayer meeting for those who were participating to come together and seek the Lord. When we came to the third week, we felt the Lord told us to have a week of prayer and *feasting*. Each day we prepared food so that those who came together could feast in the Lord's presence.

It was interesting to see the church's response. For the first two weeks, we had a good turnout. People were willing to commit time to fast and seek the Lord. When we came to the third week, however, and a feast was prepared, a strange thing happened. Nobody came! People were willing to commit time to prayer and *fasting*, but not to prayer and feasting!

To the average Christian, fasting is an unpleasant activity and therefore must be of value spiritually. Feasting, however, is a pleasant activity, so to take time to meet to eat and pray did not seem to be worthwhile!

Biblically, of course, both fasting and feasting are important. There is a time to fast and a time to feast. Both are important parts of a healthy spiritual life!

The Jews viewed all of life as a gracious gift from God and taught that God desires His children to enjoy His blessings. It is not more spiritual to be joyless! In the biblical calendar, there are days for fasting and repentance, but there are also days for feasting and being extravagant... for enjoying to the fullest every blessing God has given.

Few Christians are aware of the fact that God commanded the Jews to take a special tithe of their income each year and spend it *feasting extravagantly* in His Presence! Deuteronomy 14:25-26 instructs, "Exchange your tithe for silver... Use the silver to buy whatever you like: cattle, sheep, wine or other fermented drink, or anything you wish. Then you and your household shall eat there in the presence of the Lord your God and rejoice." The result of this extravagant celebration was that the people would "learn to revere the Lord your God always" (Deut. 14:23).

Most times of Jewish worship were times of joy and thankfulness for God's goodness. Many Christians think of a "Sabbath" observance as a solemn and serious time when pleasure must be avoided. To the Jews, the weekly Sabbath was not a day to be miserable. Sabbath was a day to relax, to enjoy family and friends, to eat good food and celebrate God's blessings. Many biblical feast days were specifically designed as fun activities to draw families together.

To the Jews, all of God's blessings are ours to enjoy, in the proper context, and with thanksgiving. Celibacy and poverty are not embraced as virtues in Judaism! Deuteronomy 28:47 taught that God wanted His people to serve Him *"with joy and gladness of heart* for the abundance of all things!"

This attitude of the early Messianic church was in sharp contrast to the attitudes of the Greek and Roman world.

In the first century, the licentious **Epicureans** said, "eat, drink, and be merry, for tomorrow we die."

The ascetic **Stoics** said, "Fast and be sober, for tomorrow we die."

The godly **Jews**—and **Messianic Christians**—said, "Eat, drink and be *thankful*, because *life* is a gift of God." (Eccl. 3:13)

That attitude was part of what made Christianity so contagious in the first century. Joyful, thankful Christians are still contagious today.

Preparing for Restoration

We've looked at a FEW of the changes the church experienced when our Jewish roots were stolen. We've seen the loss of the Jewish attitude to the BIBLE, the loss of Jewish attitude toward the HOME, the loss of the biblical attitude to GOD, and the loss of the JOY of life in God's Presence.

And there are many, many more. But I have GOOD NEWS for you: *The time has come for RESTORATION!*

In the second half of this book, we will look at specific steps that will enable you to begin to regain all that was lost!

Chapter Five
The Process of Resurrection

When Constantine outlawed Jewish practices and observances within the church, he severed the church from its Hebraic root and engrafted it into the root of pagan Greek philosophy.

If you cut a branch from a living tree and engraft it into a dead stump there may not be an immediate outward change. The branch contains enough life within itself to survive for a short while. Over time, however, as the leaves remain cut off from the life-giving sap, they begin to wither. Eventually all that remains is a dead branch.

The Lord warned Ezekiel that when pagan practices are brought into His temple, God's Presence departs. When the church abandoned its God-given Jewish heritage and embraced pagan practices, the presence and life of God departed. For a while, the effect was not obvious. In fact, the church appeared to thrive.

The church now enjoyed beautiful buildings and elaborate ceremonies, but the power and Presence of God was less and less evident. The church now lacked the spiritual power to heal the sick, cast out the demons, and win the lost.

Outwardly, the church as an institution continued to grow. Conversions had once been obtained through manifestations of the power of God. "Conversions" were now obtained through economic incentives, and eventually through military power. Whole nations were brought into "Christendom" in this way. The church gained wealth and prestige, but lost its true identity. The church the apostles had established, the Messianic Church, had ceased to exist.

Lest we think that God had completely forgotten his people, we should note that during the thousand years of the "dark ages," God did preserve a remnant.

Scriptures teach that God *always* preserves a remnant. Within the Catholic Church there have always been godly men and women like Bernard of Clairvaux and Francis of Assisi who truly loved the Lord and walked with Him.

In remote areas, around the fringes of the old empire, God also preserved remnants of the Messianic Church for many centuries.

Two of the most notable examples are the Culdees of Iona and the Waldensians.

The Culdees of Iona

One of the last vestiges of Messianic Christianity was centered on a small rocky island off the coast of Scotland--a place known as Iona. The community at Iona was founded by Columba (521-597), a Christian born of noble parents in Donegal, Ireland. Columba was a true apostle, having planted 300 churches in his native Ireland.[1]

In 563 Columba left his homeland to go on a "pilgrimage for Christ." With a group of twelve followers, Columba sailed from Ireland to Scotland, where he established a Christian community on Iona. This was a true community, not a monastery in the Roman Catholic sense. Those who lived and worked at Iona were permitted to marry and raise children. Leadership in the communities founded by Columba often passed from father to son.[2]

Initially, Iona served as a base for the evangelism for the Scotts and Picts. Through a ministry of preaching, demon expulsion, and miracles, Columba and his followers, known as the Culdees, won all of northern Scotland to the Lord in a very short time.

The accounts of Columba's ministry read like the book of Acts. Large crowds of sick were healed, and demonic powers bound and cast out. Many were won to the Lord through acts of spiritual power and the accuracy of the prophetic words Columba spoke. In scenes reminiscent of Elijah and the priests of Baal on Mount Carmel, Columba often confronted the pagan druid priests and sent them away "vanquished and confounded" by the power of God. As the result of Columba's ministry, many churches were founded and the religious, political, and social life of Scotland was permanently changed.[3]

Although counted as a saint by the Catholic Church, Columba was not in any way connected with the Church of Rome. The Culdees were, rather, a vestige of a much older version of Christianity, the Messianic Church.

The followers of Columba observed the seventh day as a Sabbath and celebrated Passover. They placed strong emphasis on each believer having a thorough knowledge of the Bible. Like the ancient synagogues, the churches Columba planted were teaching and training centers where each member was trained in the things of God.[4]

The residents of Iona purchased slaves and set them free. These freed slaves would be educated to read the Bible in Hebrew, Greek, and Gaelic, then trained to go out as missionaries. (This was in a day when even most kings in Europe could not read or write.) The message these missionaries proclaimed focused on three points, "The Father loved the world; the Son died for sinners; the Holy Spirit regenerates those who seek God in repentance and faith."[5]

Missionaries from Iona traveled throughout Europe proclaiming God's truth in the language of the people. Although often opposed by the Roman church, these missionaries continued to have an impact on European Christianity for centuries. Iona was finally destroyed by Viking raids in the eighth century, but communities planted by Culdee missionaries from Iona continued for centuries longer.

In identifying Iona as a remnant of the Messianic Church, we should not assume they thought of themselves as Jewish. The observance of Passover or the Sabbath did not seem Jewish to them, any more than reading the book of Psalms or taking the Lord's supper seems Jewish to us. For Columba, these things were simply part of normative Christianity. The things practiced by the Culdees had been part of biblical Christianity since the times of the apostles. These things only seem foreign to us because they were forcibly removed from the church in the Middle Ages.

The Waldensians

Another example of the Messianic Church can be found in the early Waldensians. The Waldensians were a community of Christians living in the remote valleys of the French and Italian Alps. (The word *Waldensian* comes from the Latin *Vallis Densa,* which means "shaded valley.")[6]

In the fourth century, when Constantine began to make sweeping changes in the church, many of the bishops rebelled. Those who resisted Constantine's changes were severely persecuted. These bishops and their followers fled for protection into the remote valleys, high in the Alps, where the Roman armies would not come.[7] They remained there for a thousand years, preserving much of the life of the early church. In the sixteenth century, their descendants joined the Protestant Reformation.

Things *stressed* by the early Waldensians include:

Observing the seventh day as a Sabbath (Waldensians
    were sometimes called the *Sabatatti*.[8])
Meeting in house churches
Memorizing the Scriptures
Preaching in the language of the people
Prophecies, visions, speaking in tongues, and anointing
    with oil for healing
Personal evangelism

Things *opposed* by the Waldensians include:

The doctrine of purgatory
Prayer for the dead
The clergy-laity distinction
Prayer to Mary and the saints
Liturgy and ritual
Pagan holidays[9]

In short, all through the Middle Ages God preserved a tiny remnant of the early church, hidden away "in the cleft of the rock" and protected from harm.

The Path to Restoration

God responded to the darkness of the Middle Ages by protecting faithful remnants of the early church. His ultimate purpose, however, was not to preserve a remnant, but to *restore* His church.

This process of restoration began through a series of revivals, or spiritual awakenings. This process began in the 14th century with John Wycliffe. Wycliffe (1329-1384) was a philosopher at Oxford University where he had the rare opportunity to study the Bible for himself. As he studied the Word, his life was transformed.

Wycliffe began to teach from the Bible and translated it into English so the common people could read it for themselves. The goal of his ministry was the restoration of the Church to its New Testament purity. He wrote, "We ask God then of His supreme goodness *to reform our church,* as being entirely out of joint, *to the perfectness of its first beginning.*"[10]

In his zeal to see the Church restored, Wycliffe became fiercely evangelistic. He trained preachers and sent them out all over England to preach wherever they could gain a hearing. They preached on the roads, in village greens, and in churchyards. His followers, known as the *Lollards*, believed that the main duty of a priest was to preach the Bible to the people in their own language. This revival in England was suppressed vigorously by the Roman church, yet the *Lollards* continued to thrive in England for several centuries.

The work of Wycliffe was built upon by Hus, Luther, Whitfield, Wesley, and many others who poured out their lives to see the church restored. Because of their sacrifice, we now enjoy much that had been lost.

The infusion of the Word of God brought life to the "dead" branches of the Gentile church. In all that has been restored, however, there has never been a restoration of the church to its original Hebrew root.

According to Romans 11, it had been God's intention for the Gentile church to be engrafted among the "living branches" of Messianic Judaism, where it could draw on the life-giving sap from the root. The problem was that, by the time of the Reformation, the natural living branches no longer existed. Messianic Judiasm had been destroyed by centuries of persecution by an anti-Semitic church. Those Jews who knew Messiah had been forced to assimilate, taking on the culture and paganized practices of the Gentile church.

For over one thousand years, Messianic Judaism, the religion of the original apostles, ceased to exist. All that remained of Judaism were the "cut off" branches of rabbinical Judaism. There were no living branches for the Gentile church to be connected to!

Then, in 1967, a momentous event occurred.

In Luke 21:24, Jesus had said, "Watch Jerusalem! When you see that city back in the hands of the Jews, you will know that the times of the Gentiles are ending. The Jewish people are about to fulfill their destiny!"

On June 7, 1967 the nation of Israel was in the midst of the Six Day War, locked in a struggle for its very survival. Hopelessly outnumbered, many experts doubted Israel could survive. The Jews had hoped Jordan would not enter the conflict, but by June 7, fierce fighting had broken out in the divided city of Jerusalem. As Jordan continued to bombard the non-Jordanian sections of the city, Colonel Mordechai "Motta" Gur, commander of the Israeli paratroopers, gave orders to his battalion commanders to occupy the old city of Jerusalem.[11]

Approaching the city from the Mount of Olives, the paratroopers entered through the Lion's Gate and fought their way through the narrow streets to the Wailing Wall, the last remnant of the old Jewish temple. There, as they stood before that ancient symbol, the hardened paratroopers wept openly. Chief Army Rabbi Schlomo Goren blew the shofar, and the announcement was made, "The temple mount is in our hands!"[12] For the first time in 2000 years, Jerusalem was in the hands of the Jews!

As the soldiers joined together to sing, "Jerusalem of Gold," the head of the Central Command, General Uzi Narkiss exclaimed with great emotion, "Never has there been such a thing... I am speechless! We all kneel before history!"[13]

Eight days later, the Jerusalem Post ran a picture of a mass gathering at the Wailing Wall with the headline, "200,000 at Western Wall in first pilgrimage since Dispersion."[14]

Those who understood Bible prophecy recognized that a major turning point in history had taken place. Jesus said when you see Jerusalem back in the hands of the Jews, you will know the times of the Gentiles are ending. It was time for God to call the Jewish people back to Messiah.

It is interesting that the modern Messianic Jewish movement traces its inception to 1967. At the start of 1967, there were no known Messianic Jewish congregations anywhere in the world, but that year Messianic Judaism was reborn. For the first time in a thousand years, living branches began to grow from the olive root. Those living branches are growing and prospering in spite of severe opposition. There are presently *hundreds* of Messianic synagogues all across America, and hundreds more in nations around the world. God is doing a miraculous work. It is the restoration of something that has been lost to the church for more than 1000 years.

As the living natural branches are beginning to grow, God is stirring the Gentile branches also. He is placing within Gentile believers a *longing* to be reconnected to their roots. Like a spiritual magnet, the living branches are drawing the church to reclaim its lost heritage. I believe we are living in the most exciting years in all of church history. The Messianic Church has returned!

As we move into this time of restoration, how can we begin to lay hold of this lost inheritance? That will be the subject of the second part of this book, "Recovering Our Lost Inheritance!"

Completed Gentiles

All over the world today, Christians are fasting and praying for a revival of the Church. Our hearts cry out for the brand of Christianity the apostles knew--a Christianity with the power to heal the sick, win the lost, and set the captives free.

Over the last few centuries, as believers have prayed and sought the Lord, God has graciously restored much that the early Church lost. Sadly, however, the Church today remains very different from the churches the apostles established.

I believe the Church will never be fully restored until we see Christianity in its Jewish context as the New Testament Church did. The attitudes, truths and practices inherent in the Jewish roots of Christianity are not foreign elements imported from a different religion. These things were given by God for our benefit. They were designed by God to give us a better understanding of our relationship with Him.

Anyone who has studied the Bible knows we cannot understand the New Covenant apart from the Old. When John the baptizer announced, "Behold the Lamb of God," he was speaking in the context of the Hebrew sacrificial system. We cannot understand John's statement, or indeed, the work of Jesus, apart from the Hebrew Bible. Likewise, we can't fully understand the events in Acts 2 without understanding the work of the Spirit described in Numbers 11 and Joel 2.

As we learn about the Jewish roots of our faith, we find passage after passage coming into clearer focus, with long-hidden significance revealed. Passages that made little sense suddenly spring to life. We gain a deeper understanding of our Covenant rights and of how God desires to relate to us.

Jews who come to know their Messiah are sometimes referred to as "completed" Jews. That's a good description. But I believe it's also true that when a Gentile Christian comes to know the Jewish roots of his faith, he becomes a "completed" Gentile!

Yeshua is not only the Savior of the world, but the Messiah of Israel--and our Messiah. By His grace, we have been made fellow citizens in that commonwealth. The more we know of that heritage, the richer and more complete we will be.

Introduction to Part Two:
Recovering Our Lost Inheritance

Over the last few years, I've been privileged to travel and minister across this nation and in many countries around the world. In the process of my travels, it's been interesting to see the changes that are occurring across the body of Christ.

The church today is in the midst of many changes. In recent years we've seen the rise of the Prophetic movement, the Apostolic movement, the Prayer movement, the House Church movement, and many, many others.

As I have gone to conferences and churches around the nation, there's one change that's been strangely overlooked by many in the church. It's a change that has taken place so subtly and so gradually that few have taken note of it, but it is a change that has massive implications for the future of the church. What I have witnessed in church after church is that, to an extent not seen since the fourth century, *the church has begun to embrace its Jewish roots.*

The change in the church's attitude toward Judaism is signaled by a host of seemingly insignificant elements. Taken individually, none of these elements is remarkable, yet taken together they form an unmistakable pattern. Let me share a few observations…

Jewish Worship. For the last twenty years, it has been obvious that Charismatic worship has tapped into our Jewish roots, often including Hebrew dances, like the Hora, and joyful choruses in a minor key. In recent years, it has not been uncommon to hear a church sing a chorus in Hebrew or address Jesus by His Hebrew name, *Yeshua*.

The Star of David. There was a time when you could tell a woman's religion by her jewelry. If she was Protestant, she wore a cross. If she was a Catholic, she wore a crucifix. If she was Jewish, she wore a Star of David. This is no longer true. In the last few years it has become common to see women who love Jesus choosing to identify themselves with the Star of David.

The *Tallit*. For most of church history, the idea of a Christian wearing a *tallit*, a Jewish prayer shawl, was unheard of! But lately, as I travel to various conferences, it's almost impossible to enter a prayer room without seeing someone wearing a *tallit*.

The *Shofar*. When I was growing up in church I didn't even know what a *shofar* was! (A *shofar* is a trumpet made from a ram's horn.) In recent years, however, it's become common to hear the blast of a *shofar* in church. Going to a charismatic church with no *shofar* is almost like going into a Catholic Church with no candles. It's become part of the standard church furniture.

The acceptance into the church of these external trappings of Judaism is incredibly widespread. A few years ago I visited the World Prayer Center in Colorado Springs, on the campus of New Life Church. As I walked into their Arsenal Bookstore, the first thing I saw was their display of *tallits* and shofars!

I recently read an account of some Christian Eskimos who went to an ancient high place on the tundra for prayer and intercession. The account described how these Eskimos stood on the open tundra, praised the Lord, prayed, …and then blew their *shofars*! Can you picture that?

Now, taken by themselves, these outward signs might be explained as simply an ecclesiastical fad. But there are deeper issues involved. As I have traveled and talked with pastors around the country, I have seen that these outward signs signal a more significant change in attitude. In fact, this embracing of our Jewish heritage has begun to affect church activities and structures in some significant ways.

"Jewish" Feasts. It's becoming increasingly common for Christian churches to add the celebration of the biblical feasts (Passover, Pentecost, and Tabernacles) to the traditional "Christian" ones. Our church first observed these feasts eight years ago and, at the time, I didn't know of another church that observed them. Since that time, I've been startled at the number of churches I've encountered that have begun these observances. As I've spoken with other pastors who have begun to observe the feasts I've found the typical response of their people has been… "This is WONDERFUL! Why haven't we done this before!"

The Jewish Sabbath. I find that more and more churches are encouraging their members to observe a Sabbath, something most American Christians have ignored for the last generation. I've talked to a surprising number of Christians who, knowingly or unknowingly, are following the pattern of the early church in observing Saturday as a day of rest (*Sabbath*), and Sunday as a day of worship.

Taking all of this together, I believe the Spirit of God is doing something! I've even tried to find a name for it. I thought about calling it the *Judification* of the church, ...but decided that wouldn't do. I jokingly suggested the re*jew*vination of the church... but my wife groaned when I said that!

It's not the *Judaizing* of the church because Judaizing was a heresy. The Judaizers taught that a Gentile had to convert and become a Jew to be saved. That's NOT what is happening today.

What is happening today is that the Spirit of God is planting a hunger in His church for the *recovery* of a lost inheritance. It is a desire on the part of the branches to be *reconnected* to their severed roots. I believe the result will be the *restoration* of the church to its true New Testament identity. It's not terribly important *what* we call it, but we need to see that something *is* happening.

Significantly, it's not happening through legalism or compulsion. For generations, there have been legalistic groups advocating seventh day worship and the observance of the feasts, but this is *different*. This is a spontaneous movement across denominational and geographical boundaries. There is no organization behind it. It is simply the Spirit of God stirring the hearts of His people. God is placing in the heart of His church a *longing* for the restoration of something that is very *old* and very *God*.

I believe God is calling His bride to reclaim her lost inheritance. God is moving His church to reconnect with her Jewish roots and the result, I believe, will be *revival*.

What Do We Do Now?

When the first half of this book was completed, I distributed copies to a number of friends to see their response. I found that nearly every one who read it had two responses.

The first response usually went something like this: "This is incredible! Why haven't we been told these things?" As pastors and church leaders read this book, their eyes were opened to things they had never imagined! They saw for the first time why the church does not walk in the power God intended it to have!

But the second response was usually this: "What do we do now?" It is important to see what we've lost, but how do we go about recovering that lost inheritance?

The Starting Point of Restoration

If you have read this far you already HAVE begun the process of restoration. The first step in restoration is to recognize that you have lost something.

In chapter four we looked at some of things the church has lost. Allow God to plant a hunger in your heart for their restoration!

Ask God to RESTORE the AWE of knowing Him! Don't be satisfied with an "intellectualized" Christianity that tries to figure out God! Let the highest goal of your life be to praise Him, serve Him, and love Him!

Ask God to RESTORE the Hebraic LOVE for His Word! The deep things of God are not just for your pastor! Learn to study the Bible. Saturate your mind with the Word! Discover the joy that comes from filling your mind with the thoughts of God!

Let God RESTORE your HOME as the center of your spiritual life! A good church can be a wonderful resource center to assist you as you walk with God! But the primary focus of a life with God is the home. Let God make your home a *miqdash meyat*, a little sanctuary! Make it a place of worship and of study. Invite friends over to eat, fellowship, worship and share testimonies!

Let God RESTORE a biblical attitude toward LIFE! Learn to enjoy God and feast in His Presence. Serve Him with joy and gladness! Let your life overflow with thanksgiving!

Let God graft you into the root, to enjoy its rich, life-giving sap! Let Him restore you to Christianity as He intended it!

As you seek restoration, here's a warning: **Don't be sidetracked into legalism!** Restoration does not come through legalism. Regaining our Jewish roots does not mean trying to live under the Old Covenant. It means experiencing the NEW covenant as the apostles knew it! It's about restoring the joy of life in God's Presence!

Here's another warning: **Don't be satisfied with the externals!** The external trappings of Judaism can be very meaningful. There is great spiritual significance in the sound of the *shofar*. It can be a very holy thing to put on a *tallit*. But just adopting these outward signs does not mean our inheritance is restored!   To dance a ring dance and sing songs in a minor key, while enjoyable, will not restore the power the Church has lost! *True restoration goes far beyond these outward signs!*

In the second part of this book we will examine some foundational issues for true restoration.   Each of the following chapters presents an element that was vital in the life of the early church, but which was lost when the church embraced paganism. These are all aspects of the "rich sap" of the olive root. I believe the truths presented in these chapters form a starting point for the restoration of the Messianic Church!

Chapter Six
The Teaching of God
A NEW Look at the OLD Testament!

*"All Scripture is inspired by God and profitable for
teaching, for reproof, for correction, for training in
righteousness; so that the man of God may be thoroughly
equipped for every good work." – II Tim 3:16-17*

The first step toward regaining our inheritance is to receive the incredible revelation God gave us through the Jewish people. When God chose the Jews, He set them apart from all other peoples by giving them a ***revelation*** of Himself. That revelation is found in the *TORAH* (which, in Hebrew means, "The Teaching of God").

The word *"Torah"* is often used to describe the first five books of the Old Testament. These books were given to set the stage for God's dealings with mankind. All of the wisdom God imparted to the Jewish people has its foundation in the *Torah*. In a broader sense, all of Scripture is the *teaching of God*. It's *all* necessary if we want to walk with Him and experience His blessings!

God gave us His *Torah* to teach us *WHO* He is and *HOW* He wants to relate to us. Understanding *Torah* is foundational to life with God! Yet most Christians only use a small fraction of the Bible God gave them. The rest has been stolen by our enemy!

The Attacks of the Enemy

Let me show you something about the way our enemy works. Satan's goal has always been to oppress God's people and hinder God's purposes in the earth. To do this, he uses two main tactics. He *lies* to us, and he *steals* from us (John 8:44, 10:10). The church today is weakened because we have *believed* the devil's lie, and *allowed him to steal* our resources.

For example, Satan has told the church, "Spiritual gifts have ceased!" By believing this lie, much of the church has cut themselves off from the tools God gave us to accomplish our mission. The result is a church that is unable to move in the power of the New Testament!

Satan's lies have weakened the church in many ways. Satan has told us: "Women can't minister" ...so half of the church sits down and stops ministering! Satan then tells the men: "Christianity is not manly" ...so the other half of the church stays home! Satan whispers: "Healing is not for today!" ...so the church is often too sick and weak to fulfill its call!

One of Satan's most effective attacks has been to steal away the Word of God (Mark 4:15)! Satan has whispered a lie to us, persuading Christians to IGNORE most of their Bible!

How Satan Steals Away the Word

One of first things most new Christians learn is that the Bible is divided into two parts, the OLD Testament and the NEW Testament:

The OLD TESTAMENT, also called the Hebrew Bible or *Tanach*, is the three-fourths of the Bible originally written in Hebrew. It describes how God worked to prepare the earth for the coming of Jesus.

The NEW TESTAMENT is the one-fourth of the Bible originally written in Greek. It describes the coming of Jesus and its results.

The two sections of our Bible are usually explained to new Christians in words like this:

"The Old Testament is written to Jews. The New Testament is to Christians."

"The Old Testament has some good Sunday school stories, but most of it is hard to understand and you shouldn't spend much time reading it because it's not for us."

The attitude communicated is that there is something inferior, substandard, or unchristian about the Old Testament! *That is the lie of the enemy!*

Satan has used that lie to prevent the church from understanding many things. When we come to a subject like the Sabbath or the biblical feasts, rather than looking into the Word to see what God has said, we dismiss the entire subject by saying: "That's OLD Testament!"

The assumption of many Christians is, "If it's Old Testament, it's wrong, out of date, and harmful!"

Many have been told something like this: "If you are really a Christian, you would never want to do something that's from the Old Testament!" Many are convinced that seriously looking into the Old Testament is somehow being disloyal to Jesus!

If that's our attitude toward the Old Testament, we need to see that we are not just rejecting the Old Testament; we are also rejecting the New Testament!

To hold a negative view of the Old Testament is to REJECT New Testament teaching, because the New Testament *teaches* us to HIGHLY VALUE the Old Testament!

A few years ago I was teaching a series through the book of Nehemiah, and a woman in our church came to me with great concern. She said, "I don't understand why we are studying the Old Testament! I thought we were a New Testament church!"

My answer was this... "We ARE a New Testament church... but the BIBLE of the New Testament church was the OLD Testament!"

Many Christians don't realize that the early church used the Old Testament as its Bible!

Suppose you were twenty-five years old on the day of Pentecost and "got saved" when Peter spoke! You were literally in the "early church" from DAY ONE! If, as a member of that early "New Testament church," you listened to the apostles' teaching and preaching every day of your life, you would be almost sixty years old before you heard your FIRST sermon from the New Testament!

For the church's first thirty years, every sermon was from Old Testament! They did pretty well with a Bible many Christians today reject!

I believe we need to repent for accepting the devil's slander against three-fourths of our Bible! It's a "New Testament" thing to study the Old Testament!

Many Christians have allowed the devil to steal away *three-fourths* of their Bible! They don't read it, teach it, or know it! IT'S BEEN STOLEN FROM THEM!

God put a SWORD in our hands... But if you cut off three fourths of a sword, all you have is a dagger! God wants you to have a full sword! A complete Bible!

Taking back what Satan has stolen!

In this chapter we want to begin to take back what the enemy has stolen. The first step in restoration is to get a "New Testament" view of the OLD Testament!

We need to look at the Old Testament the way Jesus and the apostles did! They did not view the Old Testament as inferior. They embraced it as the Word of God! Let's look at some examples of New Testament teaching about the Old Testament:

1. What the New Testament CALLED the Old Testament

Many Christians will be surprised to discover that the New Testament NEVER calls the Old Testament the *OLD* Testament! That's not a biblical term for the Hebrew Bible.

The New Testament usually just calls the Old Testament *Scripture!* Jesus and the Apostles did not hesitate to identify the Old Testament as the WORD OF GOD.

Historically, the first person to describe the Hebrew Bible as the "Old Testament" was Bishop Melito of Sardis, who wrote around AD 180![1]

The first record we have of someone calling the Greek Bible the "New" Testament is found in the writings of Irenaeus who wrote around AD 190! [2]

So our distinction between the OLD Testament and the NEW didn't take place until 150 years after Pentecost! That's at least 120 years after most of the New Testament was written! Until that time it was all just SCRIPTURE!

2. Jesus' Attitude toward the Old Testament

When we read the gospels, we discover that Jesus *loved* the Old Testament! He embraced it as God's Word and continually quoted from it!

When Satan tempted Jesus in the wilderness, Jesus resisted the devil each time by quoting from the book of Deuteronomy. (If your ability to resist the devil depended on your ability to quote from Deuteronomy, how would you do?)

In John 10:35, Jesus has this to say about the Old Testament: "the SCRIPTURE cannot be broken."

In Matt 5:18, Jesus described the *lasting value* of the Old Testament Scriptures in these words: "until heaven and earth pass away, not the smallest letter or stroke shall pass away from the Torah."

Now, some will say, "But the Old Testament is hard to understand!" It's true that there are some things in the Old Testament that seem hard to understand, but that's true of BOTH testaments!

I Corinthians tells us that spiritual truth can be divided into two categories: *meat* and *milk*. Spiritual "milk" is easily digested truth. We read it and easily understand it. We swallow it quickly and it's easy to digest. It provides nourishment for baby Christians.

Spiritual "meat," however, is harder to digest! We need to take time to chew on it! It takes time and effort and study to discover its meaning, but when we do, we find it is highly nourishing!

Both testaments contain MILK to nourish young believers! But both also provide enough MEAT to keep a mature Christian studying for a lifetime!

Most people think the Gospel of John is easy to understand. It's usually the first thing we tell new Christians to read! Yet John's gospel contains things that are so profound and deep, I have studied for years, and haven't begun to grasp them! The fact that we are not mature enough in the Lord to understand all of the Word is not a reason to reject it!

3. Paul and the Old Testament

Here's what the Apostle Paul said about the Old Testament: "Now these things (the Old Testament accounts) *happened to them* as an example, and were *written for OUR instruction*, upon whom the ends of the ages have come" (I Cor 10:11).

Look at that verse carefully! Who does Paul say the Old Testament is written for? He says the Old Testament was written for OUR benefit! Don't accept the lie that the Old Testament was just for Jews!

In II Cor 3:16-18, Paul describes what it's like when a Christian studies the Old Testament: "with unveiled face [we are] beholding *as in a mirror* the glory of the Lord!"

Paul says studying the Old Testament is like viewing the glory of God in a mirror! The Old Testament is a *reflection* of God's glory! He goes on to say that through these Scriptures, we are transformed from glory to glory!

II Tim 3:14-17 describes the value of the Old Testament this way: "*All* Scripture is inspired by God and is profitable for teaching, rebuking, correcting and training in righteousness, so that the man of God may be thoroughly equipped for every good work."

That's the value of the Hebrew Bible! If you want to be *equipped* to minister... if you want to be *taught*, *corrected*, and *trained* to walk in righteousness... you need the Old Testament as well as the NEW!

The Importance of the Old Testament

Here are several reasons why the Old Testament is important:

1. You can't UNDERSTAND New Testament without the Old! If you reject the Old Testament you won't be able to understand what the New Testament is saying! That's because the New Testament is *built* on the Old! It is *filled* with references from the Old!

When John the Baptist saw Jesus coming, he cried out, "Behold the lamb of God." That is one of the most significant statements in the New Testament. It identifies WHO Jesus is and WHAT He came to do! It points back to the feast of Passover, the sacrificial system, and the prophecies of Messiah. But if you don't know the Old Testament you can't appreciate what John is saying!

Trying to understand the Bible without studying the Old Testament is like reading the last fourth of a good novel! You may be reading some of the best parts of the book, but there will be a great deal you don't understand!

2. The New Testament INSTRUCTS US to learn the Old! If we don't study the Old Testament, we are *disobeying* the New Testament! Rom 15:4 exhorts us, "What was written in earlier times [the Old Testament] was written *for our instruction*."

God wants Christians to know the Old Testament!

3. There are RICH TREASURES waiting to be revealed in the Old Testament. Part of the reason much of the church lives in spiritual poverty is that, for much of its history, we have neglected the Old Testament! In the last 50 years, however, God has moved His church to begin studying that neglected part of the Bible. Out of that study has come incredible teachings that have changed the face of the church!

The Bible's primary teaching about praise and worship, the tabernacle of David, intercession, holiness, and many other things are found *primarily* in the Old Testament. If we refuse to read it, we will live in ignorance of many things.

I believe there are still many more treasures waiting to be revealed there! The *Torah IS* the "teaching of God." It is foundational if we want to understand the things of God. Until we think we understand everything there is to know about God, we still NEED to study the Old Testament!

4. The Old Testament is full of God's PROMISES! There are thousands of promises given in the Old Testament. In II Corinthians chapter one, Paul tells us that all of these promises are "YES" (affirmative) for us who are in Jesus! By reading the Old Testament, we discover the blessings God wants for us. As we read God's promises, faith is awakened in our hearts!

5. In the Old Testament, the church is REDISCOVERING its lost inheritance! The great truths of the Old Testament include the biblical teaching on covenant, on Sabbath, and on the celebration of God's appointed times! These are blessings God gave, but the enemy has stolen away! Through the study of the Old Testament, we are RECLAIMING these stolen blessings!

Relating to the Old Testament

The Old Testament Scriptures are a precious gift from God! *But how do we relate to them?*

The New Covenant teaches us that we are not *under* the law of the Old. Gentile Christians are not required to follow Jewish rituals to be saved! But the Old Testament is far MORE than a book of rituals and commandments! The Old Testament is a window into the heart of God:

- *The Torah* - (the first five books) gives us foundational teaching about Who God is and what He requires.
- *The Historical books* – give us many examples of Godly individuals to learn from!
- *The book of Psalms* – is the definitive book in the Bible on praise and worship.

- ***The book of Proverbs*** – teaches us God's wisdom.
- ***The Prophets*** – contain some of the greatest teaching on God ever given. (The book of Isaiah, for example, has often been called the "gospel" of Isaiah. It's teaching about the life and ministry of Jesus is just as clear as any of the four New Testament gospels!)

To reject the Old Testament is to live in self-imposed poverty! Neglecting it will cause us to miss out on many of the blessings God intended us to enjoy!

In Acts 20:27 Paul tells the Ephesian elders that his goal was to communicate: "The Whole Counsel of God!" That should be our goal also. We need the WHOLE Bible!

We need the *NEW* Testament. We need the *OLD* Testament. It's ALL one Book! It's ALL God's Word! It's ALL profitable… and it's ALL for us!

STEPS TO RESTORATION!

I would encourage you, if you have not done so, to begin to read the Old Testament Scriptures! Begin with the narrative sections. These passages tell the *story* of God's dealings with Israel. Your first time through the Old Testament, don't worry if you don't understand everything. There is much deep wisdom here, and you won't be able to grasp it all the first time through. If you get to a long section of genealogies or laws that you don't understand, feel free to skip ahead to where the story resumes. As you gain more understanding, you will want to come back to these sections and study them, but at first, just get the overview!

Another good place to start reading is in the books of Psalms and Proverbs. The book of Psalms is the central, and the longest, book of the Bible. It's designed to show you how to respond to God in prayer and praise in any circumstance of life. The Psalms are foundational for anyone who wants to walk with God. The book of Proverbs was written to instill wisdom that will enable us to prosper in life.

As you study the Old Testament Scriptures, ask God to give you a clearer picture of what He is like, and what it means to walk as one of His people!

Chapter Seven
Entering God's Rest
The Principle of the Sabbath

*"On the seventh day God ended His work... and He rested on
the seventh day from all His work which He had done. Then God
blessed the seventh day and made it holy, because in it He
rested from all His work." - Genesis 2:2-3*

Throughout the Bible, God placed great emphasis on establishing a "cycle of life" for His people. God desires to link us into cycles of blessing designed to free us from Satan's oppression and bring us into an ever-deepening experience of His goodness. There are at least two kinds of cycles described in the Bible. They are a *yearly* cycle of "feasts" and a *weekly* cycle of work and rest: the cycle of **Sabbath** (Hebrew: *Shabbat)*.

We can't really begin the process of restoration without understanding the weekly *Shabbat* cycle. In fact, the celebration of *Shabbat* is perhaps the most important thing any individual can do to begin to experience the restoration of our lost inheritance.

The Cycle of *Shabbat*

One of the primary foundation stones of Judaism has always been the observance of a weekly Sabbath, or *Shabbat*. The Jews recognize that *Shabbat* was one of God's first commands to mankind! Shabbat was instituted – not at Mount Sinai – but at the creation of the universe (Genesis 2:1-3)! Interestingly, even though God's instruction concerning *Shabbat* is widely *ignored* and *misunderstood* by Christians, it is a blessing ***desperately needed*** by all of us in our modern world!

People today are probably the *busiest* people the world has ever known. Even though the twentieth century brought the invention of incredible laborsaving devices, the result has not been a life of leisure. In fact, the pace of life has escalated greatly.

Wayne Muller describes our modern lifestyle this way: "The more our life speeds up, the more we feel weary, overwhelmed and lost. Despite our good hearts and equally good intentions, our life and work rarely feel light, pleasant or healing. Instead, as it all piles endlessly upon itself, the whole experience of being alive begins to melt into one enormous obligation... To be unavailable to our friends and family, to be unable to find time for the sunset (or even to know that the sun has set at all), to whiz through our obligations without time for a single mindful breath—this has become the model of a successful life."[1]

Our laborsaving devices cannot produce a life of rest because work always expands to fill time available. The key to rest is not found in laborsaving devices. The key to rest is found in the Word of God. True rest begins with God's gift of Sabbath.

Understanding the Sabbath

For many Christians, the word Sabbath has a negative connotation. We think of a Sabbath Day as something oppressive, a legalistic burden, a day lived under rigid rules. That's the kind of Sabbath the Pharisees promoted, and Jesus had a lot to say *against* that kind of Sabbath.

The true picture of Sabbath is a day of celebration, a day to turn the burdens of life over to God and enjoy His goodness. God intended Sabbath to be a blessing, not a burden. In Mark 2:27, Jesus said, "The Sabbath was made for man, not man for the Sabbath."

God gave Sabbath as a *blessing,* as a *GIFT*. In Ezekiel 20:12, God says, "I *gave* them my Sabbaths..."

Sabbath was one of the first expressions of God's will in the universe. On the seventh day of creation, long before the Law of Moses was given, the Creator "took a day off" from His work and rested. He didn't rest because he was tired. He rested because He wanted to *establish* the Sabbath and *set it apart* as holy. He wanted the principle of Sabbath woven into the fabric of the universe.

Our problem is that mankind has generally refused to receive God's gift of Sabbath. We have been too fearful, worried, and greedy to rest. We have ignored God's will and chosen to work seven days a week, trying to "get ahead." So when God called Moses to the top of Mount Sinai, He gave a *law* to protect the Sabbath.

The way God chose to protect *Shabbat* is very significant: When God gave the "Law of the Sabbath," He didn't give it as a *civil law* for the nation Israel. It was not one of the *ceremonial laws* governing Jewish religious ritual. It was given as part of God's *MORAL LAW* for mankind. God made the observance of Sabbath one of the Ten Commandments. That means it is just as much a violation of God's moral law to work seven days a week as it is to kill, steal, or commit adultery.

By the time of Jesus, however, the law of Sabbath had been perverted. The Pharisees turned this gracious gift of God into a legalistic burden. They kept watch over the day, condemning anyone who violated their rigid rules of prohibited activities.

Much of the New Testament teaching on Sabbath was designed to restore Sabbath to God's original intention. Colossians 2:16 sums up New Testament teaching on the Sabbath when it says, "Do not let anyone judge you...in regard to a Sabbath day." Some have read that verse and assumed it means Sabbath is not for today; that we should not observe Sabbath. But that's not what the verse says.

Colossians 2:16 doesn't say, "Don't observe the Sabbath." It says "Don't *judge each other* on how you observe the Sabbath." This verse is prohibiting a *pharisaical* observance of the Sabbath. It is returning the Sabbath to God's original intention: to be received as a gracious gift of God.

The evidence is clear that the early church regularly observed Sabbath. Origin (185-254) wrote, "After the festival of the crucifixion [Passover] is put the festival of the Sabbath, and it is fitting for whoever is righteous among the saints to keep also the festival of the Sabbath. There remains therefore a keeping of the Sabbath for the people of God" (Heb. 4:9).[2]

The *Constitutions of the Holy Apostles*, written in the 3rd or 4th centuries, states, "You shall observe the Sabbath, because of Him who ceased from His work of creation."[3]

Sabbath and "Church Day"

Some people get very uncomfortable when we start talking about Sabbath. They think if they accept the idea of Sabbath they will have to leave their church and go to one that meets on Saturday. That's a false understanding of Sabbath.

We need to see that Sabbath has *nothing to do* with what day you go to church. The early Christians met for worship *daily*, but the seventh day was still their Sabbath.

Many Christians today go to church on Wednesday night. That does not mean they are celebrating a *Wednesday Sabbath.*

Observing the Sabbath has *nothing to do* with when you go to church. We are free to worship *any* day. It's good to worship God *every* day. The Sabbath was not primarily a day of public worship, but a day of rest and enjoyment.

Which Day is Sabbath?

On what day of the week should we observe our Sabbath? Through much of church history, most of the church has observed Sunday as a Sabbath. If you've ever watched the movie "Chariots of Fire," you've seen a good picture of how the church in an earlier generation honored Sunday as a Sabbath.

Other Christians place great importance on observing Sabbath on Saturday. We know that biblically, *Shabbat* was observed from sundown Friday through sundown Saturday. That's a good pattern to follow, but I don't think choosing the "right" day of the week is as important as many suppose.

God's instruction is simply, "work for six days, then rest on the seventh." If you begin your six days of work on Monday, then your seventh day is Sunday. (Most of us think of Sunday as part of the "weekEND," and start our new week on Monday. It's interesting that this custom has become so much a part of our culture that most European calendars start the week on Monday, and list Sunday as the seventh day.)

I don't think the day is nearly as important as the fact that you *do* take a Sabbath day. (Here's an interesting observation… many Jewish rabbis take THEIR day of rest on Sunday, while most Christian pastors take their day of rest on either Saturday or Monday.)

The real problem is that *most* of the church today chooses not to observe any Sabbath at all.

In twenty-first century America, we have rejected the biblical teaching on Sabbath for the values of our contemporary culture. I recently heard a conference speaker address an audience on the need to increase our commitment to Christ. To drive home his point he shared that he recently rebuked the assistant ministers in the church he pastors. These assistant pastors wanted to take a day off every week, which this speaker took as a sign of laziness. His comment was that if the world works *seven days a week* to achieve their goals, shouldn't we be as committed as they are?

I was deeply grieved when I heard his statement. What this prominent Christian leader was saying, in effect, was "Because the world disregards the commandments of God to achieve their goals, shouldn't we do the same?" This, unfortunately, is a common attitude in the church today. The result is, while we may *go to church* on Sunday, we do not seriously advocate a *Sabbath* on *any* day of the week. We have become a church that only teaches *nine* of the Ten Commandments.

Personal Testimony

Several years ago the Lord convicted me to begin observing a weekly Sabbath. He impressed me to follow the biblical pattern, observing Sabbath from sundown Friday till sundown Saturday.

When the Lord first convicted me of this, I resisted. I said, "Lord. I can't do that." As a pastor, Saturday was often my busiest day of the week. Weekdays at our church office are so filled with appointments and administrative duties that Saturday was often the only day I had to prepare for my Sunday message.

I said, "Lord. I'm too busy. I don't have time to take a day of rest." I thought, with horror, of having to stand up on Sunday morning with no message to give.

But the Lord answered, "To say you are too busy to rest on the Sabbath is like saying you are too poor to tithe. It means you have not yet learned My ability to provide. If I tell you to rest, you CAN rest."

So I chose to cast my concerns on Him and submit to His direction. I began to welcome Sabbath as a wonderful gift of God. There have been many times that Friday evening comes and my work is not done, and I have to place it, by faith, in His hands. But He has never failed to provide what I need.

And I have found in His Sabbath one of the greatest joys of life. Often my wife and I greet each other when we wake on Friday mornings with the joyful exclamation, "Sabbath starts today." It is something we look forward to all through the week. To think that it was God's will to ordain one day a week for Sabbath has given me a whole new level of appreciation for His goodness.

Why Should We Observe a Sabbath?

I would like to give seven reasons why it's important to observe Sabbath. Sabbath is important because:

1. **Sabbath *honors God* as creator.** Sabbath observance is a tangible way of acknowledging God's greatness as Creator of the universe. As God created the universe, then rested; so we celebrate His work of creation by entering into His rest.

2. **Sabbath is a celebration of God's *provision*.** The book of Hebrews teaches that Sabbath is also a picture of Israel coming out of the wilderness into the *bountiful provision* of the promised land. Sabbath is a celebration of God's blessing. The traditional Sabbath-meal prayer over the bread expresses *wonder* that God even brings forth bread for us from the earth!

3. **Sabbath reminds us of God's *goodness*.** One of the most difficult truths for many Christians to accept is the GOODNESS of God. Many believe God is righteous and powerful, but have a hard time trusting in His goodness. Some Christians think of God as a harsh taskmaster who places excessive burdens on His people. Sabbath is an acknowledgement that God wants His people to experience and enjoy His goodness.

4. **Sabbath builds our *faith*.** It teaches us to trust that *God will provide* even when I rest. If God could create the universe in six days, He is able to handle the concerns of my life one day a week! Learning to observe Sabbath is like learning to tithe. It requires that we learn to depend on God's care and provision in a very tangible way. The man who says, "I'm too busy to rest," is like the one who says, "I'm too poor to tithe." He doesn't understand the goodness and power of God.

5. **Sabbath is a picture of *salvation*.** As we cease our daily labor and rest in His goodness, it reminds us of the basis of our salvation. Salvation is not received on the basis of our own works, but by His grace. Salvation comes when we are willing, by faith, to *rest* from our own works and receive His blessings as a gift.

6. Sabbath is a picture of *heaven*. It is a God-given foretaste of eternity, an *anticipation* of that day when we rest from our works and enjoy Him forever.

7. Sabbath releases God's *blessing*. When done as a voluntary act of obedience, Sabbath *releases* God's blessing. A few months ago I was praying for a greater release of God's blessing in our church, and God told me something very significant. He said, "If you are not experiencing what the Bible promises, it's because you are not doing what the Bible commands." Choosing to respond in obedience to God's revealed will releases blessing.

The Bible *promises* great blessing for those who will receive His gift of Sabbath. Notice the promise given in these verses:
Isaiah 58:13-14 tells us, "If you keep your feet from breaking the Sabbath and from doing as you please on my holy day, if you call the Sabbath a delight and the LORD's holy day honorable, and if you honor it by not going your own way and not doing as you please or speaking idle words, *then you will find your joy in the LORD, and I will cause you to ride on the heights of the land and to feast on the inheritance of your father Jacob*" (NIV).
Isaiah 56:6-7 says, "Foreigners who bind themselves to the LORD to serve Him, to love the name of the LORD, and to worship Him, all who keep the Sabbath without desecrating it and who hold fast to My covenant — these *I will bring to My holy mountain and give them joy* in My house of prayer" (NIV).
Interestingly, this last promise is not addressed to Jews, but is specifically given to *Gentile* believers. That's most of *us*.

What do you do on a Sabbath?

The Jews picture Sabbath as a "sanctuary in time." A time *set apart* from the rest of the week to enjoy God and His blessings.
God instructs us to *sanctify*, or set apart, the Sabbath day as holy. To *sanctify* something involves setting markers around it to distinguish it from the ordinary. When God told Moses that Sinai was His holy mountain, He instructed Moses to set markers around the mountain so no one would stray onto it accidentally.
So the first step in observing Sabbath is to establish a marker to clearly distinguish when Sabbath has begun.

From their earliest history, the Jews have sanctified Sabbath with a special family worship celebration at sundown on Friday evening.

This celebration begins with the wife offering a special prayer to welcome the gift of Sabbath, and the lighting of the Sabbath candles. The husband then offers prayer over the bread and wine, initiating the Sabbath meal. It is a special time when the father prays a blessing over his wife, and the parents pray blessings over their children. It is a time to focus on the Lord and His goodness, and to begin twenty-four hours of joy and relaxation as a family.

This special celebration is not commanded in Scripture. We can choose to sanctify Sabbath in some other way, but the traditional Sabbath meal is an example that has proven helpful to many. History tells us that the early church followed this pattern for several centuries.

Sabbath Activities.

One question I am often asked is, "What do you do on a Sabbath?"

There is no legalistic list. Leviticus 23:24-26 tells us to enjoy Sabbath-rest by avoiding our *regular* or *customary* work [NKJV and NIV]. Sabbath is a day to avoid doing what you normally do to earn your living. It means you are freed from your normal responsibilities and given time to fellowship with God and enjoy His goodness!

It's interesting that *fasting* was not practiced on Sabbath. Sabbath was NOT a day to be mournful or religious. It was a day for *feasting*. The primary purpose of the Sabbath is to *enjoy* God and His blessings. Whatever you do that promotes that goal is permissible.

I suspect that "proper Sabbath activity" varies from person to person. If you are a farmer, you wouldn't want to spend Sabbath working in your garden. But if you spend the rest of the week chained to a computer, a few hours of gardening on a Saturday morning might be a wonderful way to rest and enjoy the Lord.

Wayne Mueller described Sabbath activity as, "Time consecrated to enjoy and celebrate what is beautiful and good—time to light candles, sing songs, worship, tell stories, bless our children and loved ones, give thanks, share meals, nap, walk, and even make love. It is a time to be nourished and refreshed as we let our work, our chores and our important projects lie fallow, trusting that there are larger forces at work taking care of the world when we are at rest."[4]

As your heart is filled with praise and thanksgiving, don't neglect spending time with God! Have a relaxed time in the Word. Spend time in prayer and sing songs of praise. Enjoy God's Presence and thank Him for all of His blessings!

If you aren't sure if an activity is appropriate for Sabbath, ask Jesus. He is the Lord of the Sabbath (Mk 2:28).

Missing a Sabbath

What happens if you miss a Sabbath? Some weekends I might be ministering at a conference and don't have the option of rest. What do I do if a week comes when I cannot celebrate the Sabbath?

That's when I appreciate the grace of God. I remember that Sabbath is not a legalistic burden. When I miss Sabbath, I'm not filled with guilt. I'm filled with sorrow and disappointment. I have missed a blessing.

Let me say that again… **Sabbath is not a burden to bear, it is a blessing we are privileged to receive!** Sabbath was made for man, not man for the Sabbath.

But if you celebrate Sabbath as God intended, it will not be something you *have* to do—it is something you *want* to do. Real Sabbath observance is addictive.

God wants to make our walk with Him so enjoyable and so pleasurable that the world looks on with envy. For too long we have allowed the actions of a pagan Roman emperor to cheat us of God's blessing. We are living in the day of restoration. Allow God to restore *your* lost inheritance. *Receive God's GIFT of Sabbath.*

STEPS TO RESTORATION!

Sabbath should not be a burden, but a blessing! It is a day to enjoy God, freed as much as possible from daily worry and responsibilities.

To fully enjoy Shabbat, it's good to take time to prepare beforehand! Try to clear your schedule of responsibilities during your time of *Shabbat*. Stock up on your favorite foods. Get together with close friends and family and plan enjoyable activities. Do those things that will fill your heart with thanksgiving and praise!

If you are able to hold Shabbat from sundown Friday to sundown Saturday, I believe you will find it is a wonderful pattern. Begin with a Sabbath celebration on Friday night over your evening meal. Traditional Jewish *Shabbat* meals are often very formal affairs around the dining room table. At our home, we prefer to eat our favorite "finger foods," sitting around the coffee table in the living room! (We often watch a DVD of a good movie as part of the celebration.) The key is: Do whatever will fill your heart with thankfulness to God!

At the start of the meal, it's traditional to have the "mother of the house" light two candles and pray, welcoming God's gift of *Shabbat*. It doesn't have to be a formal, written prayer. Just a simple prayer expressing your thankfulness that God loves you enough to give you a time to rest and enjoy Him!

If you would like a "set prayer" to pray at the lighting of the candles, I would suggest the prayer the early Messianic Church probably used. Called the **Phos Hilaron** (Joyful Light), it is clearly Messianic in origin, and probably dates back to the first-century church in Jerusalem. It is considered to be the earliest surviving Christian hymn:

> Blessed are you, Messiah *Yeshua*, our joyful light,
> Pure brightness of the eternal Father!
> As we come to the setting of the sun and light the evening lamps,
> We give thanks and praise to the Father and to the Son and to the Holy Spirit of God.
> O Son of God, O giver of life,
> Worthy are You at all times to be praised with joyful voices!
> May you be glorified through all creation! [5]

In a traditional Jewish Shabbat, the father then prays a blessing over the wine and bread, acknowledging that all of our blessings come from Him. If you wish to do this, feel free to use these traditional prayers, or just pray from your heart:

Blessing over the Wine: "Blessed are You,
O Lord our God, King of the Universe!
Who creates the fruit of the vine!"

Blessing over the Bread: "Blessed are You,
O Lord our God, King of the Universe!
Who brings forth bread from the earth!"

The bread should be something special, soft and delicious. If you have never tried traditional Jewish *Challah* bread, you may want to check at a local bakery to see if it's available. It's not a sliced bread. You just tear off a piece and eat it. (At our house, we like to dip it in olive oil flavored with salt and "dipping oil" spices.) Biblically, the grain, new wine, and oil symbolize the fullness of God's blessing!

Another traditional part of Shabbat is for the father and mother to pray blessings over each child. If you do this, don't let it be a long, boring ritual. Let it be an expression of your love for your children, and an impartation of faith for their future.

The father may also pray a blessing over his wife, praising her in the presence of her children. On occasion, the father may want to read the section on the virtuous woman (Proverbs 31) over his wife.

Your goal should be to make Friday night the most enjoyable time of the week, and a time to thank God for His blessings. In a traditional Jewish home, this is the heart of worship.

Then on Saturday, Shabbat continues. It's a day to rest, read, go to the park, the beach, or a museum. The precise activities depend a lot on the ages of your children (if any) and the things your family enjoys.

In celebrating Shabbat, your focus should not be on what to *avoid*, but what you can *do* to experience God's goodness with a joyful, thankful heart!

Shabbat is a time chosen by God to meet with you each week! He wants it to be a time of great blessing, when you learn to enjoy His goodness. A typical Jewish greeting on Shabbat is, *"Shabbat Shalom!"* This greeting expresses the wish that you find complete wholeness, peace, joy, and restoration as you enjoy God's goodness on Shabbat! **May God also bless YOU with the fullness of His blessing as you celebrate Shabbat!**

Shabbat Shalom!

Chapter Eight
God's Cycle of Life
Celebrating the Biblical Feasts

"Three times a year you are to celebrate a feast to Me...
*Celebrate the **Feast of Unleavened Bread** (Passover),*
*Celebrate the **Feast of Harvest** (Pentecost), and celebrate the*
***Feast of Ingathering** (Tabernacles). Three times a year...*
appear before the sovereign Lord." - Ex 23:14-17

In the fall of 2004, I sat at my computer reading the news of a monster hurricane off the coast of Florida. The screen was filled with a satellite image of this storm: a swirling circle of destruction!

When I finished the weather report, I switched to NASA's ***"Astronomy Picture of the Day"*** website. I usually check this site daily, because it often features majestic pictures of the universe taken by the Hubble Space Telescope.

On this day, as the new picture filled the screen, I was amazed! The new image was ***almost identical*** to the picture of the hurricane! Instead of a swirling cycle of wind, however, this picture revealed a beautiful disk of stars: a spiral galaxy.

These pictures looked very similar, but there was such a stunning contrast! One was a cycle of violent storms bringing terrible destruction, while the other was a spiral of billions of stars displaying the beauty of creation!

As I switched back and forth between these pictures, God began to speak to me about *cycles.* I like to define a cycle this way:

A cycle is something that goes around
and moves you to a destination.

The universe is filled with cycles. Some are used by the enemy to bring us into a place of loss and destruction. Some cycles are given by God to bring us into an increase of His blessing. *We need to understand both kinds of cycles!*

Cycles of Destruction
Some cycles are cycles of *destruction.* There are many kinds

of destructive cycles in the world. In nature there are hurricanes. They go around and around and lead to devastation. Other cycles of destruction include cycles of addiction, poverty, unbelief, and defeat. Many people find themselves locked into these cycles and cannot escape!

A classic example of a cycle of destruction is found in the book of Judges. In Judges we find Israel locked into a *cycle of sin*. The cycle in Judges looks like this:

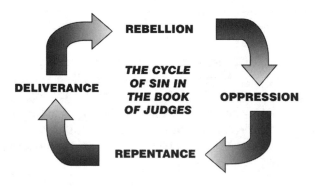

1. The people rebel against God...
2. God allows their enemies to rise up and oppress them...
3. The people repent and turn back to God...
4. God raises up a deliverer to save them from the enemy...
5. With the oppression broken, they quickly rebel again.

In the book of Judges, the people go through this cycle seven times! If you want to see an outline of the book of Judges, look down into the toilet the next time you flush. In Judges, God's people go around and around the same cycle, getting lower and lower, until they end up in the sewer!

I've known many people today who live in this same cycle. We've ministered to men and women who seek God with all their heart... when they are in *jail*! But when they are released, they quickly fall back into an old cycle of SIN.

Satan works through cycles of destruction in all of our lives. He wants to lock us into cycles that will thwart God's plan and keep us in defeat.

Cycles of Blessing

The good news is, God *also* works through cycles. Like the beautiful spiral galaxy, there are cycles that reveal God's goodness and power!

In the natural realm, there is the cycle of sowing and reaping. When you sow in good soil, you will reap much more than you sow. The result is multiplication and increase.

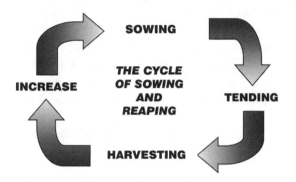

God uses cycles to bring us up to new levels of His blessing and provision. At Jericho, God put Israel into a cycle of victory. As they walked in obedience around and around that city... God brought them into a place of victory!

God wants to lock you into cycles of blessing, growth, and increase. God has a cycle of victory for you today! God wants you to break out of Satan's cycle of destruction and into His cycle of blessing!

In the Scriptures, God established some very important cycles for His people. These cycles were designed to draw us ever closer to Him. The first of these cycles was the *weekly Shabbat* cycle, established by God at the creation of the world.

God also gave us a *yearly* cycle, made up of a series of "feasts" or "appointed times." These feasts were designed to take us through key steps to *deepen* our walk with the Lord, *break* the power of the enemy, and *release* the power of God in our experience.

Learning the Appointed Times of God

Like most Christians, I grew up in church knowing little or nothing about these important cycles. In 1996, however, Chuck

Pierce—a prophet I greatly respect—had a very interesting word for our church. He told us that we needed to celebrate **three biblical feasts** that year.

From my studies in seminary, I knew the Bible devoted a lot of space to a series of feasts, but I had never taken the time to study them. I had always assumed these feasts were just for the Old Testament era, and had no relevance for Christians today.

For the first time in my life, I began to seriously study the feasts. I WAS AMAZED at what I found!

As I began to study the feasts, I discovered that the biblical feasts were part of a cycle of life that actually made up a biblical *calendar*. They were not just holidays or Jewish rituals. God called them *His* "appointed times." In a very real sense, these feasts are "appointments" with God: *times set by God* to meet with His people.

The three appointed times are described in many passages. Exodus 23:14-17 sums them up this way:

"Three times a year you are to celebrate a festival to Me...

- Celebrate the Feast of **Unleavened Bread...**
     (Passover, celebrated in early spring: March or April)
- Celebrate the Feast of **Harvest...**
     (Pentecost, celebrated in late spring: May or June)
- And celebrate the Feast of **Ingathering...**"
     (Tabernacles, celebrated in the fall: September or October)

Three times a year... appear before the sovereign Lord."

In each of these key times, God desired to meet with His people and accomplish specific spiritual transactions in their lives. Taken together, these appointed times form a yearly cycle designed to bring God's people into ever-increasing blessing. God gave specific promises to all who would observe them.

Not Just for Israel

As I studied the feasts, I was surprised to find that these appointed times were not just for the Old Testament era! God's Word repeatedly tells us that these appointed times are eternal, "for all generations," and cannot be changed. One of the sins of the antichrist (Dan 7:25) is that he would, "**try to *CHANGE* the appointed times**."

I was also amazed to discover that these feasts were not just for Jews. Zechariah promises blessings for **Gentiles** who would observe God's feasts.

As I continued to study, I learned that Jesus and His apostles regularly observed these feasts. In fact, many important New Testament events occurred in the context of these feasts:

Jesus was crucified on the Feast of *PASSOVER*.

Jesus was raised on the Feast of *FIRSTFRUITS*.

The Spirit fell during the Feast of *PENTECOST*.

In the book of Acts, we see that the early church considered these feasts very important. The church not only observed these "appointed times," but Paul actually planned the itinerary of his missionary journeys around them!

Acts 20:6-16 tells us that Paul waited to leave Philippi until *after* the Feast of Unleavened Bread, *[Passover]*. Paul wanted to celebrate Passover with the church in Philippi, but it was also important to him to be in Jerusalem for the Feast of Pentecost. Staying in Philippi for Passover forced him to rush through the rest of his journey, bypassing Ephesus, in order to be back in Jerusalem by Pentecost.

Paul took these festivals seriously! His epistles include many references to the feasts, and he assumes that all Christians will celebrate them. In I Corinthians 5:7-8, Paul exhorts the mostly-Gentile church in Corinth: "Christ, OUR Passover Lamb, has been sacrificed. Therefore *LET US celebrate the Festival...*"

Church history shows that the church continued to observe these feasts for hundreds of years! Even after Emperor Constantine outlawed their observance, it took centuries of persecution to stamp out the observance of these feasts!

Three-Dimensional Feasts

Those who like to study biblical numbers will find it interesting that there are a total of **seven** "appointed times" in the yearly cycle, but they are grouped together into **three** yearly celebrations. All **three** of these celebrations have **three** distinct dimensions. Let's look at the three dimensions of each feast:

1. Passover begins the biblical calendar. It marks the first month of the cycle of feasts. Passover is really a cluster of **three** closely related feasts. They are...

   a. **Passover**
   b. **Unleavened Bread**, and
   c. **Firstfruits**.

2. Pentecost (or *Shavuot*) is held in the **third** month of the biblical calendar. It is also a ***three-dimensional feast,*** celebrating God's blessings in three areas...

   a. God's provision of the **harvest**.
   b. God's provision of His **Word**
      (Pentecost celebrates the giving of the *Torah* on
      Mount Sinai, which took place on Pentecost), and
   c. God's provision of the **Holy Spirit** (Acts 2).

3. The Feast of Tabernacles is held in the **seventh** month, and is also a cluster of **three** closely related events. They are...

   a. **Trumpets** (also known as *Rosh Hashanah*),
   b. **Atonement** (also known as *Yom Kippur*), and
   c. **Tabernacles** (also known as *Succot*).

What is Pictured in the Feasts?

Each of these feasts has a different focus and is designed to accomplish some specific "spiritual transactions" in our lives. We might diagram them like this:

FIRST MONTH	*THIRD MONTH*	*(SUMMER)*	*SEVENTH MONTH*
PASSOVER	**PENTECOST**		**TABERNACLES**
FOCUS:	*FOCUS:*		*FOCUS:*
REDEMPTION	ABUNDANT		DWELLING IN
& CLEANSING	PROVISION		HIS GLORY

PASSOVER celebrates **redemption from sin** and **cleansing from impurity**. Each year when Passover is celebrated, we experience again the joy of being "redeemed by the blood of the lamb!"

PENTECOST is a celebration of God's **provision**. Each year at Pentecost, we *thank God* for His provision in the past and *gain faith* to experience His full provision in the year ahead!

TABERNACLES celebrates God's **Glory** – His *Presence* – dwelling with His people. In the wilderness, Israel dwelt in *tabernacles* (temporary shelters). God told Moses to make a tabernacle for Him also, and He came down and lived in their midst! Each year at Tabernacles, God wants to lead us afresh into the joy of life in His Presence!

The Feasts and Moses' Tabernacle

It's interesting that the feasts correspond to the three courts in Moses' tabernacle. The tabernacle of Moses might be diagramed like this:

OUTER COURT	HOLY PLACE	(VEIL)	HOLY OF HOLIES
FOCUS:	*FOCUS:*		*FOCUS:*
REDEMPTION & CLEANSING	ABUNDANT PROVISION		DWELLING IN HIS GLORY

In the **OUTER COURT** of the tabernacle, we find the altar and the laver. It was the place of **redemption and cleansing**, a place to be delivered from the defilement of sin.

The **INNER COURT**, or "Holy Place," was a celebration of God's **provision**. The table of showbread acknowledged God's physical provision. The lampstand pictured the provision of the Holy Spirit. The altar of incense pictured the provision of access to God through prayer.

The **HOLY OF HOLIES** was the place God's **glory** dwelt in the midst of His people. God manifested His Presence there in a tangible way, releasing His blessing into the earth.

We can see by the above diagrams that the yearly cycle of feasts was like a walk through the tabernacle. The cycle of appointed times was designed to transport us from the outermost court, through all the steps of preparation, and finally into the incredible experience of God's glory.

The Feasts and Deliverance

The yearly cycle of feasts is not only designed to draw us closer to God. It is designed to "break off" the oppression of the enemy. The yearly cycle of feasts is designed to give us a fresh experience of *deliverance* each year.

Several years ago I wrote a deliverance manual called *Set Yourself Free*, which is used by many deliverance ministries around the country. *Set Yourself Free* was written to give the keys that can help any individual gain *freedom* from Satan's oppression.

When I began to study the biblical feasts, I was amazed to discover that *many of these key deliverance principles were included as part of the observance of God's appointed times.* Those who observe these feasts, not as rituals, but as times to meet with God, will be enabled to live FREE of Satan's oppression!

The Feasts and Revival

The yearly cycle of feasts also includes a roadmap to revival! In **Appendix Three** we will see, in detail, how these appointed times are designed *to bring us into a fresh experience of revival every year.*

The Importance of God's Yearly Cycle

Why is it important to retrace the steps into God's Presence each year? It's because each of us is surrounded by temptations and influences that try to draw us away from God. Living in this world is like standing on an escalator going down. If we don't make a conscious choice to resist, the natural tendency is to sink lower and lower and end each year further from God.

That's the experience of many Christians! Most Christians who are far from the Lord didn't get there intentionally. They just drifted away, gradually succumbing to the temptations of life.

God's appointed times were designed as an antidote to that "spiritual drift!" Meeting with God in His appointed times puts you on an escalator "going up." Each year the feasts take you through key steps that draw you ever-closer into God's Presence.

Chuck Pierce described these appointed times this way: "God instituted the feasts so His covenant people would always be reminded of who He was and what He had done in the past. These feasts were also given to remember God's great acts of salvation, deliverance and healing grace. He knew that if we would remember His power displays of the past, we would have faith to see Him move today and in the future. By participating in the prescribed Feasts (Passover, Pentecost, and Tabernacles), Israel's worship would remain fresh, vibrant, and properly aligned with their Maker."[1]

For the early Messianic Church, God's appointed times formed a rich tapestry against which all of life was played out, teaching and reminding them each year of the central truths of life with God. The blessings they enjoyed were intended for you also! Allow God to restore YOU to His yearly cycle of life!

STEPS TO RESTORATION!

God's yearly cycle of feasts is designed to be a great blessing in your life. The feasts are not *commanded* for Christians, but are *given* by God as *gifts* for His children.

Many Christians don't experience God's blessings because they are "out of sync" with God's timing. Because they have not kept their "appointments" with God, they miss many windows of opportunity in their lives. Most frustrating of all, because they have not been taught about the feasts, they don't even realize what the problem is!

I would encourage you to begin celebrating the biblical feasts! If your church does something to celebrate the feasts, that's wonderful! But remember, the feasts were not primarily designed to be "church" activities. They were intended to be celebrated in the home! Why not invite some friends or family to join you in a joyful celebration of God's feasts this year?

To learn more about celebrating the feasts, I encourage you to carefully read **Appendix Three** (page 166). In Appendix Three we will look at each of the biblical feasts in detail and learn how to celebrate each one, so you can fully "enter in" to the blessings of God's appointed times!

Chapter Nine
Living in Covenant
The Key to Your Promised Inheritance!

"The LORD said to Abram, 'Bring me a heifer, a goat and a ram...'
Abram brought these to Him, cut them in two & arranged the halves
opposite each other... When the sun had set and darkness had fallen,
a smoking firepot with a blazing torch appeared and passed between
the pieces. On that day the LORD cut a COVENANT with Abram."
- Genesis 15:9-18

"Then Jonathan & David cut a covenant... Jonathan took off the robe
he was wearing and gave it to David, along with his tunic, and even
his sword, his bow and his belt... The two of them cut a covenant
before the LORD." - 1 Sam 18:3-4, 23:18

If we want to recover our lost inheritance, few things are more important than **covenant**. The Hebrew for covenant is *b'rith,* and it is one of the central truths God entrusted to the Jewish people. In Romans 9:4, Paul tells us that both "the glory and the covenants" *belong to* the Jews! Above all else, the Jews are a covenant people. They are literally *b'nai b'rith,* "the sons of the covenant."

The Jews are the only ethnic group on earth whose very identity is based on a covenant with God. God's covenants with Abraham and Moses define who the Jews are and what God has called them to become. While many ancient peoples understood covenant, no one understood covenant better than the Jews. Much of the Old Testament was written to instill in them the understanding of what it meant to walk in covenant! (Note: For a better understanding of God's covenant commitment to Israel, please see **Appendix One: God's Heart for the Jews**.)

Covenant is also the foundation of *our* walk with God. The Bible describes our relationship with Jesus in terms of a MARRIAGE. We are the bride, and Jesus is the groom! That's a covenant relationship.

God is a covenant God, and we are a covenant people. You can't understand how to relate to God without understanding covenant.

One of our biggest problems in the church is that most Christians *don't* understand covenant! We live in a society that doesn't have a concept of covenant! In our culture, we don't make covenants... we have contracts. The only form of *covenant* we have is the covenant of marriage, and most don't understand what *that* means!

Most churches don't teach about covenant. Some may use the word "covenant" but never get down to specifics on what it means. Covenant is a part of our lost inheritance.

The Importance of Covenant

Not understanding covenant makes it hard to walk with God! Many Christians think of God this way: **"God *ACCEPTS* me... but He doesn't *LIKE* me... I have to watch my step! There's an angry God in the sky, ready to stomp on me!"**

Other Christians think God's commitment to them changes from day to day, based on their behavior. Their walk with God is reminiscent of the lines children recite when they pull the petals off a DAISY...

> *He loves me...*
> > *He loves me not...*
> > > *He loves me...*
> > > > *He loves me not...*

That's no way to walk with God! You can never walk in FAITH until you understand the level of God's COMMITMENT to you!

The Value of Covenant

The men and women of the Bible understood covenant. In the world of the Bible, covenant was a common thing. Abraham, Moses, David, Peter, and Paul knew what it was to *make* covenant. They understood the penalty for *breaking* covenant. Not understanding covenant puts us at a disadvantage when we read the Bible.

One reason covenant was important in the ancient world was because the world then was a dangerous place. Warfare was constant. Every city was surrounded by a high wall to protect the inhabitants from marauding enemies. In that world, it was essential to know whom you could *trust* and who would *stand with you* in times of trouble.

The key to security in that lawless world was COVENANT. In Genesis 26:26-28, Isaac and Abimelech made peace by cutting a covenant. In Genesis 31:34, Jacob and Laban did the same. (Note: Many English translations speak of "making" a covenant, but the Hebrew always speaks of "cutting" a covenant. We will see why that's important later in this chapter.)

A loyal covenant partner provided an "insurance policy" to safeguard your future. You wanted to be in relationship with people you could *count on* when things got rough.

Covenant was always a serious business! When two individuals cut covenant, they were literally giving their lives to each other. Walking in covenant meant a sharing of danger and hardship, but also a sharing of victory and joy as they stood together in the midst of life. They were coming into a partnership that was very much like a marriage, but with no improper connotations.

Ecclesiastes expresses the benefit of covenant this way...

"Two are better than one because they have a good return for their labor. For if either of them falls, the one will lift up his companion. But woe to the one who falls when there is not another to lift him up. Furthermore, if two lie down together they keep warm, but how can one be warm alone? And if one can overpower him who is alone, two can resist him. A cord of three strands is not quickly torn apart (Ecc 4:9-12).

To gain a clearer "vision" of covenant, I'd like to suggest the following definition:
- A covenant is a solemn and binding commitment between two or more parties.
- It is a pledge of total *loyalty*. In covenant, you are permanently identifying yourself with another person.
- Covenant is a commitment that goes beyond any other commitment. It is more sacred than life itself. When you make covenant, you are literally giving your life to your covenant partner and pledging to put their needs above your own.

• Covenant is an endless partnership. It cannot be broken under penalty of death.

Why is it important that Christians today understand covenant? It's important because **our God is a God of COVENANT!** Everything God does is based on covenant. The Old Testament and the New Testament chronicle the workings of God through several covenants.

The **Abrahamic** Covenant was made with Abraham and his offspring, defining God's commitment to them as His people.

The **Mosaic** Covenant was made with Israel at Sinai defining their responsibilities as God's priestly nation.

The **New** Covenant is offered to all who believe, offering the blessings of the Abrahamic covenant to all who come to God in faith. The New Covenant is God's means of grafting all believers into the blessings of Abraham.

Our relationship with God is a covenant relationship. When you trusted in Jesus, God did not just forgive your sins and give you a ticket to heaven. God CUT COVENANT with you! The God of the universe became your covenant partner!

A Picture of Covenant

One of the best pictures of covenant in the Bible is found in the story of David and Jonathan. Their story gives a vivid picture of what covenant is all about.

In I Samuel 18, we're told that on the day David killed Goliath, Saul's son Jonathan entered into COVENANT with David. 1 Sam 18:1-3 tells us, "After David finished talking with Saul, Jonathan became one in spirit with David, and loved him as himself. Then Jonathan and David cut a covenant."

David and Jonathan UNDERSTOOD covenant! If we can see what they did that day and why they did it, we can begin to understand covenant also!

In the ancient world there was a common ceremony for entering covenant.   The description of David and Jonathan's covenant takes us through the steps in this ceremony. Understanding the steps of this ceremony can help us understand what Jesus did for us. *Let's look to see what these steps are.*

1. Counting the cost

The first step in covenant-making is always counting the cost. Covenant is a serious thing and it's not to be entered into lightly! It is TOTAL COMMITMENT.

When Jonathan "cut covenant" with David, he knew entering that covenant could cost him everything he had! (As we read the account of their lives, we see that Jonathan *did* pay a high cost for this covenant. Jonathan literally *laid down his life* to see David fulfill his destiny!) Yet Jonathan considered that the joy and benefits of covenant far outweighed the cost.

When Jesus entered covenant with us, He also counted the cost! Jesus knew what it would cost Him to enter covenant with us. Yet, Jesus did not hesitate to pay that price, because of "the joy set before Him..."

David and Jonathan knew what they were doing. This was a serious commitment, but their souls were knit together, and they were willing to pay the price!

2. Covenant Exchanges

The next step in the covenant-making ceremony involved some exchanges. I Samuel tells us that David and Jonathan did an interesting thing. They *exchanged* their ROBES, WEAPONS, and BELTS. These transactions were very significant! They symbolize the *nature* of the covenant they were making. If we understand why they made these exchanges, we will begin to understand covenant.

First, there was the exchange of robes. Jonathan took off his princely robe and gave it to David. David would have taken off his shepherd's robe and given it to Jonathan. This act pictures an exchange of *identity*.

The robe was a symbol of identity. David's robe symbolized his identity as a shepherd. His robe would have been made of course material and was probably stained, torn, and ragged from living and sleeping in the open fields. When people looked at David in his shepherd's robe, they made assumptions about who he was... "He is someone of no importance. He's just a shepherd."

Jonathan's robe, on the other hand, pictured his identity as a prince of Israel. It would have been richly embroidered and made of the finest materials. When people looked at Jonathan in his royal robes, they would have said, "He must be a prince!"

But when David and Jonathan entered covenant, they exchanged identities! As the armies of Israel gathered to observe the covenant ceremony, they would have been awed to see Prince Jonathan don David's shepherd's robe, while David stood beside him dressed as a prince!

That's part of the significance of covenant! When you enter covenant with someone you are saying, "I have so identified myself with you that what is true of you is now true of me! I will share in who you are, and you will share in who I am!"

That's what Jesus did with us! He *exchanged robes* with us! He took our sin upon himself so we could wear His robe of righteousness! He put on our robe of mortal flesh so we could wear His robe of GLORY!

Next, David and Jonathan exchanged belts. The belt was a symbol of strength. This exchange pictured an exchange of strength.

When David gave Jonathan his tattered shepherd's sash, and Jonathan gave David His warrior's belt, they were saying: "*My* strength is now *your* strength! When you are weak, I will be there for you!"

Again, that's a picture of what Jesus did when He cut covenant with us. Philippians chapter two tells us that Jesus took upon Himself our weakness, so we could put on His strength.

Next came an exchange of weapons. Jonathan would have given David his princely sword and received from David a shepherd's sling. This exchange of weapons symbolized an exchange of enemies.

In this exchange of weapons, David and Jonathan were saying, "The enemies that your weapons fought are now my enemies!" That understanding is at the heart of covenant!

The commitment of covenant is: "I will be there for you! If your enemies come against you, I will come to your defense!"

In the story of David and Jonathan, we see the depth of this commitment. Jonathan's covenant with David meant that he stood with David, even against his own father... and even when it meant the loss of his kingdom!

That also is true of our relationship with Jesus. When we come to Jesus, our enemies become His enemies. He tells us, "Vengeance is Mine, I will repay." We don't need to take vengeance against our enemies, because God has promised to be our defender.

It is also true that God's enemies are now *your* enemies. When you enter covenant with Jesus, you gain a new enemy: Satan! Covenant brings you into warfare!

3. "Cutting Covenant"

When David and Jonathan had exchanged their robes, belts and weapons, they were ready to CUT Covenant! I Samuel 18 tells us, "They *CUT* a covenant before the Lord!"

It's interesting that in the ancient world, they did not talk about "making" a covenant or "agreeing on a covenant." The word was always "cut" a covenant. That phrase accurately describes the action involved in entering covenant!

Covenant was a "blood" business! To *cut* a covenant, David and Jonathan would have killed an animal, then CUT its body in half! Once that was done, they would have stood on the bloody soil between the pieces of that animal and pledged themselves to each other in covenant.

If you can picture what this would have been like, you have a picture of the seriousness of covenant! When David and Jonathan stood between the halves of that animal, they were saying, before God, "If I fail to keep this covenant, may it be done to me as was done to this animal!"

Covenants were always made before God, calling God to witness, and God took it seriously! In Jeremiah 34:18-20, God showed how seriously he took the act of covenant! He says that those who have not fulfilled the words of the covenant they made before Him, He will treat like the calf they cut in two!

God not only treats the act of covenant-making seriously, He actually went through the process Himself! When God cut covenant with Abraham in Genesis 15, He instructed Abraham to cut the animals in half.   Then we're told: "When the sun had set and darkness had fallen... a smoking firepot with a blazing torch appeared and passed between the pieces [of the animals.]   On that day the LORD *cut* a covenant with Abram."

In the Abrahamic covenant, God manifested his presence to Abraham and caused His Presence (symbolized by the smoking firepot and blazing torch) to pass between the pieces of the animal. In doing that He was saying, "May I cease to exist if I fail to keep this covenant!" That's the depth of God's covenant commitment!

4. The Covenant Sign

At this point David and Jonathan would have done something that was a common part of the covenant-making ceremony. As a permanent sign of their covenant commitment, they would have taken a knife and made a small cut on the palm of their hand. They would have then rubbed some ashes into the cut, so that when it healed there would be a permanent mark. This mark served, like a wedding ring in a marriage, as a visible sign of covenant.

That's why, in the ancient world when two people met, a common greeting was to hold up the right hand, palm outward, to show the other person their covenant mark. When they held up their hand to a covenant partner, they were affirming their covenant commitment! They were saying, "I remember our covenant!" When they held up their palm to a potential enemy, however, it was a warning: "I have a defender! If you mess with me, you will have to deal with my covenant partner!"

Jesus has covenant mark on His hands. In cutting covenant with us, a permanent mark was made on each of His hands! It's interesting that most of the physical scars of the crucifixion were erased at Jesus' resurrection. There are no descriptions of the scars on His head and face from the horrible beating He endured. Yet the scars on His hands are still clearly visible! They are the only "man-made" thing in heaven! As He sits on His heavenly throne, those marks serve as eternal reminders of His covenant commitment! In Isaiah 49:15-16, God assures you that He can never forget you, because "He has engraved you on the palms of his hands!"

Our covenant sign involves a cutting also. It's a "cutting off" the flesh, as we choose to walk in holiness. We are then to come before Him, "Lifting up holy hands!"

5. The Covenant Meal

There is one more element in making covenant. The ancient ceremony of covenant making concluded with a simple meal of bread and wine. As the two covenant partners shared this meal, they gave the elements to each other. As they handed their partner the bread and the cup, they were saying, "I give myself to you."

That's what Jesus did at the last supper! He took bread and gave it to his disciples, saying, "This is my body!" He took the cup and gave it, saying, "This is my blood!" The apostles knew exactly what He was saying because they understood covenant!

It's interesting that we have maintained a remnant of this ancient ceremony in our modern wedding customs. What do a bride and groom do at their wedding reception? They feed each other the cake and punch! As they do it, they are symbolically giving themselves to the other!

Jesus, Our Covenant Partner

Looking at the ancient covenant-cutting ceremony, it's striking that Jesus followed each of these steps to enter into covenant with us:

1. He counted the cost. He was "the Lamb slain before the foundation of the world!" Before He ever came to earth, He knew what covenant would cost Him, but He was willing to cut covenant because of His love for us.

2. He made a covenant exchange. He took on mortal flesh so you could become a partaker of the divine nature (II Peter 1:4). He took on your infirmities and weakness so that you could walk in His strength. He took on your enemies to be your defender.

3. He provided the covenant sacrifice! In the new covenant, the covenant was not sealed with the blood of a bull or calf. It was sealed by the blood of Jesus. He was the sacrifice. It is the New Covenant in HIS blood!

4. He bears in His body the covenant sign! Through all eternity, the marks of His commitment to you will remain inscribed on the palms of His hand.

5. He invites us to reaffirm covenant at a covenant meal! Jesus invites us to meet with Him regularly to reaffirm our covenant at a covenant meal, the Lord's Supper!

Do you see the significance of what Jesus did? The God of the universe has become your covenant partner! He has eternally committed Himself to you. He has pledged Himself to stand with you. If we are faithless, He remains faithful. He promised, "I am with you always!" ...and He expects you to walk in covenant with Him!

Covenant Terms

To understand what it means to walk in covenant, there are some covenant terms we need to understand:

1. Covenant Stipulations. When you enter covenant, you pledge yourself to do some specific things. These are *covenant stipulations.*

In the covenant of marriage, covenant stipulations are expressed as **marriage vows.** In the marriage vows, each partner pledges themselves to the other in specific ways. In a traditional wedding, the minister usually asks something like this: "Will you take Sally as your lawful wedded wife? Will you love her, honor her... etc." When you say, "I do!" you are agreeing to a set of covenant stipulations!

In our covenant with God, there are also covenant stipulations. Those stipulations are found in God's Word. Our faithfulness to keep these stipulations determines whether we experience the benefits of the covenant.

That allows us to read the Bible in a new light! The Bible is a book of covenant! It explains God's commitment *TO* us, and the commitments He requires *OF* us. When we read the Bible we learn how to walk in covenant!

2. Covenant Blessings. The Bible talks a lot about blessings and curses. "Blessing" is the increase of what is good and pleasant. "Curses" represent an increase of that which is unpleasant. Most Christians desire God's blessing, but few realize that blessings and curses are directly related to covenant.

Blessings are the benefits we experience when we live in covenant. *Curses* are the negative effects we bring upon ourselves if we fail to keep covenant.

The clearest description of our covenant blessings is found in Deuternomy 28. Deuteronomy 28 spells out the blessings that come when we live in covenant with God, including health, prosperity, and contentment. The blessings enumerated are all encompassing...

"All these blessings will come upon you and overtake you if you obey the LORD your God:
Blessed shall you be in the city, and blessed shall you be in the country. Blessed shall be the offspring of your body and the produce of your ground and the offspring of your beasts, the increase of your herd and the young of your flock... (Deut 28:1-4)

The chapter goes on and on, describing the blessings that are part of our covenant inheritance. It also, however, enumerates the curses for those who are disloyal to their covenant. I would encourage you to spend time meditating on Deuteronomy 28!

Some Christians think that it is somehow wrong to want to experience God's blessings. They picture it as a selfish thing to pray, "Bless me!"

But it's God's *desire* that we walk in covenant and experience ALL of His blessings! God wants His blessing on our lives to serve as a *testimony* to the world of what it's like to know the true God.

Walking in covenant blessing is a key to successful evangelism! In Psalm 67:6-8 we read, "God blesses us, that all the ends of the earth may fear Him." God wants our lives to so overflow with His blessings that unbelievers want to find out what we have! One reason unbelievers often reject the Gospel message is that they don't see Christians walking in blessing!

3. Lovingkindness. Lovingkindness is the English translation of the Hebrew word *Chesed*. *Chesed* is is a very common word in the Old Testament. It is also translated as "kindness," or "mercy." But none of these translations express the real meaning of *chesed*.

To translate *chesed* as *kindness*, *mercy*, or *lovingkindness* makes it sound weak or sentimental. It sounds like we are saying that God is a "nice" God. That's not what *chesed* means.

Chesed is a covenant term and is a very strong word. *Chesed* is your commitment to be loyal to your covenant! It's your determination to keep your covenant promises! If a husband is tempted to infidelity, but chooses to be loyal to his wife, he is exercising *chesed. Chesed* is covenant loyalty.

God's "lovingkindness" does not mean that God is a "nice" God. It means He is absolutely committed to *KEEP HIS COVENANT* with you!

God's *chesed* is the basis for our faith! In II Chronicles 20:20-21 we find the strongest confession of faith in the Bible. Jerusalem was surrounded by an enemy and it looked like defeat was certain, but Jehoshaphat exhorted the people to put their trust in God. So the army went out to face the enemy, with singers leading the way, proclaiming: "Give thanks to the LORD, for His lovingkindness *[chesed]* is everlasting." They were saying, "We can go out against the enemy in faith, because we are trusting that God is

COMMITTED to keep his covenant!" In response to their faith, God granted a supernatural victory!

Chesed is the root of the New Testament concept of love. Biblical love is not an emotion, it is a commitment. Ern Baxter once said we would understand the New Testament better if we went through and crossed out the word "love" and replaced it with LOYALTY.

4. Friend. There is one more covenant term we want to look at. It's the word "friend." For most of us, a friend is someone we enjoy being with and doing things with. It's someone we "hang out" with, or go to a ball game with. That's *not* what the Bible means when it talks about friendship. Biblically, the word "friend" means "covenant partner." A friend is someone you have given your life to!

In John 15:15 when Jesus said, "I no longer call you servants... I call you **FRIENDS!**" He was saying, "I have committed myself to you as your covenant partner!"

Horizontal and Vertical Covenant

When God cut covenant with us, He not only brought us into covenant with Himself, He joined us in covenant with each other! The New Covenant is both a *vertical* and a *horizontal* covenant.

The *vertical* component of our covenant is **John 3:16**. Jesus *laid down His life for us.*

The *horizontal* component is **I John 3:16**. "He laid down His life for us; and we ought to lay down our lives for the brethren."

The outflow of our covenant with God should be that we walk in covenant with each other. That's what we see described in the book of Acts. The early Messianic Church understood covenant and walked in covenant!

It's interesting that both components of covenant are represented in the Lord's Supper. The cup – the blood of Jesus – is the *vertical* component. His blood cleanses us from sin and brings us into covenant with God! It is the New Covenant *in His blood!*

The bread – the body of Jesus – is the *horizontal* component. I Cor. 10:16-17 tells us: "Since there is *one bread*, **we who are many are *one body*;** for we all partake of the one bread."

When we take the Lord's Supper, we are literally pledging ourselves in covenant to the Lord, and to our brothers and sisters. That's the basis of true unity. In the body of Jesus, you are *covenant partners* with every believer in Jesus. All the blessings and responsibilities of covenant apply! The body of Jesus is "knit together" by covenant.

Within His body, God then links us with specific brothers and sisters to walk out the joys and responsibilities of covenant. As we walk in covenant, the body of Jesus is empowered to accomplish the works of Jesus in the earth.

God created us to be covenant people. It is *through covenant* that believing Gentiles are "grafted in" among the natural branches. It is *through covenant* both Jew and Gentile are knit together into one body to enjoy the blessings of Abraham. That's the basis for the ONE NEW MAN.

God is calling us to become men and women of covenant... to walk in covenant with Him, and with each other. He is calling us to be a people of loyalty and integrity! There has been so much disloyalty and betrayal in the church, God's heart is broken. God wants to *restore us* as His **covenant people:** People who understand covenant, walk in covenant, and experience all the blessings of His covenant!

STEPS TO RESTORATION!

Part of walking in covenant involves learning your own identity in Him! You are not a "poor miserable sinner" existing from moment to moment at the mercy of an angry God! God *loved* you and *chose* you for Himself! God has *committed Himself* to you! You are in covenant with the God of the Universe!

Begin to study the Word to better understand your covenant blessings and your covenant commitments. Thank God for His *Chesed*, His *faithfulness* to you! Learn to trust Him more.

Covenant is a "knitting together." On the human level, ask God to show you *who* He has knit you to. We are supposed to love everyone, but there will be certain individuals God will "knit you to" in covenant.

Become a man or woman of covenant! Choose to become a person of loyalty, integrity, and commitment! *Walk in covenant and experience the blessings of covenant in your life!*

Chapter Ten
Walking in Holiness
What Most Christians Don't Know About HOLINESS!

"You are to be HOLY... because I, the LORD, am holy." – Lev. 20:26

The next foundational truth we want to look at is **holiness**. God gave the Jewish people a great deal of revelation about holiness. It's foundational to their identity! The Jews were designated by God as a HOLY nation (Ex 19:6)!

In Leviticus 20:26 God commanded the Jews, "You are to be HOLY... because I, the LORD, am holy." Most Jews, even today, have a pretty good idea what it means to be holy.

Ignorance of the Holy

Surprisingly, most Christians don't have a clue what holiness is! We read about Holiness, talk about it, and sing about it, but very few have taken the time to learn what it is.

Over the years, Christians have developed a variety of strange ideas about holiness. One common idea was that holiness meant "being DIFFERENT from the world." Back in the 40's and 50's, Christians who wanted to be holy tried to *look* different. They walked around in hair and clothing styles that were at least ten years out of date and thought that made them holy!

Some Christians thought they needed to SOUND different! In the 60's, the idea of having a guitar in church was unheard of. The guitar was a "worldly" instrument, often played by unbelievers! Being HOLY meant worshipping with an organ or piano.

Some thought holiness meant avoiding the activities of the world. Christians made up lists of "worldly" activities to avoid... "Don't smoke, drink, cuss, or chew, or run with those that do!" They often also added: "No movies, roller-skating, make-up, or card playing either!" The idea was that if you avoided the activities of the world, that made you HOLY.

Fortunately, the idea that *being different* makes you holy has gone out of style. Christians today tend to think holiness means being "good." They think if they live a life that is righteous and moral, they will have achieved holiness. But that also misses the mark.

Living a good life, while important, is *not* what makes you holy. Stop and think of some of the things God calls "holy." God called the burning bush *"holy."* That does not mean the burning bush *sinned less* than the other bushes! God called Sinai His "holy" mountain. But Sinai did not become HOLY by being more MORAL than other mountains!

Holiness is not a matter of being good or moral! It's in a different dimension entirely.

What is Holiness?

Several years ago John Dickson, our worship leader at Glory of Zion, made an interesting comment. He said, "The opposite of holy is not *sinful* or *evil*. The opposite of holy is *ordinary*."

That statement surprised me. Like many Christians, I had always used "holy" as a synonym for "righteous." To live a "holy life," I had assumed, meant that you lived a good, moral life, avoiding sin as much as possible.

When I heard John's statement, I decided to study "holiness" for myself to see what it meant. I was amazed at what I found!

I discovered that I had lived forty-five years as a Christian, attending church every Sunday, and graduating from one of the finest seminaries in the world, *without ever learning what holiness is!*

As I studied the original Greek and Hebrew words and saw how they were used in the Bible, I discovered that John was absolutely right! Holiness doesn't mean "free from sin." Holiness means "set apart from the ordinary" or "elevated above the norm." The best one-word definition of "holy" is the word *"special!"* To treat something as holy is to honor it as special!

We see that in the first chapters of Genesis. The first time God called something HOLY was in Genesis 2 when God blessed the seventh day and designated it as "HOLY."

Calling the seventh day holy did not mean that days one through six were worldly, bad, or sinful! The first six days were *good* days. God said they were *very* good. But they were not *holy.* They were just *ordinary* days. God set the seventh day apart from the rest and said, "This day is SPECIAL."

In Leviticus 10, God gave Aaron instructions for serving at the tabernacle. He warned Aaron to be careful to "distinguish between the HOLY and the COMMON." God was saying, "Don't take what is SPECIAL and treat it as ORDINARY!"

If Aaron had brought his laundry to the tabernacle, washed it in the laver, and hung it up on the ark of the covenant to dry, he would have been violating the holiness of the tabernacle! He would have been taking some very special things and treating them as ordinary!

Being *holy* is being "set apart from the ordinary." If something is "holy," it is designated for special purposes and deserving of special treatment. To treat something as HOLY means that you treat it with HONOR.

When Linda and I got married, we got two sets of dishes: our "good china" and our "everyday" dishes. We really loved our everyday dishes. They were gold and orange with big flowers... a very popular style back in the '70s! We used those dishes every day. We treated them very casually. Sometimes we ate dinner from them on the living room floor while watching TV. We were not always careful when we put them in the sink. Because of the way we used them, they eventually became so chipped and worn we had to throw them away and buy *new* everyday dishes!

Our "good china," on the other hand, was beautiful and elegant. It was reserved for special occasions. When we used it, we treated it with great care and always put it back in a special cabinet. It is still as beautiful today as the day we got it.

Our everyday dishes were very nice, but they were ORDINARY. Our good china was SPECIAL. If I took a bowl from our good china and set it down on the floor to hold food for our dog, my wife would be justifiably upset! I would be taking something special and treating it is ordinary! I would be failing to show those special dishes the honor they deserved!

Walking in holiness is not about being good or different; it's about showing HONOR! It's about treating what is SPECIAL in a special way!

The Importance of Holiness

In Deuteronomy 23:14, God gives this warning, "The LORD your God walks in the midst of your camp, to protect you and deliver you and give your enemies over to you; Therefore your camp shall be *HOLY*, that He may see no unclean thing among you, and turn away from you."

Holiness is very important to God. If we fail to walk in holiness, we will cause His *Presence* to withdraw!

Holiness is the secret to walking in God's Presence and power! In the Word, God has designated certain things as holy. He asks us to treat these things in a special way. ***When we honor what is holy, we walk in holiness, and His Presence abides with us!*** *Holiness is a KEY to a Supernatural Life!*

How Holiness Works

In His Word, God has designated certain things as holy. In calling these things *holy*, He was saying, "Give special HONOR to these things. Don't treat them as ordinary."

When God designated these things as HOLY, God connected them with covenant principles. If we HONOR what God calls holy, we link into those covenant principles and are brought into a supernatural dimension of life.

Let's look at some examples of things the Bible calls holy. In His Word, God identifies all of these things, and many others, as holy:

God's Word	The Tithe	Other Christians
Apostles	Prophets	Spiritual Leaders
Marriage	His Name	Places of Worship
Your Body	The Sabbath	Israel

Choosing to HONOR these things (by treating each of them as SPECIAL) will set us apart from the ordinary. God's promise is that when you honor what is holy, you will tap into covenant blessings and experience a supernatural dimension of life. Let's look at some examples...

Holy Money. Did you know money could be holy? Some money is! In fact, God has designated a tithe (1/10th) of your income as holy. Lev. 27:30-32 tells us, "A tithe [tenth] of everything belongs to the LORD; it is HOLY to the LORD."

That means, when you earn ten dollars, one of those dollars—a tithe of your income—is holy. This applies to all forms of income.

If you are a farmer, one tenth of your produce is holy! If you raise cattle, one tenth of your calves are holy. (So there *really is* such a thing as a HOLY COW!)

Malachi three tells us HOW to honor the tithe as holy. We honor it as holy when we "bring the whole tithe into the storehouse..." The tithe was to be brought into the temple storehouse to support those who minister in the things of God.

God then connected the tithe to a covenant promise. He said, if you will treat the tithe as holy, "...I will throw open the floodgates of heaven and pour out so much blessing you will not have room enough for it" (Mal. 3:10-11).

Now, when God designates the tithe as holy, we have a choice: We can honor the tithe as holy (treat it as special), or we can choose not to honor it! We can treat it like the rest of our income.

The choice is ours. You will not go to hell for not tithing! But *honoring* the tithe as holy will set you apart from the world in your finances.

Honoring the tithe allows you to tap into covenant principles and opens a door to supernatural provision.

Holy Time. God designates one-seventh of your *time* as holy.

Genesis 2:3 tells us, "God blessed the seventh day and made it HOLY." In the Ten Commandments, God instructs, "Remember the Sabbath day by keeping it HOLY." (Ex 20:8-11)

Now, observing a Sabbath is not a requirement for salvation! You can work seven days a week and still get to heaven! As a matter of fact, if you work seven days a week, you may get to heaven *faster!* You can literally work yourself to death!

But honoring the Sabbath links you into a covenant principle of blessing. God promises: "If you call the Sabbath a delight... & *honor* it... you will find your joy in the LORD, and I will cause you to ride on the heights of the land and feast on the inheritance of your father Jacob" (Is 58:13-14).

Holy Places. Places where God manifests His Presence are holy *places*. The burning bush was holy. Mt. Sinai was holy. The tabernacle and the temple were holy. Places of worship are holy.

Honoring a holy place links us into God's covenant blessing. In the book of Haggai, we learn that the people of Judah had neglected work on the temple to build their own houses. The result was that God's provision was withheld. They never had enough!

Solomon, on the other hand, showed great honor to God's temple! He depleted his resources to build it. The result was that he experienced overflowing abundance for the rest of his days.

When we honor what is holy, we tap into blessing!

Holy People. God designates many kinds of people as holy. Apostles & prophets are holy (Eph. 3:5). The Jewish people are holy. Your brothers and sisters in the Lord are holy. Your husband, wife, parents & children are holy to you.

The Bible gives instructions on how to honor each one of these in an appropriate way. It also gives a promise: If you honor those God calls holy, you receive God's blessing!

Learning about holiness gave me an interesting insight on a passage that had long troubled me. It's the story of Elijah and the widow in I Kings 17:13-15.

This account took place at a time of famine in the land. God sent Elijah to Zarephath and told him that a widow there would provide for him. Elijah arrived in town, only to discover that the widow was preparing her last meal. She was at the end of her resources! She had just enough to make one small meal for herself and her son, and then she would starve!

In that tragic situation, Elijah makes an incredible demand: He tells the widow, "Feed me first! Then you and your son can eat!" Of all the nerve! How could Elijah go up to a starving woman and ask her to feed him before she feeds herself and her son!

But Elijah understood the things of God. He knew that if the widow would honor a prophet, she would unlock the flow of God's blessing! God promises: "honor a prophet... and receive a prophet's reward" (Mt. 10:41). *Elijah was giving the woman an opportunity to enter into the miraculous!*

As the woman chose to honor God's prophet, God began to miraculously multiply her resources! She and her son enjoyed supernatural provision in the midst of famine!

A Picture of Holiness

I believe the internet provides us with a wonderful picture of how holiness operates! Suppose you were "surfing" the internet, and came across the following:

> When we honor what God calls **holy**, our lives are linked to covenant principles, resulting in a great release of blessing.

See anything familiar? If you were on the internet and saw that line on your computer screen, you would know that the word **holy** is a "hyperlink." A hyperlink is *special* text that is usually underlined and in a different color from the rest of the paragraph.

But a hyperlink is not only special because it's underlined and in a different color. It's special because it is linked to things you cannot see!

You can click your mouse on other words in that paragraph, and nothing happens. But if you click on the hyperlink, WHOLE NEW PAGES OPEN UP TO YOU!

That's a picture of how holiness operates. You can choose to *honor* many things in life:

A Sports Team	A Rock Group	An Author
A Movie Star	Your Hobby	A Brand of Computer

or... What God Calls **Holy**

When you show honor to most things, you receive no benefit! But when you choose to honor what is holy, new realms of **blessing** open up to you! Honoring the holy sets us apart from the world and lifts us up into a supernatural realm where we tap into the covenant blessings of God.

The Source of True Holiness

Where does holiness come from? Stop to think about the things God calls holy. What made the burning bush holy? What made Mount Sinai holy? What made the "most holy place" holy?

The answer is: *The Presence of God!*

Now think about this: When you trusted in Jesus, God's Holy Spirit came to live inside you. God's Presence is in *you* right now. That means, *YOU* are holy! You are a *saint*, a HOLY ONE.

You are holy right now. You are holy no matter what you do.

Remember, holiness is not sinlessness!

Most Christians confuse holiness with righteousness. Righteousness is being CLEAN. It means you have removed the defilement of sin from your life. God wants us to walk in righteousness.

But holiness is in a different dimension. Holiness is being SPECIAL. Because you have trusted in Jesus, you are holy, even when you are sinning! In First Corinthians, Paul writes to the church at Corinth to correct their many problems. The problems in the Corinthian church included immorality, drunkenness (at the Lord's Supper!), factions, etc. In writing concerning their sin, however, the very first thing Paul does is to remind the Corinthians that they are HOLY (I Cor. 1:2)!

You ARE holy! God wants you to begin walking in holiness!

Earlier in the chapter I used the illustration of our good china. Our good china is *special*. Sometimes when we finish eating a big meal, our good china is not very pretty! It is covered with bits of food! It's dirty. It needs to be cleaned. But it's still special. It's still our good china.

Our everyday dishes are ordinary. We keep our everyday dishes very clean, but they are still ordinary. That's the difference between holiness and righteousness.

Righteousness is being clean.

Holiness is being special.

Our good china is special whether it is clean or not. Because our good china is special, we treat it carefully, even when it's dirty. We are careful to wash it, to restore it to its beauty.

You are God's "good china!" You are special to Him, even when you are not walking in a way that pleases Him.

Jews today are STILL God's HOLY NATION …even in their unbelief!

Walking in Holiness

Walking in Holiness begins by knowing that God has made you holy:

- You are a saint ("holy one") - Rom 1:7.

- You are not a mere human - 1 Cor 3:3.
- You are indwelt by God's Spirit - Rom 8:9.
- You are a partaker of God's nature - II Pt 1:4.
- The power of resurrection is in you - Rom 8:11.
- You have a purpose and a destiny - Jer 29:11.
- You've been given supernatural abilities and are called to live as a supernatural being! - I Cor 12.

As God's HOLY man or woman you can begin to WALK in the realm of holiness! You learn to show HONOR! You learn to treat as special what God calls HOLY (including yourself)! As you HONOR what is HOLY, you enter into the supernatural favor and blessing reserved for God's Holy People.

"How do I walk in Holiness?"

Holiness is all about showing honor. Honor is a little-known concept among Christians. Some Christians love to gossip and criticize. They dishonor one another and their spiritual leaders. Then they wonder why they don't walk in God's blessing and power!

Walking in holiness means showing honor where honor is due. It means showing honor to your parents because they were God's chosen instruments to bring you into the world. It means honoring your spouse as your covenant partner. It means showing respect to those God has established as your spiritual leaders.

Walking in Holiness means showing honor to God's name. It means treating the Sabbath as a "set apart" day. It means treating your own body as a holy temple for God's Presence. It means honoring marriage by speaking highly of it. It means treating other Christians as special, just because they know Jesus! It means showing honor to the Jews as God's chosen people.

As you walk in HOLINESS, showing honor where it is due, God's PRESENCE invades your life and His BLESSING is released!

STEPS TO RESTORATION!

Holiness is not about legalism, being different, or being good! Holiness is all about showing honor! Honor has not had a big place in our Christian vocabulary. But God wants us to begin to think in terms of showing honor!

First, learn to honor **God**. He is the *most* holy. One way to honor God is found in the principle of Firstfruits. We honor God by giving Him the *first* of our increase. In the Old Testament when it was time for harvest, the *first sheaf* of wheat gathered in the field was taken to the temple as a "Firstfruits offering." This was in addition to the tithe. A Firstfruits offering does not have to be large, but it is a special way of honoring God by giving Him the first of what we receive!

In our family, we began to practice "Firstfruits giving" several years ago. Whenever we saw an increase in our income, we took the first of that increase and gave it as a Firstfruits offering to honor God. The results were incredible. We saw God begin to pour out blessing on our finances as we showed Him special honor in this way!

We also honor God with the first of our time. At the first of every month, the Jews had a special "New Month" (New Moon) celebration. The people would gather at the head of the month for a time of praise, prayer, and feasting before God. It was a way of honoring God by choosing to dedicate the *first* of the month to Him!

Our church has begun a monthly "Firstfruits Harvest Celebration" to honor God at the start of each month. If your church doesn't do something like this, why not have a special "praise night" in your home, to feast and celebrate God's goodness at the head of each month? When we choose to give God what is first in our lives, we honor Him as holy.

It's also important to honor the people and things that God has designated as holy. Ask God to show you how to honor what is holy in your life.

As we walk in Holiness, we are enabled to experience more and more of God's power and blessing!

Chapter Eleven
The Dwelling Place of God
The *"Jewish Roots"* of Revival

*"Let them construct a sanctuary [a special "set-apart" place]
for Me that I may DWELL among them." – Ex 25:8*

*God's purpose was to bring together Jew and Gentile into **one new
man**... fitted together and growing into a holy temple in the Lord,
becoming a dwelling place of God." – Eph 2:15, 21, 22, paraphrased*

As I write this chapter in the city of Jerusalem, I can look out
my window and see Mount Zion, where the Holy Spirit fell on the
day of Pentecost (Acts 2). That was the "birthday" of the early
church. On that day, God's **Glory** [Heb: ***Kavod***) came down and
filled the church! Through the outpouring of the Holy Spirit, the
very LIFE of God was released to dwell among His people. The
results included signs, wonders, overflowing joy and excitement, and
the ingathering of a massive worldwide harvest.

Sadly, the church today rarely experiences that kind of life!
We read the accounts of the early church and long to "experience
God" as those early Messianic Christians did! That's why the church
today cries out for *revival*! The word "revive" literally means, "to
restore to LIFE!" When we pray for revival, we are confessing that
we have LOST the life God intended us to have. We are admitting
that the church is now dead!

We ***enter revival*** when God's LIFE is restored! Revival is
when God's POWER and GLORY come down and fill His temple.

Revivals in History

I've spent many years studying the great revivals of history.
True revival is not a week of evangelistic meetings. It is a
supernatural move of the Holy Spirit that can sweep through
churches, cities, and nations! Revivals are wonderful times! During
times of revival, the life of God is restored to His church! There is
repentance of sin, salvation of the lost, and an overflow of praise and

worship. Most of all, there is an overwhelming sense of God's Presence dwelling among us.

The *Presence of God* is the hallmark of true revival. As you read historical accounts of revival, you repeatedly come across phrases like this:

"There was an overwhelming sense of the Presence of God."

"His sacred *Presence* was everywhere."

"God came down into that room."

"The power of God seemed to descend on the assembly with an astonishing energy that bore all down before it."

One of my favorite "revival stories" took place during the Welsh revival. During the Welsh revival, the Spirit swept across the country with such power that thousands were saved. Crime and drunkenness ended. The territory was transformed!

In the midst of the excitement, two children were overheard talking about the changes taking place in their village. One child commented, "I don't understand what is happening!"

The other child responded, "Don't you know? *JESUS lives here now!"*

That's revival! It's the Presence of God coming to live with His people in a very real and tangible way.

The church has known many times of revival but, unfortunately, most revivals in modern history have been short-lived. The average "major" revival lasts less than five years. The Presence of God comes… but quickly leaves! People spend the rest of their lives talking about the great things that happened "back in the revival!"

The church has not understood how to KEEP the Presence of God in our midst! We don't understand what BRINGS His Presence and what CAUSES His Presence to leave!

The early church knew a different level of revival! When the Spirit fell at Pentecost the LIFE OF GOD came to dwell in the church. The early church was filled with life! The church experienced REVIVAL for more than 300 years! It experienced sustained multigenerational revival! It UNDERSTOOD how to live in God's Presence!

Where did they learn that? I believe the knowledge of how to relate to God's Presence came through the church's Jewish roots! Biblical Judaism was the religion of God's Presence! It was all about **hosting the Presence of God in the earth** ... first at the tabernacle of Moses, then at David's tabernacle, and finally at the two temples.

Much of the Old Testament was written to teach the Hebrew people how to experience God's Presence on a continual basis. No one understood the Presence of God more than the ancient Jews!

Sadly, many Christians today don't understand the Presence of God at all. That's why we have a hard time entering, and staying in, revival!

Understanding the Presence

When we talk about the "Presence of God" coming in revival, some Christians are confused. They ask, "Isn't God always present everywhere?" The answer is "Yes!" ... and "No!" To understand God's Presence, we need to see that the Bible describes **four levels** of God's Presence:

1. God's Omnipresence – Omnipresence means that God is always present everywhere. No matter where you go, God is there with you. Even though you may not be able to sense His Presence, you know from His Word that He is always aware of what is happening to you, and is always there to hear your prayers.

2. God's Indwelling Presence – While the Bible teaches that God is always present everywhere, it also says that He lives in *you* in a special way. If you believe in Jesus, His Holy Spirit dwells in you in a way that is distinct from His general presence everywhere.

3. God's Manifest Presence (His Glory) – While God is always present everywhere, it is also true that God sometimes reveals Himself in ways you can *feel* with your physical senses. Sometimes, you hear His voice. Sometimes you may see a visible "cloud" of light. Sometimes there is just a "knowing" that God is present with you in a very personal way. When God manifests His Presence in a tangible way, we call that His GLORY.

You may have been driving in your car and the Holy Spirit came and ministered to you. You began to weep! You knew God was there! Maybe you were alone in your bedroom and God "showed up!" Most of us have had experiences like this, and the result is often a major change in our spiritual life! In those times, when we experienced God's Presence, many of us found salvation, healing, empowering, and comfort.

Sometimes the tangible Presence of the Holy Spirit shows up in church. It may be for a few minutes, a few days, or even weeks. You know, "God is HERE!" For as long as His Glory is present, the church comes alive! Many find salvation, healing, and deliverance. There is an overflow of joy!

4. God's DWELLING Presence – The fourth level of God's Presence is when God causes His manifest Presence to DWELL CONTINUALLY in a given location. When God's Presence is continuously manifested in a given place, we call that His *Shekinah Glory.* (The word *Shekinah* comes from the Hebrew word, *shakan,* which means, "to dwell." God's *Shekinah Glory* is His *Dwelling Presence.*)

In the Jerusalem temple, God's *Shekinah Glory* dwelt in the midst of Israel for generations!

God wants His *Shekinah* to dwell in His church NOW!

Hosting God's *Shekinah*

One of the most amazing verses in the Bible is Exodus 25:8. In this verse, God told Moses...

> "Let them construct a **sanctuary** for Me that I may DWELL among them."

This verse is amazing for two reasons. First, because it tells us that God WANTS His Presence to *dwell* with us. God DESIRES that His *Shekinah* rest among us, releasing His blessing in our midst.

The second amazing thing in this verse is that God gives US the responsibility to prepare a place for Him. The word *Sanctuary* meant "Holy Place" or "Special Place." God wants us to experience His glory, but His Presence must have a specially prepared place to dwell. In the Old Testament God taught the Jews how to prepare a place for His Presence! The Jews followed these instructions and experienced God's Presence on a CONTINUAL basis:

- God appeared to Israel as a pillar of cloud & fire (Ex. 13:21)!
- At Moses' Tabernacle His Presence came down and filled the place (Ex. 40:34-35).

- Through Israel's time in the wilderness, God's Presence was tangibly present (Deut 29:5).
- At David's Tabernacle, God's *Shekinah* was visibly present. David writes, "I have seen You in the sanctuary and beheld Your power and glory!" (Ps 63:2).
- The Jerusalem temple was the "place of His Presence!" At the dedication of the temple, God's glory came down in such power that the priests could not stand up (II Chron 5:14)!
- Every year, when the high priest went into the holy of holies, he knew that behind the veil he would encounter the burning purity of the PRESENCE OF GOD!

Because of the Presence of God in their midst, Biblical Judaism was also the religion of God's *power!* Where His Presence dwells, His power is released! We must not confuse Biblical Judaism with the dead branches of Rabbinic Judaism! *Biblical Judaism was a SUPERNATURAL religion!*

In the Old Testament Scriptures, signs and wonders were common. There were many angelic visitations, visions and prophetic words! In the days of Elijah and Elisha, there were schools to train prophets (II Kings 2:3; 4:1; 4:38).

Prophecy, deliverance and supernatural healing were common elements of Judaism, even in New Testament times. Shortly after Jesus' birth, He was taken to the temple where He was greeted by Anna, a Jewish *prophetess*, who had been supernaturally alerted to His coming (Luke 2).

In Jesus' day, ministries of healing and deliverance were not uncommon among the Jews. Jews were well known in the ancient world for their ability to cast out demons. The Jewish historian Josephus tells of Eleazar, who expelled a demon in the presence of the Roman emperor Vespasian. Jesus also acknowledged the existence of Jewish exorcists. In Matthew 12:27 when Pharisees accused Him of casting out demons by the power of Satan, Jesus asked, "by whom do your sons cast them out?"

A Galilean Jew named Hanina ben Dosa was well-known for his healing ministry. When the son of Rabbi Yohanan ben Zakkai was taken ill, Yohanan called for Hanina, who prayed fervently over his son. As a result, the son was totally healed.

When Rabbi Gamaliel's son was afflicted with a high fever, students were sent to Hanina's home in Galilee. Hanina went into his chamber, prayed, and upon returning, said, "Go home, his fever has departed from him." When the students came back, Gamaliel confirmed that his son had been cured. [1]

It should not surprise us that there was supernatural healing among the Jews. Many of the biblical *promises* for healing are given in the *Old* Testament (Ex. 15:26, Psalm 41:3, Psalm 103:3, etc). When the Glory of God is present, there is always healing and deliverance!

The Jews understood the BENEFITS of dwelling in God's Presence! In Psalm 42, the psalmist expresses his longing for God's tangible Presence: "As the deer pants for the water brooks, so my soul pants for You, O God" (Ps 42:1).

The Jews knew that the entire territory is blessed when the Presence of God dwells among His people! Leviticus 26:4-12 lists some of the benefits that occur when God "makes His dwelling" among His People...

- "I shall give you rains in their season, so
  the land will yield its produce."   *(Productivity)*

- "You will eat to the full and live securely."   *(Security)*

- "I will turn toward you and multiply you..."   *(Increase)*

- "I will walk among you and be your God."   *(Knowing Him!)*

Many Christians have seen the set of videos produced a few years back by George Otis, Jr. These videos, called *Transformations* and *Transformations II,* document how, in modern times, the coming of revival has brought transformation to territories in incredible ways! They show that the Presence of God not only brings repentance and salvation, it actually brings economic prosperity, a decrease of crime, and even physical changes in the land. That's just what the Bible promises!

This is nowhere seen more clearly than in the biblical teaching about ZION. In the Bible, *Zion is the place God's Presence dwells among His people* (Ps 76:2). When you study what the Bible has to say about Zion, you discover that God's Presence in Zion brought some interesting changes in the whole region:

1. From Zion, God's BLESSING was released to His people:
   Ps 128:5 – "May the LORD bless you from Zion."

2. From Zion, God's REVELATION was made known to the world:
   Isa 2:3 – "Torah (the teaching of God) will go out from Zion."

3. In Zion, God's AUTHORITY was established in the earth:
   Ps 110:2 – "The LORD will extend your mighty scepter from Zion; you will rule in the midst of your enemies."

4. Zion was a place of REFUGE and PROTECTION:
   Isa 14:32 - "The LORD has established Zion, and in her His afflicted people will find refuge."

5. Zion was a place of HEALING *and* FORGIVENESS:
   Isa 33:24 – "No one living in Zion will say, "I am ill"; and the sins of those who dwell there will be forgiven."

6. Zion experienced abundant PROVISION:
   Ps 132:15-16 – "I will bless her with abundant provisions; her poor will I satisfy with food."

7. Zion was a place of unrestrained JOY:
   Jer 31:12-13 – "They will shout for joy on the heights of Zion… maidens will dance and be glad, young men and old as well. I will turn their mourning into gladness; I will give them comfort and joy instead of sorrow."

The Biblical teaching about Zion is this: Where God's PRESENCE dwells there is…

BLESSING
REVELATION
AUTHORITY
PROTECTION
HEALING
SALVATION
PROVISION
and JOY!

The Jews understood this! They knew their CALL was to host the Presence of God! They believed that by hosting God's Presence in the temple, they were releasing God's blessing to the entire earth! One Jewish rabbi commented: "If the Romans understood the blessings mankind received from the temple, they never would have destroyed it!"

Keys to Hosting God's Presence in the Earth

God taught the Jews HOW to dwell in His Presence! That was one of the primary purposes of the Old Testament Scriptures. In the Scriptures, God reveals several KEYS to hosting God's Presence in the earth. Let's look at three of these:

Key # 1: Avoiding Idolatry

The first issue that must be dealt with if we are to enjoy God's *Shekinah* is the issue of idolatry! God's Presence cannot dwell in the presence of idolatry.

One of the saddest passages in the Bible is found in the book of Ezekiel. In Ezekiel 8-11, we see God's glory departing from His temple! Ezekiel explains that Israel's **idolatry** was *driving God's Presence away.* But God's *Shekinah* didn't leave all at once... it left slowly, by stages...

In Ezek 8:6, Ezekiel is told, "Do you see what the house of Israel is doing here, *things that will DRIVE ME far from My sanctuary?"* God then begins to show him pictures of Israel's idolatry.

In Ezek 9:3, the departure begins. God's *Shekinah* Glory moves from the inner court (the Holy of Holies), to the threshold of the sanctuary, and stops. God *waits* to see if Israel will notice that He is leaving and repent!

In Ezek 10:19, God's departure enters its next stage. His Glory moves from threshold to the eastern gate... and *waits* again! But still there is no repentance of idolatry.

In Ezek 11:23, God's *Shekinah* is seen moving out of Jerusalem, across the Kidron Valley, to the Mount of Olives. There He *waits* again! He gives Israel one last chance to turn from their idols!

I believe Ezekiel reveals God's heart for His people. He *cannot* dwell where there is idolatry, but He doesn't leave in anger.

He leaves in sorrow. God longs for His people to repent so His Presence may return!

Idolatry drives God's Presence away! That's a picture of the church in the fourth and fifth centuries… as idolatry came in, God's Presence and power departed!

When REVIVAL breaks out, God responds to our prayers and allows His glory to return. His Presence comes to "visit" His people once again! We experience His life and power! But if God finds idolatry in the church, REVIVAL ENDS QUICKLY! Idolatry *always* drives God's Presence away!

Key # 2: Establishing Holiness

A second issue involved in hosting God's Presence is *holiness*. God's *Shekinah* DEMANDS holiness. God told Moses to prepare a "*holy* place" so He could dwell among the people!

Lack of holiness drives God's Presence away! In Deuteronomy 23:14, God warns, "For the LORD your God walks in the midst of your camp, to deliver you and give your enemies over to you; therefore your camp shall be HOLY, that He may see no unclean thing among you, and turn away from you."

God devoted much of the Old Testament to teaching the Jews about holiness. Even today, most Jews understand holiness.

As we saw in the last chapter, most Christians don't even understand what holiness is! Holiness is not a part of our thinking. Many Christians have such an independent spirit, they don't want to *honor* anything!

In much of the church today, we disregard God's holy days and appointed times. We dishonor our parents. We criticize and ridicule our spiritual leaders.   And then we wonder why God's Presence departs from us so quickly!

Holiness is an absolute necessity if we are to dwell in God's Presence

Key # 3: Continual Worship

A third issue for maintaining God's Presence is that there must be a CONTINUAL SACRIFICE of prayer and praise.

Psalm 22:3 (NASB) tells us God is ENTHRONED on the praises of His people! Where God is praised… His Presence comes! Where He is praised *continually*, His Presence *dwells*!

Continual prayer and praise was one of the first things God taught the Jews! When God told Moses, "Let them construct a sanctuary for Me, that I may DWELL among them" (Ex 25:8), He revealed HOW a special place was to be prepared for His Presence. He promised: "Follow the pattern I give you, and My Presence WILL dwell with you!"

God's Pattern for the Tabernacle

Moses' tabernacle was a tent constructed to host the Presence of God. Each element pictured an aspect of prayer and worship. As you read God's instructions for this tabernacle, God repeatedly stressed that it must be a place of *continual* prayer, praise, and worship! Notice God's instructions concerning the elements of the tabernacle:

1. The Altar of Burnt Offerings. The burnt offering was an act of WORSHIP, "expressing commitment and complete surrender" (NASB Study Bible). It was the Old Testament equivalent of Romans 12:1-2! When you offered a burnt offering, you were symbolically placing yourself on the altar and giving yourself totally to God! God's instruction about the altar of burnt offering was this:

Lev. 6:8 - "The fire is to be *kept burning...*"
Lev. 6:12 – "The fire on the altar shall be *kept burning*..."
Lev. 6:13 – "Fire shall be *kept burning continually* on the altar."

2. The Table of Showbread. The table of showbread was a grain offering. On it, bread was set each week as an act of worship, thanking God for His goodness and provision. Concerning this table, God instructed:

"Take fine flour and bake twelve cakes with it... you shall set them on the pure gold table before the LORD... *Every Sabbath day* ... set it in order before the LORD *continually.*" (Lev. 24:5-8)

3. The Golden Lampstand. The lampstand was a symbol of the Holy Spirit among His people releasing revelation from God.

Lev. 24:2-4 instructs: "Make a lamp *burn continually*... keep it in order from evening to morning before the LORD *continually*; it shall be a *perpetual* statute... keep the lamps on the lampstand before the LORD *continually.*"

4. The Altar of Incense. The burning of incense was a symbol of the prayers of God's people.

Exodus 30:7-8 instructs, "Burn fragrant incense on it... burn it *every morning* ... [and] at twilight. There shall be *perpetual incense* before the LORD throughout your generations."

Do you see a pattern here? In each part of the tabernacle, *expressions of praise and prayer were to be* **continually** *lifted up to the Lord!* God wanted the tabernacle marked by...

- Continual Worship
- Continual Thanksgiving
- Continual Fellowship with His Spirit, and
- Continual Prayer

The Jews took this very seriously. Generation after generation, they maintained continual worship in the tabernacle and later at the temple! Every morning, there was a morning sacrifice to God. Every evening, an evening sacrifice. Every day there were regular times to light the incense. It was a place of continual worship!

The Jews also offered continual offerings of praise, prayer, and worship at David's tabernacle. When David brought the ark into Jerusalem, he pitched a tent for it and stationed musicians and singers to surround the ark with praise continually.

During the Babylonian captivity, Israel had no temple, but every faithful Jew offered a sacrifice of prayer and praise three times a day. These times of prayer were based on the times of morning and evening sacrifice in the temple, and the daily burning of incense. We see the importance Daniel placed on this practice in Daniel chapter six. Daniel was willing to be thrown to the lions rather than give up his regular hours of prayer!

By New Testament times, offering God a "continual sacrifice" of prayer and praise was a standard part of Judaism! It was a normal part of life for *every* observant Jew. Jesus and the apostles lived their lives observing these regular daily prayer watches. These set times are still observed by many Jews today!

Not long ago I was waiting for a flight at the airport in Zurich, Switzerland. In the waiting room, I noticed three Orthodox Jews. They stood out clearly from the crowd because of their beard, hairstyle, and manner of dress. While these men had not been sitting together, they all did something very interesting. At about the same time, all three got up from their seats and walked over to the window that faced toward Jerusalem. They all put on their prayer shawls and began intently praying, prayer book in hand.

While their appearance and actions probably seemed odd to most of those present, I knew exactly what they were doing. This was one of their daily times for prayer! They were engaging in a practice that was at least 2500 years old, going back to the time of the prophet Daniel! I would not choose to display my prayer life in public as they did (Jesus instructed us not to pray "on the street corner" to be noticed, but to seek a more private place.) Yet I was impressed by how seriously these men took their commitment to offer up a continual sacrifice of prayer.

The early church took this seriously also! In Acts 3, we see Peter and John going up to the temple for the *hour of prayer.* History reveals that the church had several set times each day to offer up a sacrifice of prayer and praise. Interestingly, these were the same hours of prayer the Jews observed! A continual sacrifice of prayer and praise was part of their Jewish heritage.

The church placed great importance on offering up this continual sacrifice of prayer and praise to God! Note the following passages...

- Luke 24:53 - They stayed *CONTINUALLY* at the temple, praising God.
- Acts 1:14 - They were *CONTINUALLY* devoting themselves to prayer.
- Acts 2:41-43 - They were *CONTINUALLY* devoting themselves to... prayer.
- Acts 2:46-47 - They *CONTINUED* to meet together in the temple courts... praising God.
- Heb 13:15 - Through Jesus, therefore, let us *CONTINUALLY* offer to God a sacrifice of praise...

As the Jews had done before them, the church practiced continual prayer in every location. For more than 300 years, the church considered this their highest priority!

Out of that continual *ministry to God*, the power flowed! As the church obeyed God's instructions to maintain a continual sacrifice of prayer and praise, God's glory came and dwelt in their midst! Miracles happened! Prophetic revelation was released, and the territory changed!

For three hundred years, the church experienced continual revival! But then, in the days of Constantine, the church rejected its Jewish roots. Idolatry was allowed to fill the church. The church no longer functioned in holiness. Continual prayer became a dead ritual and ultimately ceased. The result was that *the Glory of God departed!*

The Watch of the Lord

We are living in a day when God is restoring His Presence to the church. God wants the church again to experience continual revival! God is cleansing His church of impurity and idolatry. He is teaching us about continual prayer.

One of the most interesting teachings in the church today is the renewed emphasis on the WATCH OF THE LORD. In many locations around the world, God has burdened the hearts of Christians to establish prayer rooms where 24-hour prayer and praise are lifted up to the Lord. Christians sign-up to be part of a daily or weekly "Prayer Watch" so that a continual sacrifice of prayer may be offered!

The "Watch of the Lord" is not a new fad in Charismatic Christianity. It is the restoration of an ancient pattern. God is calling His church to observe the watches of prayer observed by Jesus, the apostles, and the early church. He is calling His church to once again offer that continual sacrifice before Him!

That's a legacy of our Jewish Roots! If you would like to learn more about establishing regular prayer watches, I would highly recommend the book, *Ordering Your Day*, by Chuck Pierce (available from Glory of Zion).

A Case-Study of Continual Prayer

Does a continual sacrifice of prayer really help maintain continual revival? Let's look at an example of a place where this practice was observed.

One of the greatest revivals in modern history began in the little German village of Herrnhut. I have visited Herrnhut, and even today it is a very small village in eastern Germany, hard to find on a map! Yet something took place there that literally shook the world!

In the early 1700's, a group of Moravian refugees came into Germany, fleeing the thirty-year's war in their native Moravia. A German nobleman, Count Nicholas Von Zinzendorf, gave them permission to settle on his estate, and they founded the village of Herrnhut.

Herrnhut quickly became a haven for Protestant refugees from across Europe. There was a great deal of division and strife between the various factions at Herrnhut, so Count Zinzendorf invited the entire village to come together for a communion service at the Lutheran church in the nearby village of Bertholdsdorf.

That service was held on August 13, 1727. As the Moravians crowded into the church, Zinzendorf climbed the stairs to the high pulpit and began the service...

Suddenly the Holy Spirit FELL!

No one present at that service ever told exactly what happened, except to say the place was filled with signs, wonders, and miracles! They left that place changed! Strife and confusion were gone! They burned with love for Jesus and each other ... and a passionate commitment to reach the world! GOD had invaded Herrnhut!

In the days that followed the outpouring, the leaders met to discuss what to do next! Uppermost in their minds was the question of how to keep the Presence of God in their midst. They didn't want to lose what they had received!

In the midst of this, Zinzendorf remembered God's instruction about the tabernacle! He said, "We must keep the fire on the altar!"

In response to this directive, the Moravians divided up the day and night into watches and started 24-hour prayer at Herrnhut! As they continued in prayer, twenty-four hours a day, seven days a week, the *Shekinah* glory of God dwelt in their midst. The Moravians continued that cycle of 24-hour prayer for over one hundred years!

The results of that prayer meeting sound like something from the book of Acts! From the little village of Herrnhut, missionaries were sent out all over the world! At that time, the church in Europe sent out an average of one missionary for every 5000 church members! In Herrnhut, it was one missionary for every *sixty* church members! Within a few years, there were missionaries from Herrnhut in North America, South America, Greenland, South Africa, among the aborigines of Australia, and even in Tibet!

One Moravian convert was a young Englishman named John Wesley. Wesley was saved through the ministry of Moravians from Herrnhut. Shortly after his salvation, Wesley traveled to Herrnhut, "caught" the revival, and brought it back to England, where it became known as the "Evangelical Revival" or the "Wesleyan Revival." It literally changed the nation! Many thousands were saved. Slavery was abolished. Drunkenness and crime dramatically decreased. Many historians feel that this revival probably saved England from the kind of bloody revolution France endured!

As the Moravians at Herrnhut continued to lift up their continual sacrifice of prayer, revival spread around the world! Men like George Whitfield brought the revival across the Atlantic to America, where it was called "The First Great Awakening." Revival swept the American colonies. Church attendance doubled!

Benjamin Franklin described the effects of the Great Awakening this way: "From being thoughtless and indifferent about religion, it seemed as if all the world was growing religious! One could not walk through a town in an evening without hearing psalms sung in different families in every street!"

That revival changed the face of America! Most of the men involved in the writing of our constitution were men whose lives had been dramatically changed by the Great Awakening! America owes part of its godly foundation to a group of Moravians in the village of Herrnhut who "prayed the price" to keep the fire on the altar!

God *always* desires for His Presence and power to dwell among His people! God's word to us is the same word He gave the Jews: "Let them construct a sanctuary for Me that I may dwell among them" (Ex 25:8).

The church is to be a sanctuary of living stones where God is continually enthroned on the praises of His people! Out of His Presence dwelling among us flows the supernatural power to change the world!

STEPS TO RESTORATION!

Ephesians 2:12-22 tells us that the ultimate goal of the ONE NEW MAN is *revival!* When Jew and Gentile are fitted together, Paul says, they form a holy temple... *a dwelling place of God!* God is calling you to be a vital part of that temple today!

Ask God to show you any areas of *idolatry* in your life. Be sensitive to His Spirit and deal with those issues He shows you.

Learn to walk in *holiness*. Be careful to show honor where it is due.

Develop regular *times of prayer*. Ask God to show you how to establish a "continual sacrifice" of praise in your life. (Note: "continual praise" does not necessarily mean "twenty-four hours a day" praise, although that is a wonderful goal. To the ancient Jews—and the Messianic Christians—continual praise meant maintaining regular watches of prayer and praise each day.)

If your church, or a group in your area, is establishing regular watches for prayer and praise, I would encourage you to participate. God wants His people, in every place, to offer up *a continual sacrifice of praise and prayer.*

When we offer up continual prayer, we are **preparing a sanctuary** for His Presence. *If you build it, He will come!*

Chapter Twelve
The Restoration of All Things.
Becoming the One New Man

*"Repent and return, so that your sins may be wiped away, in order that times of refreshing may come from the presence of the Lord; and that He may send Jesus, the Messiah appointed for you, whom heaven must receive until **the time for the restoration of all things** about which God spoke by the mouth of His holy prophets." - Acts 3:19-21*

The church today seems but a pale shadow of the one the apostles knew. We plant a new church and diligently nurture it, but in twenty years it may only reach a few hundred people. If a church reaches a few thousand, we consider it a highly successful church.

The average church in America has *less* than one hundred members and is decreasing. Most church growth in America comes from membership transfers. When one church is growing, you usually find others that are shrinking. As of five years ago, *no county in America* had seen a net increase in church attendance in twenty years. The "unsaved" community in America is not being reached. Of those few who respond to our evangelistic outreach, only 5-10 percent are still involved in church a year later.

A few churches around the world have seen remarkable success, but that success is usually linked to a specific leader or local setting, and the techniques have not transferred well to other cultures.

For generations, men and women have sought to discover the secret of the early church's success. There have been many attempts to restore the New Testament church and many of these have seen a measure of success.

The Protestant Reformation restored the doctrine of salvation and put the Bible back in the hands of the people. This was a major step forward, but it did not fully restore the church.

The great revivals of the 18th century restored an emphasis on a godly lifestyle. 19th century restoration movements focused on the structure of the church, seeking more biblical forms of church government.

In the 20th century, the Pentecostal and Healing movements restored the gifts of the Spirit. Through the Charismatic and "Jesus" movements, we saw the restoration of expressive, Spirit-led worship. Through the "Body life" movement came the restoration of every-member ministry. Presently, the house church movement, prayer movement, prophetic and apostolic movements are all seeking to restore the power and life of the early church.

I believe all of these movements have been raised up by God and are restoring pieces of the puzzle. All of these are *essential* if the church is to be restored.

Yet, in all of this, there is a key element missing. In all the efforts at restoration, almost everyone has ignored the most basic fact of the early church's identity: We have not yet seen the church restored to its Jewish roots.

But we are living in a day when that foundation stone is being restored.

The Days of Restoration!

We are living in the days of restoration!

Acts 3:21 promises that, before the return of Jesus, God will bring a great move of restoration in the earth. It will be a time when God will literally restore all things! That's also a Jewish concept! The Jews believe in a coming time when all the universe will be restored. The Hebrew for that restoration of all things is, *"Tikkun Ha 'Olam!"* I believe that time of restoration has begun!

Part of that restoration is seen in the rise of Messianic Judaism. God is restoring the Jews to their Messiah!

But God also desires restoration for His church! God's Presence cannot dwell in a paganized church! He is calling the church back to its roots. He is restoring our lost inheritance! He is calling His church to BECOME the "One New Man" where Jew and Gentile together feast on the riches of God's new covenant!

In Ephesians chapter five, God pictures the church as the Bride of Christ. The promise is given that, in preparation for His coming, God will do an incredible work to prepare His bride! He will wash His bride with the Word to purify her, that He may present her to Himself as a glorious bride, without spot or wrinkle.

I believe we are living in the day these verses describe. God is preparing His bride! He is restoring His CHURCH! I believe we are about to see the church rise up in a power and glory we have not witnessed since the first century. It will not look much like the church we have known. Many in the traditional church will be the first to oppose it! But for those who are hungry for God, it will be the fulfillment of their deepest longings!

We live in the most exciting days in all of history! God's power is being restored! His Spirit is being poured out! God is inviting YOU to join in the process of restoration!

Let God Restore You to Your ROOTS!

Let God Restore You to His PRESENCE!

The MESSIANIC CHURCH has returned!

Appendix One
God's Heart for the Jews

One of my favorite biblical stories is the parable of the lost son. It's the story of the young man who took his inheritance and squandered it in a far country (Luke 15:11-32). When his money was spent and his friends had deserted him, he was forced to take a job feeding livestock on a pig farm, a horrible fate for a young Jewish boy.

One day, when the son was tempted to fill his empty stomach with pig feed, he "came to himself" and realized that even the lowest servants on his father's farm lived better than he. Thus enlightened concerning the *goodness* of his father, he headed for home, prepared to humble himself and plead for employment on the family farm.

But the son had underestimated his father's goodness. The father had anticipated his son's return and was eagerly searching the horizon for some trace of his wayward boy. At the first sight of his son, the father ran to him and threw his arms around him. Before the son could express his well-rehearsed speech of repentance, the father had put a robe on his shoulders, a ring on his finger, and ordered a lavish feast to celebrate the son's return.

This story is a beautiful account of repentance and restoration, but few Christians have really grasped its meaning. The real point of the parable is not the repentance of the lost son or the goodness of the loving father. In Jesus' telling of the parable, the real focus is on the older brother, sitting outside the party pouting, refusing to join in the joyful celebration of his brother's return.

The older brother had lived in the father's house and received the father's love. All the father's blessings were his, freely given. Yet in spite of his daily experience of the father's goodness, he had never come to know his father's heart. He had been so preoccupied with his own position and responsibilities that he had failed to share the father's love for his wayward brother.

I believe this story gives us a painfully accurate picture of the church's attitude toward the Jewish people. Gentile believers in Jesus enjoy all the blessings of the Father's house. We rejoice in our Father's love, but we have failed to understand our Father's heart.

Much of church history has been characterized by a satanically inspired hatred of the people God loves as the "apple of His eye."

Even where anti-Semitism has been repudiated, the church has frequently been blind to the true significance of the Jewish people. Many evangelicals view the Jews as simply one more ethnic group to penetrate with the gospel, one more religious community to convert and bring into the church.

This attitude, though well intentioned, has been almost as harmful as anti-Semitism, for it fails to honor the special place the Jewish people occupy in God's heart.

We live in a day when I believe it is essential that we gain a biblical picture of God's heart for the Jewish people. A failure to understand God's heart and purposes for Israel will leave us, like the older brother, sitting outside the party that is about to begin.

God's Covenant with Israel

To comprehend what God is doing in the world today, we need to see that the Jews are unlike any other nation, any other race, and any other people, in all the earth. Of all the peoples of the earth, the people of Israel are the only ones whose identity is founded on a covenant with God himself

The giving of that covenant is described in Genesis 15. In Genesis 15:4-7, God gives Abram three promises. He promises Abram an heir--a *son* coming from his own body. He promises that Abram's offspring would become a great *nation*. And finally, He promises that Abram's offspring would possess a specific *territory,* the land of Israel.

Now, in the preceding chapters, God had repeatedly given Abram those same promises. Abram's problem was that *he hadn't seen any of it happen!* He had already waited a long time for the promises, and his faith was close to faltering. So Abram asks the Lord for some assurance that the promises would be fulfilled.

In response to Abram's demand, the Lord tells Abram to bring a cow, a goat and a ram. He has Abram slaughter these animals, cut their bodies in half, and arrange the pieces opposite each other on the ground. Then, when the sun has set, Abram sees a smoking firepot with a blazing torch appear and pass between the pieces. We are told that, on that day, the Lord "cut" a covenant with Abram.

In the ancient world, when you wanted to give someone

absolute assurance of your intentions, you did not make a promise. You *cut* a covenant. You took an animal, killed it, and literally *cut* it in half. The person making the covenant would then walk between the two halves of the animal. As he did this, he was saying, "This is how serious I am in my promise. May the Lord do to me as I have done to this animal if I do not keep my promises to you."

This was taken very seriously. It established a *blood* covenant, made before God, in which a person offered his life as pledge-- asking God to take his life if he failed to keep his agreement (Jer. 34:18-20).

When God "cut" this covenant, He was saying, "This is how serious I am, Abram. I will *cut covenant* with you. You divide the animals and I will pass between them. In cutting this covenant, this is My pledge... May I cease to exist if I fail to keep the promises I make to you!" That was God's covenant with Abram. It's on the basis of that covenant that the Jewish people exist.

As we read the Bible, we need to hear the heart of God as He expresses His covenant love to the Jewish people.

In Deuteronomy 32:9-10, He says, "The Lord's *portion* is His people, Jacob his *allotted inheritance*. ... He guarded him as *the apple of His eye*."

In Genesis 12:3, God promised the Jews, "I will bless those who bless you, and whoever curses you I will curse; and all peoples on earth will be blessed through you." Through the ages God has remained true to that word. You can trace the rise and fall of nations by how they have treated the Jewish people. God blesses those that bless them. He curses those that curse them.

The obituary of the Jewish people has been written many times and it has always been premature. There is no other race in human history that has been as persecuted and oppressed as the Jewish people. Time after time, powerful rulers have risen up with plans to exterminate the Jews, yet the Jews have survived.

Nations that were mighty in Abram's day have passed from the scene. Have you ever met a Perizzite or a Kenite? Do you know where the descendants of the Hittites have been scattered? Have you ever heard of a Russian Amorite, a Spanish Jebusite, or a German Girgashite? These were well-known nations and people-groups in Abram's day, but today they are lost and forgotten. Yet you can go to almost any nation in the world and identify the seed of Abraham.

Against all odds, the Jews have survived! The very existence of this people is a testimony to God's supernatural work to fulfill His covenant.

Israel and the New Covenant

It's important to note that God's promises concerning Israel are not limited to the First Covenant. The New Covenant Scriptures also speak of Israel's unique position before God.

In Romans 3:1-2, the apostle Paul writes, "What advantage, then, is there in being a Jew? ... Much in every way!"

This is not a Jewish prophet writing. This is the Apostle Paul, the apostle to the *Gentiles.* Writing to a predominantly *Gentile* church in a *Gentile* city, Paul asks, "What advantage is there in being a Jew?"

How would *you* answer that question? Do the Jews have an advantage with God? Do they have a special position in God's sight?

Paul's answer is, "Much in every way!"

"First of all," he writes, "they have been entrusted **with the very words of God.**"

Paul says that when God chose to reveal Himself in Scripture, He entrusted that revelation to Jews. He could have chosen Americans, Russians, Moabites, or Hittites, but He didn't. He chose to reveal His eternal, unchanging Word through only one group of people, the Jews.

Did you know your Bible is a *Jewish* book? Every book in your Bible was written by *Jews.* Most of it was also written *to* Jews.

Some time ago, I had our church do a little experiment to show them how Jewish the Bible is. I first asked them to open their Bibles to Acts 15.

I explained that Acts 15 is a pivotal chapter in the Bible because in Acts 15 God gives the church some fantastic new revelation. In this chapter, God reveals for *the very first time* that a *person does not have to become a Jew to walk in relationship with God!*

This was a revolutionary truth, and one that some of the early church had a difficult time accepting. Until Acts 15, if you wanted to relate to the God of Israel, you had to be circumcised, convert to Judaism, join the synagogue, and keep the ritual law. From the time Moses picked up his quill to write Genesis 1:1 until Acts 15, everything in the Bible *assumes* that, if you are walking with God, you are a JEW! But in Acts 15, God reveals that Gentiles can know Him without first becoming Jews!

I then asked the congregation to hold their place at Acts 15 and turn to the book of Hebrews. It may surprise you to realize that the book of *Hebrews* was written to *Hebrews!* Messianic Jews! It's about how Jesus, the Jewish Messiah, fulfills the Hebrew Scriptures.

I pointed out that if you start at Hebrews and read the rest of the Bible, almost everything else was written specifically to Messianic Jews.

James was clearly written to Jews. James 1:1 is addressed "to the *twelve tribes* scattered among the nations."   James 2:2, if translated *literally,* reads, "Suppose a man comes into *your synagogue...*" (Many English translations translate this word as *"assembly,"* but the Greek text says *synagogue.)* The Book of James was written to *Messianic Jews* who were meeting in *synagogues.*

Many Bible scholars believe the epistles of Peter, John, and Jude were also written to Messianic Jews. Most of the book of Revelation focuses on God's future plan for the Jewish people. So almost everything in the Bible from Hebrews on is thoroughly *Jewish.*

I now was ready to complete the experiment. I had the people hold their thumb at Acts 15, and their index finger at Hebrews chapter one. I pointed out that the pages they held between thumb and index finger represented pretty much *all of the Bible* that was addressed *specifically* to Gentile Christians. It represents less than one tenth of the Bible!

Did you know your Bible is such a Jewish book?

Now, I'm not saying the whole Bible isn't for all of us. *All* of the promises and blessings of God belong to *every* believer in Jesus, whether Jew or Gentile. But God wants us to know those blessings came *through* the Jews. The Jews have the *great advantage* that they **have been entrusted with the very words of God.**

In Romans 9:4-5, Paul continues to list the advantages of the Jewish people. "Theirs is the adoption as sons; theirs the divine glory, the covenants, the receiving of the law, the temple worship and the promises. Theirs are the patriarchs, and from them is traced the human ancestry of Christ, who is God over all, forever praised! Amen."

Paul says from *the Jews* we have received the Bible, the covenants, and the promises. *From the Jews* we have the revelation of God's character in the law. *Through the Jews* we have the godly examples of men like Abraham, Moses and David. *And from the Jews* we even have Jesus.

Do you realize that every good thing you have received from God in the spiritual realm you have gotten through Jews? That's what Paul is saying. I believe Jesus, Himself, summed it up when He said in John 4:22, *"Salvation* is of the **Jews**." If you are saved, it's because you have "linked in" to something that God poured out upon the Jewish people.

No wonder Satan hates the Jewish people and has tried so diligently to destroy them! They are the race of people through which God has poured out His blessing upon the earth. It is through them that the plans and purposes of the devil have been frustrated again and again. And I believe the Bible teaches that in these last days, the people of Israel will come into their finest hour!

Has God Divorced His Wife?

One of the subtlest forms of anti-Semitism in the world today is a doctrine called *replacement theology*. And it is, unfortunately, rampant in much of the church today. Replacement theology says, "Yes, God gave these promises to the Jewish people! He married Himself to the Jewish people in solemn covenant. They were His people, His bride. But they rejected the Messiah, so God rejected them! God cut them off. They are no longer His people. God divorced his first wife, Israel, and married the *church."*

That is basically what replacement theology teaches. And there are a surprising number of Christians who believe it.

Some time ago, I attended a conference in a large church in another city. The pastor of this church is an influential man in the Charismatic community. If I mentioned his name, you would probably recognize it.

As I looked around the inside of the building, I saw it was decorated with the flags of many nations. Having a heart for missions, I was intrigued. I walked around the auditorium between the conference sessions and looked to see how many of the flags I could identify. I saw Russia, Argentina, Mexico, Australia, and many others. I noticed, however, that one flag was conspicuous by its absence. They had no flag of Israel.

When I mentioned the omission to my companion, he explained, "Oh the pastor here is into replacement theology. *He doesn't believe Israel is significant"* That statement *stunned* me! It took my breath away! I was dumbfounded! Here is a godly man, a national leader in the church, who believes the God of Abraham has turned His back on the Jews!

Why was I so shocked? It's because replacement theology is not just an attack against the *Jews.* It's an attack against the *character of God.* To say that God has rejected the Jewish people goes against everything He has revealed about His character and nature.

In Isaiah 44:21-22, the Lord promises, "O Israel, *I will not forget you.* I have swept away your offenses like a cloud, your sins like the morning mist. *Return to me, for I have redeemed you."* That is the cry of God's heart to the Jewish people. Even in their unbelief and disobedience, His love never ceases.

In Jeremiah 31:35-36, we find some amazing statements: "This is what the LORD says, **He who appoints the sun to shine by day, Who decrees the moon and stars to** shine by night. **'Only if these decrees vanish from** my sight,' declares the LORD, 'will **the descendants of Israel ever cease to be a nation before me."'**

This is earthshaking. God stakes the whole universe on His commitment to Israel! He says, "Do you want to know if I am finished with Israel? Look out the window and see if the sun is still shining! Walk out at night and see if the moon and stars are still in their places. So long as those decrees are still in place, you can know that I have not forsaken My people Israel!"

In verse 37, He goes on to say, "'**Only if the heavens above can be measured and the foundations of the earth below be searched out will I reject all the descendants of Israel because of all they have done,'** declares the LORD." That's the level of God's covenant commitment to the Jewish people!

In Romans 11, Paul deals with the question, "Did God reject His people?" Paul's answer is, "By no means!" Paul seems irritated that such a question would even be asked!

In Romans 11:25-29, Paul explains the unbelief of Israel in the present day. He says "a *partial* hardening has happened to Israel *until* the fullness of the Gentiles has come in and so *all Israel will be saved."*

Paul says that Israel's unbelief, first of all, is *partial.* Not all of Israel is in unbelief. God always preserves a remnant. In Elijah's day, Elijah thought he was the only one in Israel still faithful to God. But God said "I've preserved 7,000." God *always* preserves a remnant! There have *always* been Jews that have known their Messiah.

Secondly, Paul assures us that Israel's hardening to the Gospel is *temporary.* It will only last until the fullness of the Gentiles has come in.

God tells us that the final outcome is *assured...* that all of Israel *will* be saved! That Israel, as a nation, will one day turn and embrace their Messiah! They will ultimately fulfill their priestly role as a light to the Gentile nations, and the result will be the greatest revival in human history. Paul describes the return of the Jews to Messiah as bringing "life from the dead" for the Gentile church (Rom. 11:15)!

This is one of God's primary goals in history, and it *will* be accomplished. We will never comprehend what God is doing in the world if we fail to recognize His heart and plan for Israel.

Why does God still love the Jews? Paul says it's because "the gifts and the calling of God are irrevocable." God made a covenant with Abraham 4,000 years ago and it does not matter what the Jews have done. He still loves them. He still reaches out to them. And He assures us that they *will* respond!

Appendix Two
The Jewishness of the Early Church

This book presents a view of church history that is radically different from that which many have been taught. For this reason, many who read it will have legitimate questions about the historical data to support this view. While this book is not intended as a scholarly treatise, I have written this appendix to briefly outline this evidence. I regret that space limitations do not allow a fuller recounting of this evidence.

The Traditional View of Church History.

H.L. Elison's article in *Eerdman's Handbook to the History of Christianity* describes the Church's connection to Judaism this way: "At first Christians were regarded as a Jewish sect by both Jews and Gentiles... After the Jewish revolts against Rome (AD 66-73, AD 132-35) most Christians disassociated themselves from the Jews... From this time few Jews converted to Christianity."[1]

This is typical of the treatment of our Jewish roots in most history books. Out of a total of 656 pages, Christianity's relationship to Judaism is dismissed in one brief paragraph. The implication is that the church's Jewish heritage is irrelevant, and was quickly dismissed by the apostles when they established the Gentile church.

At least two factors have contributed to this interpretation of church history:

1. Few primary sources for the early Messianic Church survive. Through the 1000 years of the dark ages, the only ones preserving ancient manuscripts were the monks of the Roman Church, most of whom embraced a replacement theology and viewed any expression of Messianic Christianity as heretical. Their goal was not to preserve Messianic sources, but to destroy these "heretical" writings whenever possible. We know that in the Eastern Church there were many books written by Messianic authors. Eusebius even quotes from a second century Messianic Jewish historian. Unfortunately, these works have not survived.

Most of the descriptions of the early Messianic Church that have survived come from those who opposed it.

2. By the time post-reformation church histories were written, Jewish influences in the church were so thoroughly eliminated that historians did not consider it important to investigate our Jewish origins. It was assumed that the Apostles had rejected Judaism and established the church as a Gentile organization.

As a result, most modern historians have approached the data with the assumption that the relationship between the church and Judaism was short-lived and unimportant.

I believe a closer inspection of the historical data, however, pictures an early church that embraced its Jewish heritage even in the midst of severe persecution for many hundreds of years.

Space will not allow the full recounting of this evidence, but I have tried to outline below the four major lines of evidence which point to an early church that was far more "Jewish" than most of us have been led to believe.

Evidences for a "Jewish" Early Church

1. Evidence of Christian Participation in the Synagogues.

According to historical records it was common for early Christians, both Jew and Gentile, to attend the local synagogue on Sabbath and other holidays, in addition to attending church on Sunday.

There are numerous New Testament references to Christians meeting at the Temple (Acts 2:46, 3:1, 5:42, 24:17-18, etc.) and attending synagogues (Acts 13:14-42, 14:1, 17:2, 17:10, 19:8, etc.). In the book of James, Christians are described as meeting in synagogues to worship. (James 2:2, if translated literally, reads, "Suppose a man comes into your *synagogue*..." Many English translations translate this word as *"assembly,"* but the Greek text uses the word *synagogue.*) In Acts 15, the Jerusalem counsel *assumed* that the Gentile converts would attend the Jewish synagogue to hear the *Torah* read each Sabbath (Acts 15:20-21).

It has traditionally been taught that around CE 90, the Jews added the **Birkat ha-Minim**, to the synagogue liturgy. This benediction—a curse on heretics—was thought to be directed against Christians to drive them from the synagogues. Many have assumed that this brought about the final break between the church and Judaism. More recent scholarship has shown that the original text of the *Birkat* was probably pre-Christian (even late Maccabbean) in origin, and was not initially used against the Christians. Specific wording against Jewish Christians was not added to the *Birkat ha-Minim* until much later, possibly as late as the fourth century.[2]

Eric Meyers, Professor of Religion and Archaeology at Duke University, comments that, contrary to popular opinion, Jews and Christians "lived side by side for several hundred years." He continues, "I'm not sure the tensions most people associate between Jews and Christians really occurred before the fourth century, when Christianity becomes the official religion of the Roman Empire under Constantine. All of these tensions are exaggerated." Meyers describes tensions between Jews and Christians in the first few centuries as an internal *family* conflict, "between cousins and brothers and sisters."[3]

There are many indications that synagogue participation by Christians was still common in the second century. Mark Nanos, in his book, *The Mystery of Romans*, writes, "Evidence indicates that in Rome Christianity and Judaism were inseparable... perhaps until the middle of the second century," and, "There are many indications that community interaction [between Jews and Christians] continued to be the case well into the second century."[4] In another place he writes, "It is possible that the Christians in Rome continued to be part of the Jewish communities and synagogues for a long time."[5]

Bargil Pixner, writing in the *Biblical Archaeology Review,* cites several second-century references to Christian worship in Synagogues.[6]

Christian attendance at synagogues is mentioned by *Ignatius of Antioch*, the *Shepherd of Hermas*, and other second century writers:

"When a man who has the Spirit of God comes into a synagogue of righteous men... and intercession is made to God by those men, then the prophetic Spirit fills the man, and the man speaks to the multitude as the Lord wills" (*Shepherd of Hermas*). [7]

"Stand rightly. Let there be frequent synagogue gatherings, ask every man [to them] by his name. Do not despise slaves, either male or female" (*The Epistle of Ignatius to Polycarp*)." [8]

Amazingly, the practice appears to have continued in some locations as late as the fifth century. Dr. Wayne Meeks, Professor of Biblical Studies at Yale University, recently commented, "As late as the 4th and 5th century, we have evidence of Christians still existing within Jewish communities, and we have evidence of members of Christian communities participating in Jewish festivals. The preacher of Antioch and later of Constantinople, John Chrysostom, complains in a series of eight sermons to his congregation, that "you must stop going to the Synagogue, you must not think that the Synagogue is a holier place than our churches are."[9]

Why would the early Christians attend a Jewish Synagogue? I believe there are at least two reasons. First, they attended synagogue because that had *always* been a part of the Christianity they knew. They had never known or imagined a Christianity that was not closely tied to the Jewish community.

I believe the relationship of the first century church to the synagogue is comparable to the relationship that existed between the charismatic movement and the denominational churches in the '60s. While a number of new charismatic churches were planted during those years, that was not the norm.

Wherever possible, charismatics chose to remain members of the traditional churches. They worshipped in their Lutheran, Episcopal, or Catholic churches on Sunday, but on a different night of the week met in smaller "prayer groups" to celebrate their own distinctive beliefs. They viewed themselves as part of the larger congregation, but had an evangelistic zeal to introduce the rest of the body to their own special focus.

The rest of the congregation sometimes viewed the charismatics with suspicion and uncertainty, but for the most part accepted them as part of the larger community.

If we can accept this as a rough analogy of the early church and synagogue, I believe it gives us a basis to re-evaluate the early church's decision to worship on Sunday.

Many have assumed that the early Christians' choice to worship on Sunday grew out of a *rejection* of Judaism. I would like to suggest that the opposite may be true. I believe the early church's choice to meet on Sunday was an outgrowth of their *commitment* to Judaism. They met as Messianic believers on *Sunday*, because they were *already committed* on Saturday. Saturday was the day they met with the Jewish community to worship the God of Abraham and hear His Word!

A second reason why Christians would have attended Synagogue was to hear the Scriptures read and taught.

In Romans 3:1-2, the apostle Paul states that the Jews have a great *advantage*, because "they have been entrusted **with the very words of God.**"

To the early Christians, the synagogue was the repository of the Scriptures. The sacred scrolls were rare and very expensive. Few Gentile Christians could have owned even one book of the Bible. Their knowledge of God's truth depended on hearing it read at the synagogue.

As we pointed out earlier, Acts 15 assumes the Gentile converts would attend synagogue to hear the *Torah* read.

Even as late as the 4th century, when the Christian scholar Jerome wanted to learn to read the Hebrew Scriptures, he studied at the schools of the rabbis![10]

Nanos writes, "How would they learn the Scriptures and the way God deals with His people apart from involvement in the Jewish community? For the Scriptures were read and interpreted only in the synagogues, and primarily on the Sabbath at that! How else would they learn the ways of righteousness, as there was no New Testament for them? ... We must come to grips with the fact that outside the Synagogue environment the early Christians would have had little opportunity to learn the Scriptures."[11]

2. Quotes from early writers indicating that observance of Jewish Sabbaths and feasts continued well into the fourth century.

A second line of evidence for the Jewishness of the early church comes from the continued Christian observance of "Jewish" Sabbaths and feasts.

There is abundant evidence that the church celebrated the Sabbath and the biblical feasts well into the fourth century and beyond. Here are a few quotes about the early church's observance of the Sabbath:

> *Origen* (185-254) wrote, "After the festival of the crucifixion [Passover] is put the festival of the Sabbath, and it is fitting for whoever is righteous among the saints to keep also the festival of the Sabbath. There remains therefore a keeping of the Sabbath for the people of God (Hebrews 4:9)."[12]

> *The Constitutions of the Holy Apostles,* written in the 3rd or 4th century, states, "You shall observe the [seventh day] Sabbath, because of Him who ceased from His work of creation." [13]

> *Socrates Scholasticus* (late 4th century) wrote, "For although almost all churches throughout the world celebrate the sacred mysteries [Lord's Supper] on the Sabbath of every week, yet the Christians of Alexandria and at Rome, on account of some ancient tradition, have ceased to do this." [14]

The method of observing the Sabbath varied from place to place. In many places, churches worshipped on Sunday while observing Saturday as a day of rest. In a few places, the Church worshipped on Saturday instead of Sunday. The most common practice, however, seems to have been for churches to worship on both the Jewish Sabbath *and* on Sunday.

> *Cassian*, in the *Antiquities of the Christian Church,* says that among the Egyptian churches, services of the Lord's Day and the Sabbath were always the same. In another place he observes that in Egypt and Thebes, believers met to celebrate Communion on Saturday *and* on the Lord's Day. [15]

> *The Catholic historian, Sozomen* (early 5th century), describes the worship of the church in these words: "The people of Constantinople, and almost everywhere, assemble together on the Sabbath, as well as on the first day of the week, which custom is never observed at Rome or at Alexandria. There are

several cities and villages in Egypt where, contrary to the usage established elsewhere, the people meet together on Sabbath evenings, and although they have dined previously, partake of the mysteries [Lord's Supper.]"[16]

Coleman writes: "The last day of the week was strictly kept in connection with that of the first day for a long time after the overthrow of the temple and its worship. Down even to the fifth century the observance of the Jewish Sabbath was continued in the Christian church, but with a rigor and solemnity gradually diminishing."[17]

3. Evidence from Church Council Decrees (4th through the 8th centuries).

One of the best evidences for the continuation of Jewish influence comes from the decrees passed against it. As we read repeated decrees against "Jewish" practices in the church, we must ask, "What conditions would have existed in the church to prompt such decrees to be passed?" Church counsels did not ban a practice unless they were threatened by it. The church did not pass decrees against Buddhist practices because Christians in Rome, Alexandria, and Antioch were not participating in Buddhist practices. Yet, as we saw in chapter three, council after council felt it necessary to repeatedly levy harsh penalties against Jewish practices. The fact that these decrees were passed testifies that such practices as the Sabbath observance and the biblical feasts were still common in the church. Notice again the wording in these examples:

Eusebius, in communicating the decrees of Nicea (325), sternly commanded his readers to "*have nothing in common*" with the Jews, to "*withdraw ourselves*" from participation in Jewish practices and customs, and unite in "*avoiding all participation*" in Jewish conduct.[18] It is clear from his wording that Eusebius was greatly distressed that Christians in his day were still participating in these Jewish customs.

The council of Antioch (A.D. 345) decreed, "If any bishop, presbyter or deacon will dare, *after this decree*, to celebrate Passover with the Jews, the council judges them to be anathema from the church."[19] This decree testifies that fourth century local church leaders, twenty years after Constantine's decree, were still celebrating Passover with the Jews. It expresses the alarm of the council that celebration of feasts with Jews was still a common practice!

As we study the decrees of the various church councils, we find decrees such as these continued to be issued *as late as the eighth century!* Note the following examples:

THE COUNCIL OF LAODICEA (A.D. 365) - "It is not permitted to receive festivals which are by Jews, nor to hold a festival together with them."[20] "Christians must not Judaize by resting on the Sabbath, but must work on that day... but if any be found to be JUDAIZERS let them be ANATHEMA from Christ."[21]

THE COUNCIL OF AGDE, FRANCE (506) – "Clerics must not take part in Jewish festivals."[22]

THE COUNCIL OF NICEA II (787) – "[Those who] openly or secretly keep the Sabbath and follow other practices in the manner of the Jews are not to be received into communion, nor into prayer, nor into the church."[23]

I believe this is an indication of the value the early Christians placed on their Jewish heritage, that for hundreds of years they clung tenaciously to these roots in the face of severe persecution.

4. Perpetuation of Jewish customs in churches not affected by Constantine's edicts.

A fourth line of evidence for the Jewishness of the early church comes from the continuation of Jewish practices in areas not affected by Constantine's decrees.

A study of the medieval church reveals that, around the fringes of the old empire in areas where Constantine's decree could not be readily enforced, groups of believers continued to maintain distinctively Jewish elements of their faith. These groups include the Waldensians of the remote alpine valleys in France and Italy; the Celtic Christians in Ireland, Scotland, Wales; the Eastern churches of

Persia, China, and India, as well as the African churches in Ethiopia. Chapter Five describes the Waldensians and the Celtic Christians of Iona. Here are a few additional examples:

The Abyssinian (Ethiopian) Christians

The Ethiopian Christians claim the gospel was brought to them by the Ethiopian eunuch (Acts 8). For centuries, these churches were almost totally isolated from the European church. Beginning in the seventeenth century, repeated and violent attempts were made by the Jesuits, under the patronage of Portugal, to convert or subdue them.[24] In spite of this, the Ethiopian church, even today, retains a very strong Jewish influence. Some descriptions of the Ethiopian church:

"The Jewish Sabbath and Sunday, are religiously observed. Indications of Jewish influence, besides Sabbath observance, are the practice of circumcision, and distinction between clean and unclean animals, etc."[25]

"For more than seventeen centuries the Abyssinian Church continued to sanctify Saturday as the holy day of the fourth commandment."[26]

The Church in Persia

Another church cut off from the influence of Constantine was the church in Persia:

"The Chaldean Christians, called by their opponents *Nestorians*, trace their descent from the earliest of all Christian missions, the mission of Thaddaeus to Abgarus."[27]

Coleman writes of the Nestorians, "They observe the 'festivals of our Lord' and the Sabbath-day, on which they do no labor. ... The Sabbath-day they reckoned far above the others."[28] He also states that "they burn incense on the Sabbath and feast days."[29]

Schaff comments, "The Nestorians eat no pork and keep the Sabbath. They believe in neither auricular confession nor purgatory."[30]

The Church in India

Tradition attributes the founding of Christian communities in the southwestern part of India (Malabar) to the apostle Thomas. When Portuguese explorers arrived in India in the seventeenth century, they found upwards of a hundred Christian churches already established. Disturbed that these churches did not follow the customs of the Roman Church, they tried to convert them by the power of the Inquisition.[31]

> According to Dellon's *Account of the Inquisition at Goa,* 1684, the St Thomas Christians were accused by the inquisitors of "having Judaized," which was defined as, "having conformed to the ceremonies of the Mosaic law, such as not eating pork, hare, fish without scales, etc., of having attended the solemnization of the Sabbath, having eaten the Pascal Lamb, etc."[32]

> Schaff writes, "Widespread and enduring was the observance of the seventh-day Sabbath among the believers of the Church of the East and the St. Thomas Christians of India. It was also maintained among those bodies which broke off from Rome after the Council of Chalcedon, namely the Abyssinians, the Jacobites, the Marionites, and the Armenians."[33]

Taken together, I believe these four lines of evidence present a picture of a church that clung tenaciously to many of the customs of her Messianic roots for close to a thousand years, despite ongoing persecution. In remote locations, such as Ethiopia, where Jewish customs were not opposed by systematic persecution and inquisition, they have, in fact, persisted to the present day.

The conclusion of this study is that the early church did not, as many have been taught, reject her Messianic roots. These roots were violently cut off through the decrees of the pagan emperor Constantine and his successors. While the 16th century reformers restored much that the church had lost, they never re-engrafted the church into its original Messianic root. I believe that process has, in our day, finally begun.

Appendix Three
Celebrating the Biblical Feasts

In chapter eight, we saw that God has given us a yearly *cycle of life,* made up of a series of "feasts" or "appointed times." God's intention was that, as you repeat this cycle each year, you would be drawn ever-closer to Him, to experience more and more of His blessing in your life.

.   When it comes to these appointed times, however, we have a problem: Most of us are totally ignorant of them!

We know all about our traditional holidays. We know how to celebrate the Fourth of July. We know how to celebrate Thanksgiving. We know how to celebrate Christmas.

These holidays have been part of our culture and part of our lives. It's part of our lives to have picnics and watch fireworks on the Fourth of July. No one needs to teach us to eat turkey and watch football on Thanksgiving!

But when it comes to God's appointed times we are ignorant. We *don't understand* God's appointed times!

Most of us have never celebrated them. The few who *have* celebrated them were often taught to observe them as legalistic rituals, where the true spiritual power was lost!

We don't know *what* God's appointed times are! We don't know *when* they are! Most of us have no idea how to *celebrate* them to enter in to the purposes of God!

To put the biblical feasts in perspective, it's helpful to understand what the Bible means when it talks about a feast or festival.

In the New Testament, the word for these celebrations is the Greek word "*heorte,*" which means "Festival" or "Special Day."

In the Old Testament, several Hebrew words were used of the Appointed Times. One word used is "*mo'ed,*" which simply means "an appointed time." It designated an occasion fixed by divine appointment to meet together with God.

Another Hebrew word used for these special days is "*hag,*" which is taken from the verb "to dance," and means, "An occasion of joy or gladness."

A third Hebrew word used of God's appointed times is "*hagag.*" This word has a variety of meanings:

- *To celebrate a special day.*
- *Rejoicing!*
- *The festive attitudes & actions of celebrating a feast.*
- *Wild and unrestrained actions, like the behavior of a drunken person.* (*On the feast of Pentecost, the apostles so overflowed with the Spirit that they appeared to be drunk.*)
- *Festive dancing and celebrations, as of a victory over enemies in battle.*

From looking at these words, we can begin to get a sense of what holding a festival to the Lord, such as Passover or Tabernacles, was to be. It was a time of rejoicing and celebration with unrestrained joy such as you would experience when you were victorious in a battle!

This gives us real insight into the heart of God! God could have made His appointed times to be times of sorrow. He could have made them times of severe fasting and repentance.

Some people think that's what God desires for His people! Many Christians assume God wants us to show our devotion to Him by being *miserable.* That's not in the Bible! There ARE times for fasting and self-denial, but MOST of God's appointed times are times of FEASTING! God wants us to know that He desires that His children ENJOY Him and experience His GOODNESS!

The feasts of God are times for celebration. But in the midst of the *celebration*, God wants to do an incredible work of *transformation* in our lives.

The **purpose** of this appendix is to give you an ***understanding*** of God's appointed times so you can experience the full blessing of God in each one. I want you to see these feasts, not as legalistic rituals, not as a new set of holidays, and not as traditional "Jewish" celebrations. I want you to see them as they really are: ***appointments with God!***

I want you to experience the joy of meeting with God, allowing Him to break off the enemy's oppression, and drawing you into a fresh experience of His blessing!

May God bless you greatly as you "enter in" to God's yearly CYCLE OF LIFE!

Appendix Three – Part One
The Feast of Passover
Redeemed by the Blood of the Lamb!

"Take a lamb for each household... and on the 14th day of the month, slaughter them at twilight. Then take some of the blood and put it on the sides and tops of the doorframes of the houses... That same night they are to eat the meat roasted over the fire, along with bitter herbs, and bread made without yeast... Eat it... with your cloak tucked into your belt, your sandals on your feet and your staff in your hand. Eat it in haste; it is the LORD's Passover." - Ex 12:3-14

The first of God's festivals is Passover. Passover begins God's yearly cycle. The Feast of Passover is designed to set us on a course that will draw us closer to God and into a fresh experience of His glory each year.

In the early church, Passover was considered the most important celebration of the year. God wants it to be a blessing in your life also!

Understanding Passover

It's sad to say, but most Christians today know very little about Passover. We don't know what it is or how to celebrate it.

If you are not familiar with Passover, here's a one-sentence summary of what Passover is all about:

> **"Passover is the celebration of God's love and power in delivering His people out of the hand of their enemy."**

Passover is not to be just a religious ritual or a holiday. It is a time set by God for specific **SPIRITUAL TRANSACTIONS** to take place. It's a time...

- To **praise God** for His work of deliverance in the past.
- To **seek Him** for a fresh release of deliverance today.
- To **gain faith** for His work in the future.

For the Jews, Passover was a celebration of God's power in setting them free from slavery in Egypt. They had been in bondage, under bitter oppression. They cried out to God and He delivered them *through PASSOVER.*

Christians also have a deliverance to celebrate! We have also been in bondage, under the oppression of a cruel enemy… SATAN. Passover is a vivid picture of how God delivered *US.*

To understand Passover it is good to ask, what was "passed over" at Passover?

The answer is: the *ISRAELITES* were passed over!

The time had come for God's JUDGMENT to fall. It would have fallen on everyone, but God gave the Israelites a way of escape. The key to their rescue was not in an army. It was not in some great, heroic deed, but in a pure, spotless LAMB.

God instructed each family to kill a lamb, drain the blood, and put the blood of the lamb on their doorpost of their home. When the blood of the lamb was placed on the doorpost, God accepted the death of that lamb in place of Israel's firstborn. The angel of death *passed over* them.

Many things happened at Passover:

- By the blood of that lamb, Israel was *REDEEMED!*
- The judgment of God was turned away from them!
- The gods of Egypt were judged, their power broken!
- Israel was released from oppression & bondage!
- They were set free to enter God's promise!

The Celebration of Passover

A typical Jewish Passover meal today consists of several elements, each designed to recreate the sights, sounds, emotions, and even the tastes of the original Passover night. Elements on the table at a traditional Passover meal usually include:

Chazeret, a "Bitter Vegetable" (mentioned in Num 9:11), a reminder of the bitterness of slavery.

The shankbone of a lamb, used to represent "The Lamb that was sacrificed."

Karpas, or parsley, usually dipped in salt water and eaten, to recall the "salty taste of the tears" shed by the Israelite slaves.

Haroset (a mixture of apples & cinnamon), picturing the "mortar or clay" used by the Israelites in their time of slavery.

Maror or "bitter herbs" (usually horseradish). The bitter taste brings tears to the eyes and is, again, a reminder of the "bitterness of slavery."

A roasted egg, included as a symbol of mourning.

These elements in a typical Passover celebration are designed to take us back in time to **RELIVE** God's miracle. As we *see* and *taste* these elements, we remember the cruelty and pain of slavery in Egypt. We taste the bitterness of oppression, but then we remember that God brought deliverance. *By the blood of the Lamb He set His people free!* By His great power Israel became the people of God!

Passover is a very significant celebration for Jews, but it's also for Christians.

WHY is Passover important for Us?

Passover is important to Christians for several reasons:

1. It's important for us because we are spiritually united with Israel. Romans 11:17 says that when we came to Jesus, we were **grafted** into Israel, and share in all the blessings God gave them. Ephesians 2 says that at one time we were "excluded from citizenship in Israel," but now we are "fellow citizens" with them. We join with the Jews in celebrating Passover because we are spiritually united with them.

2. Passover is important because it is part of God's plan of salvation for you. Apart from Passover the Jews would have died as slaves in Egypt. Jesus could not have been born and, as a result, there would be no salvation for us. We would have ended up in hell!

3. Passover is important because God designed Passover as a celebration of Jesus. I Cor. 5:7 says, "Jesus is our Passover Lamb." God could have had Jesus die at any time of the year but He chose to have Him die at Passover. God chose Passover because Passover was GIVEN to teach us about Jesus. Through Passover, we come to understand what His death accomplished.

Passover is all about Jesus!

- He came as the Lamb of God.
- His blood redeems us.
- By His death, judgment was turned away and the power of the enemy was broken.
- We were released from bondage and oppression.
- We were set free to enter into God's promise.

Everything in Passover is a picture of Jesus! Every element points to Jesus!

Picture in your mind what took place on the original Passover night: In obedience to God's command, the father of the house took blood from the Passover lamb and put it in a bowl. He went to the door of his home, dipped a branch of hyssop into the blood, and applied it first to both doorposts of the home. Then he dipped the hyssop into the blood again and reached up to apply blood to the lintel also.

Now stop and think about what is taking place. First the father moves the hyssop **from side to side** to apply blood to both doorposts. He then **lowers the hyssop down** into the bowl and **reaches up** over his head to apply blood to the lintel. Can you see what this Israelite father is doing at the front door of his home? It's a gesture you've probably seen Roman Catholics do when they pray. At Passover every father in Israel made **the sign of the cross** in the blood of the Lamb! What a dramatic picture of Jesus! *God's deliverance ALWAYS comes by His cross and by His blood!*

Through Passover, the Jews became the people of God. But Passover is *also* how WE became the people of God!

The Message of Passover

One of the strongest confessions of faith you can make is this:

"I am redeemed by the blood of the Lamb out of the hand of the enemy."

I remember hearing Derek Prince share that in leading people into deliverance, he often had them make that profession. If he could get them to declare, in faith, "I am redeemed by the blood of the Lamb out of the hand of the enemy." That was often enough to break the power of demonic forces from a believer's life!

That's the message of Passover! The message of Passover is summed up in that one sentence: "I am redeemed by the blood of the Lamb out of the hand of the enemy!" Israel knew what it meant to be delivered by the blood of the lamb! At Passover, God wants you to experience the reality of this also.

At Passover, God wants you to experience the reality of His deliverance. It's a time to thank God for His deliverance in the past.

It's also a time to enter into His deliverance for you now in every area of life. I Corinthians 5:7-8 says, "For Christ, our Passover Lamb, has been sacrificed. Therefore let us celebrate the festival..." *Passover is a celebration of deliverance!*

Preparing for Passover

In studying how Passover is observed, it's interesting that there was a special time of *preparation* for Passover. Before Passover could be celebrated, the people were to cleanse their homes from impurity. This is still done today in observant Jewish households. Every Jewish woman diligently searches her home, looking on every shelf, in every drawer, and in every cabinet to find any trace of *leaven*. (Leaven is often used to symbolize sin and impurity.) If any leaven (impurity) was discovered, it was removed before the Passover celebration could begin.

This is good for us to do today. Before experiencing God's deliverance, it's important to search your home and remove impurity.

Chuck Pierce has written a very helpful book called ***Protecting Your Home from Spiritual Darkness*** (Regal Books) which describes how to go through your home and remove defilement and impurity. (You can also find information on cleansing your home in my book, ***Set Yourself Free***, published by Glory of Zion.) We have received many, many testimonies of how ridding a home of spiritual darkness has broken demonic oppression and released the blessing of God over the home.

God wanted this *breaking of demonic oppression* to be a yearly part of His cycle of life! Here are some suggestions for preparing your home for Passover:

1. Dedicate your home to the Lord. Pray and invite the presence of God into your home. Ask the Lord to use your home for His purposes.

2. Take a Spiritual Inventory of your home. Ask God to give you discernment as you look at what you own. Go through your house, room by room, and let the Holy Spirit show you any objects that should not be in your home. Particularly note the following:
- Objects depicting false gods.
- Objects used in Pagan worship, occult practices, or witchcraft.
- Objects exalting or promoting evil.
- Objects related to past sin.

- Objects that have become idols in your life.

3. Cleanse your home of ungodly objects. Deuteronomy 7:25 says such objects should be destroyed by fire. Take what can be burned and burn it in an appropriate place. If it cannot be burned, pass it through the fire (as a symbolic act of obedience) and then destroy it by whatever means is appropriate, such as smashing or flushing. *NOTE:* **If you have a roommate or spouse, do not remove items belonging to them without their permission!**

4. Ask forgiveness. Once you have destroyed the object, renounce any participation you or your family have had with that object, and ask God to forgive you.

5. Cleanse each room and cleanse the land. Go through your house and repent for any known sin that has been committed in each room. Pray that the Lord would heal any trauma caused by the torment of demonic forces in your home. Pray over your property as well.

6. Consecrate your home and property to God and His service. Declare Joshua 24:15 over your home, *"As for me and my household, we will serve the LORD!"*

7. Fill your home with glory. Take communion at home as a family. Sing praises and pray in your home. Testify about the good things God has done for you. Speak the Word in your house. Read the Psalms aloud. Play praise music on your CD or tape player. Keep your house bright. Cultivate a mood of hope in your home. Refuse any influence that would extinguish the brightness of God's glory. **When you have removed all spiritual defilement, speak a blessing over your house and invite the presence of God to fill it!**

Celebrating Passover

There is no one "right" way to celebrate Passover. The primary goal is to remember the greatness of God's deliverance. At the end of this section I have included a brief outline of a Passover service that can be used in a family or small group setting over a meal. Feel free to make copies of this outline and use it in your celebration if you would like.

As you complete your Passover celebration, be sure to thank God *that you are redeemed out of every old cycle, that bondage is broken, and that you are set free by the blood of the Lamb to enter the promise!*

Redeemed by the Blood of the Lamb!
A Passover Seder

by Dr. Robert D. Heidler

*The traditional Passover Seder involves a leisurely meal with many elements.
While there is value in preserving this tradition, we will use a shorter version to
more closely follow the Biblical instruction that this be a meal "eaten in haste."
The basic outline of this Seder has been followed by the Jews for thousands of years.
It is likely that Jesus and the apostles followed an order very similar to this when
they met in the upper room to celebrate their Passover meal.*

*If you are celebrating Passover in a "home group" setting, the group leader should read
the sections designated for the father, and assign others to fill the roles of the "mother of
the house" and the child. Hints for preparation are found at the end of this outline.*

LIGHTING THE PASSOVER CANDLES
The mother of the house lights two candles, and prays:
"Blessed are You, O Lord our God, King of the Universe, who
has brought us safely through another year and blessed us with
Passover, as a celebration of Your goodness. We thank you
tonight for Jesus, our Savior and Messiah, Who is the Light of
the World" (Ex. 12:14, 27).

INTRODUCTION
The Father reads: "Now this day will be a memorial to
you, and you shall celebrate it as a feast to the Lord;
throughout your generations you are to celebrate it as a
permanent ordinance. It is a Passover to the Lord who passed
over the houses of the sons of Israel in Egypt when He struck
the Egyptians" (Ex. 12:14, 27).

All participants: At one time we Gentiles "were separate
from Christ, excluded from citizenship in Israel and foreigners
to the covenants of the promise... But now in Messiah Jesus we
who once were far away have been brought near through the
blood of Christ."

The Father reads: "Consequently, we are no longer
foreigners and aliens … Through the work of Jesus we

Gentiles are heirs together with Israel, members together of one body, and sharers together in the promise (Eph 2:12-13, 19; 3:6).

All participants: "When the hour came, Jesus and his apostles reclined at the table. And He said to them, 'I have eagerly desired to eat this Passover with you before I suffer'" (Lk. 22:14-15).

THE UNLEAVENED BREAD IS BROKEN

The Father reads: The three loaves of unleavened bread in one napkin are called a Unity. This symbolizes the unique unity of God: Father, Son, and Holy Spirit.

At this point in the Seder, the father breaks the middle piece of matzo, which represents Jesus, the second person of the Trinity. The breaking symbolizes His death. One half of the matzo is wrapped in a napkin and hidden under a pillow, picturing Jesus' burial. This piece is called the Afikoman. The father puts the other piece back into the napkin.

This ancient ritual is followed by Jews all over the world today. No one knows where it came from, or what it means, it is just "tradition." As believers in Jesus, however, the meaning is obvious. As we do this, we celebrate the death of Jesus, our "Passover Lamb."

THE INVITATION

The Father reads: Let all who are hungry come and eat… "For Jesus, our Passover Lamb, has been sacrificed. Let us therefore celebrate the feast…" (I Cor. 5:7-8).

A Child Asks: "Why is this night different from all other nights? What does this celebration mean?"

The father reads: "It will come about when your children say, 'What does this celebration mean?' that you shall say, 'It is a Passover to the Lord who passed over the houses of the sons of Israel when He smote the Egyptians, but spared our homes'" (Ex. 12:24-27).

All participants: All Israel suffered as slaves in Egypt, but the Lord delivered them out of the hand of the enemy by His mighty hand and outstretched arm.

The father reads: In the same way, all of us were held in slavery and bondage to sin. Through Jesus, our Passover lamb, God delivered us. He set us free to live for Him.

All participants: So Passover is a celebration of God's love for all mankind. It celebrates Israel's release from slavery in Egypt and the redemption of all mankind from slavery to sin.

The father reads: Now the Lord said to Moses and Aaron, Speak to all the congregation of Israel, saying, "On the tenth of this month they are to take a lamb for each household. Your lamb shall be an unblemished male a year old. You shall keep it until the fourteenth day, then kill it at twilight. Moreover, they shall take some of the blood and put it on the two doorposts and on the lintel of the houses where they eat it. And they shall eat the flesh that same night, roasted with fire. They shall eat it with unleavened bread and bitter herbs.

"You shall eat it in haste-it is the Lord's Passover. For I will go through the land of Egypt on that night and will strike down all the first-born in the land of Egypt, both man and beast; and I will execute judgments against all the gods of Egypt -- I am the Lord. And the blood shall be a sign for you on the houses where you live. When I see the blood I will pass over you and no plague will come upon you to destroy you when I strike the land of Egypt.

"Now it came about at midnight that the Lord struck all the first-born in the land of Egypt. Pharaoh arose in the night, he and all his servants and all the Egyptians; and there was a great cry in Egypt, for there was no home where there was not someone dead. Then he called for Moses and Aaron at night and said, 'Rise up, get out from among my people, both you and the sons of Israel; and go, worship the Lord, as you have said'" (Ex. 12:1-13; 28-31).

All participants: Blessed is He who kept His promise to Israel. The Lord brought an end to bondage, and fulfilled His promise to Abraham: "Know for certain that your descendants will be strangers in a country not their own, and they will be enslaved and mistreated four hundred years. But I will punish the nation they serve as slaves, and afterward they will come out with great possessions" (Gen. 15:13-14).

The father reads: Rabbi Gamaliel, who taught the apostle Paul, said: "He who does not speak forth these three essentials of the Passover Seder has not discharged his duty: namely, the Passover Sacrifice, unleavened bread, and bitter herbs."

THE BITTER HERBS

The father lifts up the bitter herbs and reads: These are the bitter herbs which we will eat.

The participants say: They picture the bitterness and sorrow of Israel, when they were held captive in Egypt and oppressed by their cruel masters (Ex. 1:14).

Pass the bitter herbs while the father reads: These bitter herbs symbolize the bitterness of slavery and Israel's miserable existence in Egypt. To us as Christians, the eating of bitter herbs also reminds us of our lives before we knew Jesus. They are symbolic of the bitter cup our Lord tasted on our behalf. The horseradish brings tears to our eyes as we taste it and remember.

THE PASSOVER SACRIFICE

The father holds up the lamb and reads: This lamb pictures the lamb slain in Egypt, to set Israel free from bondage.

The participants say: "The Lord passed over the houses of our fathers in Egypt. As it is said, 'It is the Lord's Passover, for He passed over the homes of the Children of Israel, when He killed the Egyptians; He passed over our homes and did not destroy us'" (Ex. 12:27).

Pass the lamb around while the father reads: The children of Israel were told how to protect themselves from the last plague. Each family was to take a lamb and kill it and drain the blood into a basin; and then take a bunch of hyssop and dip it in the blood and strike the upper lintel and two side doorposts of the house where they eat it. In doing this, they made the sign of the cross at each door.

All participants pray: LORD, we thank you that you gave Israel a place of protection under the blood of the Passover lamb. We now take this meal with thankful hearts, remembering Your faithfulness and love for Your people. We pray that all men and women everywhere would discover the place of blessing and protection you have provided under the blood of Jesus, who is the perfect Passover lamb.

EAT THE PASSOVER MEAL

Following the meal, the Seder continues with...
THE UNLEAVENED BREAD
The father reads: In Passover, we not only remember the lamb slain in Egypt. We also celebrate the true Lamb of God, the Messiah, who was sacrificed to bear the sin of the world. The Prophet Isaiah wrote:

"Surely He took up our infirmities and carried our weaknesses, ...He was pierced for our transgressions, He was crushed for our iniquities; the punishment that brought us peace was upon Him, and by His wounds we are healed. We all, like sheep, have gone astray, each of us has turned to His own way; and the LORD has laid on Him the iniquity of us all.

"He was oppressed and afflicted, yet He did not open His mouth... He was cut off from the land of the living; for the transgression of My people He was stricken. It was the Lord's will to crush Him and cause Him to suffer, and though the LORD makes His life a guilt offering, He will see His offspring and prolong His days... He poured out His life unto death, and

was numbered with the transgressors. For He bore the sin of many, and made intercession for the transgressors" (Isa. 53:1-12).

The participants say: "The next day John saw Jesus coming to him, and said, 'Behold, the Lamb of God who takes away the sin of the world'" (John 1:29).

The father takes out the Afikoman *and reads:* This is the broken piece of matzo that was hidden early in our Seder.   The unleavened bread is a picture of the body of Jesus. It is made of pure flour and water without yeast. When the dough is prepared, it is pierced and striped with a pointed tool.   The prophecy of Isaiah 53:5 declares: "He was pierced for our transgressions, he was bruised for our iniquities: the chastisement of our peace was upon him; and with his stripes we are healed."

When this loaf was broken at the start of the service, it symbolized Jesus' death. When the loaf was wrapped in linen, it spoke prophetically of the wrapping of His body in linen after the crucifixion. When the broken and wrapped bread was put under the pillow, it symbolized His burial in the tomb of Joseph of Arimathea (Matt. 27:57-60). Now after the meal is over, the pillow is removed, picturing the stone that was removed by the angel (Matt. 28:1-2). The matzo is unwrapped and held up for all to see. This symbolizes the resurrection of Jesus.

The participants say: "On the first day of the week, at early dawn, they came to the tomb... they found the stone rolled away... Two men suddenly stood near them in dazzling clothing; and said to them, 'Why do you seek the living One among the dead? He is not here, **HE HAS RISEN'"** *(Luke 24:1-6)!*

The father breaks the Afikoman into small pieces, and they are passed to each participant.

The father says: This is the place in the Passover celebration which was recorded in the Gospel of Luke, "Having taken some bread, when He had given thanks, He broke it, and gave it to them, saying, 'This is My body which is given for you; do this in remembrance of Me'" (Lk. 22:19).

The father prays a blessing... "Blessed are You, O Lord our God, King of the Universe, Who brings forth bread from the earth, and Who gave us Jesus, the bread of life."

All eat from the broken matzo.

THE CUP OF REDEMPTION

The Father reads: At this point in a Passover celebration, a cup of wine is poured. It is the third cup of wine poured in the traditional Passover meal, and it is the most significant.

The father lifts the cup and says: This cup is called the Cup of Redemption. At this point in the Passover, Jesus lifted the cup and said, "This cup is the new covenant in my blood; do this, whenever you drink it, in remembrance of me" (I Cor. 11:25). This was the original context of the Lord's Supper.

The Father prays, *"Blessed are You, O Lord our God, King of the universe, who brings forth the fruit of the vine, and who gave the blood of your Son Jesus for our redemption."*

All drink the Cup of Redemption.

At this point, a section of the book of Psalms, called the **Hallel***, is sung to praise God for His provision of redemption. This is the song Jesus and His disciples would have sung in Mark 14:26 to close their Passover meal.*

THE HALLEL

Father: Not to us, O LORD, not to us,
Participants: But to Your name be the glory,

Father: Why do the nations say,
Participants: "Where is their God?"

Father: Our God is in heaven;
Participants: He does whatever He pleases.

Father: But their idols are silver and gold,
Participants: Made by the hands of men.

Father: They have mouths, but cannot speak,
Participants: Eyes, but they cannot see;

Father: They have ears, but cannot hear,
Participants: Noses, but they cannot smell;

Father: They have hands, but cannot feel,
Participants: Feet, but they cannot walk;

Father: Those who make them will be like them...
Participants: And so will all who trust in them.

Father: O house of Israel, trust in the LORD;
Participants: He is their help and shield.

Father: The LORD remembers us and will bless us:
Participants: He will bless those who fear the LORD...

Father: May the LORD make you increase,
Participants: Both you and your children.

Father: May you be blessed by the LORD,
Participants: The Maker of heaven and earth.

Father: Give thanks to the LORD, for He is good;
Participants: His love endures forever.

Father: The LORD is my strength and my song;
Participants: He has become my salvation.

Father: The stone the builders rejected
Participants: Has become the capstone;

Father: The LORD has done this,
Participants: And it is marvelous in our eyes.

Father: This is the day the LORD has made;
Participants: Let us rejoice and be glad in it.

Father: Blessed is He who comes in the name of the LORD.
Participants: From the house of the LORD, we bless you.

Father: The LORD is God,
Participants: And He has made His light to shine upon us.

EVERYTHING SHALL BLESS HIS NAME!
The father says: To You alone do we give thanks, O Lord!
Though our mouth were full of song like the sea,
and our tongue of rejoicing like the multitude of its waves,
and our lips of praise like the breadth of the horizon,
and our eyes were shining like the sun and the moon,
and our hands were spread like the eagles of the sky,
and our feet light as the hinds' we could never thank You
enough, O Lord our God, for the good You have done for us.

The father says (triumphantly): "We have been redeemed by
the blood of the Lamb!"
All say: "Out of the hand of the enemy!"

The father says: "Our redemption is complete!"
All say: "Bondage has been broken!"

The father says: "We have been released from captivity!"
All say: "We are set free to enter the promise!"

All participants pray: Holy One of Israel, we thank You for
Your gift of salvation. We pray Your blessing on Your church,
and on Your people Israel. We pray for the peace of
Jerusalem. We pray that all of Israel be saved and come to
know Messiah Jesus.

The father reads: "And they returned to Jerusalem with great
joy and were continually in the temple, praising God" (Luke
24:52-53).

All the participants joyfully shout:
"NEXT YEAR IN JERUSALEM!"

[This traditional Jewish ending to the Passover celebration is optional!]

PASSOVER MEAL PREPARATION HINTS:

Be sure to have these essential elements for the Passover meal: **Matzo** (unleavened bread), **Horseradish** (bitter herbs), **Wine** (or grape juice), **Lamb** (& other dishes for a complete meal).

Also needed: A copy of this **Seder** for each person. 2 **candles** & matches, 2 white **napkins**.

Before the celebration: Put three unbroken matzos in the folds of one napkin. You will use the other napkin to wrap the Afikoman before you hide it. Have a small **pillow** ready, as a place to hide the Afikoman.

Have a **child** – or the youngest adult present – prepared to ask the questions at the start of the celebration: "Why is this night different from all other nights?" and "What does this celebration mean?" (The rest of the celebration is the answer to these questions, passing on the remembrance of our redemption from one generation to the next!)

Appendix Three – Part Two
The Feast of Pentecost
The Feast of the Open Heavens!

"The morning of the third day there was thunder and lightning, with a thick cloud over the mountain... Moses led the people out and they stood at the foot of the mountain. Mount Sinai was covered with smoke, because the Lord descended on it in fire. The smoke billowed up from it like smoke from a furnace, the whole mountain trembled violently... the Lord called Moses to the top of the mountain." - Exodus 19:16-20

"When the day of Pentecost had fully come, they were all together in one place. Suddenly there came a sound from heaven like the rushing of a violent tempest blast and there appeared tongues as of fire distributing themselves, and rested on each one of them. And they were all filled with the Holy Spirit and began to speak with other tongues, as the Spirit was giving them utterance." - Acts 2:1-4

Recently our friends, John and Sheryl Price, were driving into Middletown, Ohio to attend a Global Harvest prophetic conference. As they were driving into town, they noticed a very strange cloud formation in the sky. It appeared to be a word written in Greek letters. John and Sheryl puzzled over this, so Sheryl got out some paper and attempted to draw what they were seeing. She brought it to me at the conference and asked me if it really was a Greek word.

When I saw what Sheryl had written, it really did look like a Greek word! I have a lot of Bible study tools on my laptop, so I looked it up and this is what I found:

What she had written was "*Schizo.*" *Schizo* is a Greek word that means, "to rend, tear violently, open or unfold."

In studying the Bible, the first mention of a word is often very important, so I looked up the first place *schizo* was used. I discovered that it was in Mark 1:10 when, at the baptism of Jesus, the heavens were "torn open" *(schizo)* and the Spirit descended as a dove!

So as John and Cheryl are driving into Middletown for a prophetic conference, *God writes **SCHIZO** across the sky!* **What an** *incredible prophetic sign!*

What was God saying? I believe He was telling us *He is about to OPEN THE HEAVENS!* **We are on the verge of a major move of the Holy Spirit!**

If that is true, it means we live in days when *Pentecost* is very important! PENTECOST is the feast of the open heavens.

Just as PASSOVER is God's "appointed time" to deliver his people, Pentecost is the appointed time for the heavens to open!

If we want to understand and experience "open heavens," we need to understand Pentecost. When most Christians think about Pentecost, they think about the outpouring of the Spirit in Acts chapter two. But Pentecost didn't *begin* in Acts 2. Pentecost was a biblical feast instituted by God in the Old Testament Scriptures.

The Feast of Pentecost is described in Leviticus 23:15-16, Numbers 28:26-31, and Deuteronomy 16:9-12. The Israelites were told, "From the Feast of Passover count off seven weeks (forty-nine days) then on the fiftieth day have a festival before the Lord." In Hebrew this feast is called *Shavuot* which means "feast of weeks." In the New Testament it is called "Pentecost" which is Greek for "fifty days."

Three Dimensions of Pentecost

There are three levels of significance for Pentecost, and each level represents a new expression of God's blessing. **The three levels picture three things God wants to accomplish in our lives when the heavens open!** Each level is a doorway we must pass through to enter into the release of God's power. If we understand the three dimensions of Pentecost, we will catch a glimpse of what God wants to do in our lives.

The first level of Pentecost is receiving God's blessing of *abundant provision.* Pentecost celebrates the release of provision from God to meet our physical needs. In ancient Israel the hardworking farmers worked week after week to prepare the soil and plant the seeds in hope of a harvest, but they had no ability to make the earth produce. If the Lord did not open the heavens, they would have no crops. But as they trusted Him, God opened the windows of heaven and rain poured forth. The result was: The earth brought forth its harvest.

The Jews recognized that our physical provision is a wondrous act of God's grace. Every Sabbath, the father of the house lifts a freshly baked loaf of bread before the Lord and blesses (thanks) God for His bountiful provision: **"Blessed are You, O Lord, our God, King of the Universe, *Who brings forth bread from the earth!"***

From the first sheaf of every new harvest, the Jews would bring a thanksgiving offering to the temple, acknowledging that God opened the heavens to bring forth their bread from the earth. This was a praise offering – offered by faith – offered *before* the full harvest was gathered. **That offering was brought to God at *Pentecost!***

The first dimension of Pentecost was a celebration for the release of God's provision. Pentecost was celebrated by praise and by giving. On Pentecost, the Israelites would express their praise by bringing "burnt offerings, grain offerings, drink offerings, sin offerings, fellowship offerings, and freewill offerings." The picture is a massive outpouring of GIVING! Every kind of offering imaginable!

It's interesting to note that this is what the disciples would have done the evening before "Pentecost morning." The night before the Spirit fell they would have brought offerings to the temple to thank God for His physical provision.

Pentecost is, first of all, a time to open your heart to God through joyful giving and praise. *As we do this, it positions us to receive!* To prepare for Pentecost, ask God how to express your thankfulness in a way that will open your heart to Him!

The second level of Pentecost is *supernatural revelation*. Pentecost was the day God opened the heavens to reveal His Word.

When Israel left Egypt, God did not take them directly to the Promised Land. He had some very important things to communicate to them, so He led them southward down the Sinai Peninsula to Mount Horeb (or Sinai).

Fifty days after Passover, God directed Moses to come up to the top of the mountain. There the heavens opened and God gave him *Torah.*

What is *Torah*? Some call it the "Law" and picture it as a list of nasty "thou shalt nots." Some think it is just a big old scroll.

The word *Torah* really means **"the teaching of God."**

Torah is the revelation of God's will, God's love and God's character. Although the word *Torah* is most specifically used of the first five books of the Bible, in a real sense *all* Scripture is "*Torah.*"

On Pentecost, God revealed His heart to His people! Pentecost celebrates the release of God's revelation. At the time Jesus lived, part of the celebration of Pentecost included staying up all night studying the Bible! It was a way of "receiving His Word anew."

Acts chapter 2 says, "When the day of Pentecost had fully come, they were all together in one place." When morning dawned on Pentecost, the disciples were already gathered together. What were they doing? As observant Jews, they would have brought thank offerings to the temple the night before, then gone to the upper room and stayed up all night studying God's Word!

Don't you wonder what they would have studied? We know that Jesus had recently promised the release of His power when the Spirit was poured out. I believe, in light of that, they would have studied Scriptures about the outpouring of God's power.

They might have read the passages about God coming down in fire on Mount Sinai, or Ezekiel's vision of the Lord coming in a whirlwind with darting flames of fire. They almost certainly would have studied the account of the Spirit's outpouring in Joel 2, where the end-time release of the Spirit was to be accompanied by prophetic utterance along with great signs and wonders.

As they filled their minds with God's Word, I believe God prepared them for the *third level* of Pentecost.

Then... "When the day of Pentecost had fully come," **the heavens were torn open!** The power of God was released into the earth-realm!

The Third Level of Pentecost Is the Outpouring of the Holy Spirit. As fire came down on Mt. Sinai, the FIRE OF HIS GLORY now came upon the disciples. They were clothed with His power. The gifts of the Spirit were energized. The anointing of God equipped them to see the sick healed, the oppressed delivered, the Gospel boldly proclaimed, and the world changed.

That is what the Church today longs for. The Church all over the world is crying out for a new Pentecost, but because we don't understand Pentecost, we don't know how to prepare for it.

The apostles understood Pentecost. They knew how to enter into the blessing of an open heaven. They celebrated God's provision with thank offerings and praise. They acknowledged that "He brings forth their bread from the earth." *When we come before God seeking new blessings, it's important to acknowledge the blessings we have already received.*

The apostles filled their minds with His Word by devoting an entire night to studying and pondering God's *Torah. As we meditate on the Word, we attune our minds to think the thoughts of God. Faith is released* to receive a fresh move of the Spirit.

As the apostles celebrated God's previous blessings at Pentecost, they positioned themselves to receive something new.

Pentecost is about three things: God's abundant provision, His supernatural revelation, and the release of His power and authority "on earth as it is in heaven." All are available for us to receive when the heavens open. *God is telling us to PREPARE for the open heavens!*

Preparing for Pentecost

Here are three steps to prepare for Pentecost:

1. Learn to celebrate God's provision.   Don't take any blessing for granted! Marvel that God loves you so much that He brings forth bread from the earth! *Be filled with praise!* Praise Him with your testimony. Praise Him in singing. Develop a lifestyle of thanksgiving.   Praise Him in thank offerings.   Celebrate God's goodness through lavish giving. *Praise opens heaven for fresh blessing to rain down!*

2. Celebrate God's revelation.   Thank God that He has revealed Himself to us and that He wants us to know His mind and heart. *Fill your mind with His Word!* Receive his revelation afresh! Allow the thoughts of God to reprogram your thinking processes! Memorize His promises. Observe how He worked in the lives of the men and women who trusted Him. Hunger and thirst for spiritual bread. *Let FAITH arise!*

3. Prepare for a fresh release of His Spirit. Stay in step with Him, positioned to receive when the heavens open.   Obey His directives. Walk by faith. *Know that God is opening the heavens!*

When the Day of Pentecost comes, RECEIVE His Promise by faith! Spend time with Him. Gather with friends and family who are seeking Him. *Enjoy His Presence! Rejoice in His goodness! Thank Him for His Holy Spirit! Declare that His power and authority are being released in the earth!*

Celebrating Pentecost like the Apostles

In celebrating Pentecost, why not follow the example set by the apostles?

Set apart an extended time to be with God! You can plan a private "retreat" to spend time alone with the Lord. You may wish to gather with family or friends for a "Pentecost party" to seek a new release of His power! Spend time thanking God for what He has done. Sing praises to Him. Share testimonies. Prepare a thank offering.

Spend time in His Word. Study the accounts of God's power and miracles in the Bible. Read a book about the great revivals of history! Thank Him that He never changes!

Pray for a fresh release of the Spirit. If you are with friends, pray over each other for a fresh outpouring and an increased experience of His blessing. *Receive the fire of God and the energizing of His gifts!* (For more information about receiving the ministries of the Holy Spirit, see my book, *Experiencing the Spirit,* available from Glory of Zion.)

Praise God that He has released His power in the earth!

Appendix Three – Part Three
The Feast of Trumpets
God's "Wake-Up Call"

*"On the first day of the seventh month you are to have a day of rest,
a sacred assembly commemorated with trumpet blasts... The tenth day
is the Day of Atonement... On the fifteenth day of the seventh month the
Lord's Feast of Tabernacles begins..."* - Leviticus 23:24, 27-28, 34

In God's calendar there are three major "appointed times."
The year begins with **Passover**, which initiates God's yearly cycle.
In the third month comes **Pentecost**, the feast of the open heavens.
Then comes the long hot summer. When fall comes, God moves us
into the climax of the yearly cycle, the celebration of His GLORY at
the feast of **Tabernacles**.

Tabernacles, held in the seventh month of the biblical calendar,
is really a cluster of three feasts. The seventh month begins with the
Feast of Trumpets. This feast begins the most important series of
days in the biblical calendar.

Interestingly, the Feast of Trumpets is also called *Rosh
Hashanah*, the "Head of the Year." Rosh Hashanah is the "Birthday
of the World," the "Anniversary of Creation."

This confuses some people. Some ask, "Why does *the head of
the year* begin in the **seventh month?**" The answer is that there are
two different cycles in God's calendar.

The first cycle is the "Cycle of Blessing." In God's original
plan, each Feast of Trumpets was to begin a new year of peace,
health, joy, and provision in God's presence.

A problem arose when sin entered the world. Sin took us *out*
of God's cycle of blessing and *into* a cycle of sin and death. In the
cycle of sin and death, the new year no longer brought peace, health,
joy, and provision. Now each new year brought more fear, loss,
infirmity and death.

So God initiated a NEW cycle, the "Cycle of Redemption."
This cycle began seven months earlier at Passover. When God
instituted Passover He said, "This will now be the beginning of
months."

The Cycle of Redemption rescues us from the effects of sin and restores us to God's original plan. We celebrate God's *redemption* at Passover and His *provision* at Pentecost. We affirm our deliverance from the hand of the enemy and receive afresh God's power and revelation. When the Cycle of Redemption is complete, a door is opened to experience every blessing we had lost.

The trumpet blast at *Rosh Hashanah* is the signal to shift out of the old cycle and enter the presence of God. *The seventh month in the cycle of redemption becomes the first month, the "head of the year," in a new year of blessing!*

Countdown to Revival

The fall feasts were given *to create a pathway into God's glory.* They give us a four step countdown to bring us into His presence:

- *The Feast of Trumpets – A Wake-up Call.*
- *The Days of Awe – A Time for Seeking Him.*
- *The Day of Atonement – A Day to be Restored.*
- *The Feast of Tabernacles – A Week to Experience Glory.*

These feasts have always been important, but I believe Tabernacles is the *key feast* for the church today. We live in a day when God wants to draw us into His presence in a unique way. **It is time for His power and blessing to be poured out.** *He wants us to experience His GLORY.*

The fall feasts provide the pattern for revival for any individual or nation. God established His calendar to take us through this countdown every year, drawing us closer and closer each year into His presence.

The starting point is the Feast of Trumpets. God gave one commandment for this festival: All His people should **listen** to a blast of trumpets! The blast of the trumpets is a call to *awaken*! The Hebrew name for this feast, **Yom Teruah,** means, "The day of the awakening blast!"

We sometimes *need* a wake up call! We need to be called to alertness. We need a call to enter the new season.

A wake-up call almost always comes before revival! This is

true for NATIONS and for INDIVIDUALS.

Many have heard about the great revival in Argentina. Back in the 90's many of us thrilled at the wonderful accounts of what the Spirit was doing in that nation. Like many others I was privileged to go to Argentina and visit that revival firsthand. Many in America began to call out to God, in prayer and fasting, that we could see a revival like that here.

But the Argentinian revival did not come without a wake-up call! Argentina suffered a devastating defeat in the Falkland Islands war, followed by a crushing collapse of their economy. Alarmed at the devastation hitting the nation, pastors and Christian leaders began meeting together, praying in desperation for God to do something in their country. In the midst of that unified outpouring of desperate prayer, THE HOLY SPIRIT FELL!

The Falkland Island war was a wake-up call for the nation of Argentina! Many times a disaster or economic collapse will drive people to seek God, resulting in revival. This is true for individuals as well as nations.

God doesn't want us to wait till disaster strikes to enjoy His presence, so He invented a less painful wake-up call! It is the blast of the ram's horn!

Have you ever been startled by the sound of a trumpet blast? It does something inside you. **You wake up!** *God designed the sound of the trumpets to pierce our soul and call us to attention!*

The Feast of Trumpets is designed to be a time when the sound of the trumpet awakens your spirit. When you hear the trumpet blast, ask God to show you anything in your life that would hinder His work in you!

The Days of Awe!

The ten days after Trumpets are called the "Days of Awe." They are also called days of "*Teshuvah.*" **Teshuvah** is a Hebrew word that means "to turn" and "to return." It means *repentance*, but it is also the word for "springtime."

When God gives you a wake-up call, it's time to *turn* from anything that hinders your walk with God. It's time to *return* to God! Through these days of *repentance*, we enter a season of *springtime!* It's a season to experience a fresh release of the life and blessings of God.

You may have started the last year close to God but ended up "drifting" and getting off course. You may have neglected key appointments with Him. You may have become ensnared by sin.

When the trumpet blast calls you to alertness, it's a time to **turn** and ***return***. It's time to draw close to God and experience full restoration!

This ten-day period is part of God's "countdown to glory." If you have listened to the trumpet blast, something has awakened in your spirit. The response should be a time of seriously seeking the Lord. ***Here are some things to do during the Days of Awe:***

1. Praise Him and Read His Word!   It's important during this season to spend some extended times alone with God. Open your heart to Him in praise. Spend time reading and meditating on His Word. While it's *always* important to seek God and spend time with Him, ***the Days of Awe are a time set by God when His Spirit is ready to meet you in some unusual ways.***

I believe a key verse for the Days of Awe is Jeremiah 29:12-13, "Then you will call upon Me and come and pray to Me, and I will listen to you. You will seek Me and find Me when you seek Me with all your heart!"

The New Testament equivalent is James 4:8, "Draw near to God and He will draw near to you!" God says that if we will draw near to Him, seeking Him with all our hearts, He will draw near to us!

There are times when we need to make "seeking Him" our most important priority! During much of the year, many people take a quick twenty minutes a day with the Lord, offering up a short prayer and reading a few verses of Scripture. While that is not a formula for spiritual health, it may "get you by" in the midst of a busy schedule.

But we also need extended times with the Lord, when we can open our hearts to Him, and have Him open His heart to us. That's what these days are for!

2. Let God Reveal Old Cycles!   As you spend time in fellowship with God and meditating on His Word, ask Him to show you any cycles of destruction in your life. Are you trapped in recurrent debt, infirmity, or loss? Do you find that your heart has grown cold and that you no longer feel the closeness to God you once felt? If God shows you old cycles in your life, ask Him to show you His strategy for freedom!

3. Ask God to Reveal any Sin in Your Life. All of us have blind spots, areas of sin we are not aware of. Those areas of sin hinder the work of the Spirit in our lives. So during the Days of Awe, ask the Lord to reveal hidden sin. When God reveals sin, He also gives us grace to gain victory over it.

4. Draw Close to God! Let Him quicken your Spirit and awaken a new level of LOVE for Him in your heart!

When you have diligently sought the Lord during the Days of Awe, you are ready for the **DAY OF ATONEMENT!**

The Day of Atonement is a day to put all your sins under the blood of the Lamb and be fully restored to God and His purposes. Isaiah 44:22 says, "I have wiped out your transgressions like a thick cloud, and your sins like a heavy mist. *Return to Me, for I have redeemed you!"*

Observing the Feast of Trumpets

The Feast of Trumpets sets your feet on the path to revival! On the Feast of Trumpets, ask God to awaken your spirit to seek Him. Ask Him to *prepare you* for the Days of Awe and the Day of Atonement! Ask Him to bring you into a fresh experience of His GLORY!

God's instruction for observing this feast is to HEAR the sound of a *shofar (a ram's horn)*! You may not understand completely why that is important, but it is! God designed the sound of the *shofar* to awaken something in your spirit.

If you know of a church or messianic synagogue that celebrates this feast, go and listen to the *shofar!* If you don't know of a place where a *shofar* will be blown, listen to a CD of a *shofar* blast! (A CD recording, *Sound of the Shofar*, may be purchased at the Glory of Zion website, www.glory-of-zion.org.) Ask God to *shift you* when you hear the trumpet sound! As you listen to the trumpet blast...

Let go of old forms of security!

Break out of old habits!

Repent of old ways of thinking!

When the trumpets sound... *SHIFT!*

Appendix Three – Part Four
The Day of Atonement
Experiencing Restoration!

"The tenth day of this seventh month is the Day of Atonement... when atonement is made for you before the LORD..." - Leviticus 23:27-28

"Take two goats... and present them before the LORD...
Cast lots for the two goats, one lot for the LORD and the other lot for the scapegoat... Slaughter the goat of the sin offering and bring its blood inside the veil, and sprinkle it on the mercy seat...
Aaron shall lay his hands on the head of the live goat, and confess over it all the iniquities of the sons of Israel... and he shall lay them on the head of the goat and send it away..." - Leviticus 16:5-34

God wants us to begin every year with a tangible experience of His Presence. The fall feasts give us a four-step "countdown" to experience God's Glory. These steps are...

1. The Feast of Trumpets - A wake-up call! A time set by God to call you to attention.

2. The Days of Awe – An extended time of seeking Him.

3. The Day of Atonement – A time for your fellowship with God to be restored.

4. The Feast of Tabernacles – An appointed time to experience God's Presence.

That countdown represents God's desire for us every year. At the start of each year, God wants us to wake-up! He wants us to put off passivity, lethargy and distraction, and ***seek Him*** for ten days! After the days of seeking Him, He wants you to deal with anything that would hinder your fellowship. God wants to use this time to restore you to full fellowship with Him!

The Day of Atonement is a day to REPENT and be RESTORED. It's a time to deal with anything in your life that would hinder fellowship with a holy God. It's a time to receive a fresh anointing of the LIFE of God. Heb. 12:1 is a perfect description of the Day of Atonement. It says, "Let us throw off everything that hinders and the sin that so easily entangles, and let us run with perseverance the race marked out for us."

Importance of the Day of Atonement

The Day of Atonement is the HOLIEST day of the year. The word "Holy" means, "set apart, special; unlike any other." The Day of Atonement is the most "special" day of the year. It's a day *appointed by God* for a very important purpose.

Unlike the other "appointed times" in God's calendar, the Day of Atonement is not a FEAST, but a *FAST! The Day of Atonement is not a day to rejoice and celebrate. It's a day to humble yourself before God by fasting.*

It was REQUIRED of all Israel to observe the Day of Atonement. This was not an optional observance. God took this day very seriously

Another thing to note about the Day of Atonement is that it was designated a *lasting ordinance* for all generations. **Four times** God specifically tells us that this is *not* a temporary ordinance. The coming of Jesus *fulfilled* this ordinance, but it did not abolish it! In fulfilling this ordinance, Jesus opened it to all who believe and FILLED it with fresh significance. This observance was designed by God to bless His people *in all generations!* God desires that we experience His atonement afresh every year.

The Day of Atonement was designed to answer the question, "How can a sinful man enjoy fellowship with a holy God?"

Originally, it was the day the High Priest entered the Holy of Holies. If you understand what happened on that day it will change your life!

The Bible teaches that we were created to dwell with God. The desire for His PRESENCE is built into us. Without it, there is something missing. Apart from God's presence, there's an emptiness inside that nothing else can satisfy.

Our problem is that when sin entered the world, it cut us off from His presence. God hates sin. He hates what it does to us. He hates the sickness, pain, suffering, and loss it produces. Sin is a violation of His character. It robs Him of what He deserves. The book of Romans tells us that the wrath of God is aroused against all sin.

Because of that, sinful man can't come into God's presence. When a sinful creature enters the burning purity of God's presence, it's like a wad of paper thrown into a blast-furnace. It's *consumed*. When Uzzah touched the ark, he fell down dead. In Moses' tabernacle and again in the Temple, a thick curtain called "The Veil" was used to separate the people from the place of God's presence. Sinful man cannot come freely before God. When sinful men come into the presence of God, they die!

To restore fellowship, sin had to be covered. That's what atonement does! When atonement is made, every sin, every failure of the past is covered! When atonement has been made, you can face the future with no guilt, no regret and no shame. Atonement opens the door to His presence. When atonement is made, we can come to Him freely and experience His glory!

A Tale of Two Goats

The original ceremony for the Day of Atonement involved two goats.

The first goat is called "The goat for the Lord." Leviticus 16 describes the ceremony this way: "The high priest shall take two male goats for a sin offering... He shall take the two goats and present them before the LORD. He shall slaughter the goat of the sin offering and bring its blood inside the veil, and sprinkle it on the mercy seat... And he shall make atonement."

In the sacrifice of the first goat, God was saying, "The wages of sin is death, but I will let this goat die instead of you!" This was a vivid picture of the horror of sin. As the High Priest killed the first goat the meaning was clear to every Israelite, "This goat is being killed to cover my sin."

When the blood of this goat was placed on the Mercy Seat, atonement was made. It provided a covering for sin.

For centuries God gave His people visible proof of their atonement. It was the Jewish custom to tie a red sash to the door of the Temple each year on the Day of Atonement. When the sacrifice for atonement was accepted by God, the red sash turned white. This took place year after year.

According to the Jewish Talmud (*Talmud Bavli*, Yoma 39b), something alarming took place forty years before the destruction of the temple. *In the year A.D. 30, (40 years before the temple's destruction in A.D. 70) the red sash stopped turning white.* **The sacrifice of atonement was no longer accepted by God!**

Why did the sash stop turning white in A.D. 30? It's because in *that year*, Jesus of Nazareth (*Yeshua*) was sacrificed in Jerusalem.

The offering of God's perfect sacrifice made the yearly sacrifice of a goat unnecessary. The temple rituals had found their fulfillment in Him!

Jesus is now the atoning sacrifice. He shed His blood to make atonement. Romans 3:24-25 tells us that redemption *came* by Christ Jesus! God presented Him as a "sacrifice of atonement."

He put HIS blood on the Mercy Seat. As High Priest, He entered the most holy place by His own blood, having obtained eternal redemption (Heb. 9:12).

The "Goat for the Lord" pictures the sacrifice of Jesus! He died to pay your penalty. He covered *all sin* for *all time* in *one* sacrifice. If you have trusted in Him, YOU ARE FORGIVEN. God can say, "As far as the east is from the west, so far have I removed your sin from you!" He can also pronounce, "Your sins and your lawless deeds I remember no more!"

Through the blood of Jesus atonement has been made! Your past is covered! God's wrath has been turned away! *God calls you into His presence again!*

Cleansed to Approach a Holy God

There is another issue that must be dealt with before you can come boldly into His presence. God's WRATH against sin was dealt with by the blood of Jesus, but there is also the issue of man's "uncleanness" before God.

Sin makes us FEEL defiled and guilty. It makes us uncomfortable to be around God. You don't WANT to come into His presence. If you owed me $10,000 and didn't have the money to pay your debt, you would feel uncomfortable around me. You would feel awkward if I came up and tried to speak to you. You would probably decline an invitation to come to my house for dinner. In the same way, when we know we have sinned, we feel uncomfortable in God's presence.

God had a goat for that too. The second goat was called the SCAPEGOAT. It was a goat for the people. It gave them an opportunity to confess their sins and was a tangible picture that sin was removed. Leviticus 16 says, "*Aaron shall lay his hands on the head of the live goat, and confess over it all the iniquities of the sons of Israel*... and he shall send it away into the wilderness... the goat shall bear on itself all their iniquities to an uninhabited land."

As the Israelites saw Aaron confess their sins and symbolically place them on the goat, then watched that goat taken out to the wilderness to die, it was a tangible reminder that their guilt had been taken away.

We have a "new covenant equivalent" to the scapegoat. It's called confession of sin. I'm not talking about confessing to a priest, as is done in some churches; I'm talking about confessing our sins to God.

I John 1:9 says, "If we confess our sins He is faithful and just to forgive us our sins and cleanse us from all unrighteousness." We don't need a goat, but we still need to confess our sins to gain assurance that our guilt has been removed.

- **The sacrifice of the first goat pictures what Jesus accomplished on the cross.**

- **The sending of the second goat pictures what we do when we confess our sins to God.**

The word "confess" literally means "to agree with." Confession means coming into agreement with God about our sin. It means admitting that we have sinned and that it was wrong. It means viewing sin as God does.

God promises that if we will come into agreement with Him over our sin, He will act, on the basis of Jesus' blood, to cleanse us and fully restore our fellowship.

Anyone who is married knows exactly what this feels like. If I have offended my wife, and her feelings are hurt, there will not be much fellowship between us. My offense brings a barrier. There has been defilement in the relationship.

I will continue to be very uncomfortable in my wife's presence until I swallow my pride and go to her to confess my offense and ask forgiveness. When I have confessed and she has forgiven, the relationship is restored. Confession brings cleansing, healing, and restoration.

To come freely into God's presence you need to know that Jesus' blood has paid your debt. In the courts of heaven, the penalty has been paid and your case has been closed. You also need to know that your defilement is removed. You need to admit you were wrong and receive the forgiveness Jesus has already purchased. When that is done, you are free to enjoy God's presence. That's what the Day of Atonement is all about.

The Day of Atonement is a day to put all your sins under the blood of Jesus and be fully restored to God and His purposes. Isaiah 44:22 says, *"I have wiped out your transgressions like a thick cloud, and your sins like a heavy mist. Return to Me, for I have redeemed you!"*

Starting the New Year Fresh

Here are two crucial steps to observing the Day of Atonement:

1. Be sure you have accepted Jesus as your "Atonement." If you are not sure you have trusted Him and received His "atoning sacrifice" for your sin, go to Him in prayer right now:
- It's not a matter of joining a church.
- It's not promising to do better.
- It's accepting that HE has done it all!
- It is knowing your past is wiped clean, and you are restored to God by the sacrifice of Jesus.

2. Be sure you are cleansed and restored to fellowship with God:
- If you are aware of any sins in your life, CONFESS them.
- Claim God's promise of I John 1:9.
- Thank Him that you are forgiven and cleansed.
- KNOW that all defilement is removed and that you can come joyfully into His Presence.

The Day of Atonement is not a day for joyful celebration, but it DOES open the door for the most joyful celebration of the year, *the Feast of Tabernacles.*

As you observe the Day of Atonement, I would like to suggest a "Day of Atonement" exercise.

Many Christians have never experienced the blessing of confessing their sins. They've never known the peace that comes when you know you are completely FREE of all guilt before God. Some Christians have NEVER confessed their sins. They have so much unconfessed sin in their lives they would not even know how to begin confessing it. There is such a backlog of sin they are no longer even *conscious* of the individual acts of sin they have committed. They just have a general "guilty" feeling.

Some time ago, in my Sunday message, I asked our church members the question, *"How many of you sinned already this morning?"* Every hand went up. Every one was sure they had sinned before they got to church that morning.

Next, I asked, "How many of you *know* what sin you committed?"

Ninety-five percent of the hands went down. Only a handful of people could point to a specific act of sin they had committed. The rest just felt *guilty*.

Many Christians live most of their lives that way. Their conscience is so overloaded, they feel *guilty* all the time. That's NOT how God intended you to live. When you feel guilty, you can't freely come into God's presence to experience His love. God doesn't want you to live with a cloud of guilt over your head. When you sin, He wants you to admit your guilt, be forgiven, and walk in joyful relationship with Him.

If you "feel guilty," but don't know where to begin in confessing your sin, I have good news for you. **God wants you to experience the reality of His forgiveness *NOW!*** At the end of this chapter is a sheet titled *"EXPERIENCING ATONEMENT."* I call it a *repentance exercise*. It's a brief transaction between you and God to remove your backlog of guilt. You can go to bed tonight knowing you are completely free from guilt. I urge you, as strongly as I can, to take the time to do this exercise!

Repentance Exercise Instructions

When the Day of Atonement comes, set a time and place where you know you can be alone with God, undisturbed, for at least an hour. For many, the best time will be just before bed at night or early in the morning.

As you come before the Lord, bring your Bible, a pen, and paper (or you can use the *"Repentance Exercise"* sheet at the end of this chapter). Begin by reading Psalms 32 and 51, where David shares his testimony of confessing sin. Thank God for His love and ask His Spirit to minister to you.

Next, ask God to bring to mind any sins He wants you to

confess. Pray as David did, "Search me, O God, and know my heart; test me and know my anxious thoughts. See if there is any offensive way in me" (Psalm 139:23)! As God brings your sins to mind, write them down. Make a list of your sins. When God stops bringing sins to mind, ask Him, "Is there anything else?"

As He shows you more sins, write them down also. Write down *every* sin He shows you. Don't be in a hurry and don't try to make excuses. If you can't fit all of your sins on one sheet of paper, use a second sheet. The goal is to make your list as complete as possible.

When nothing more comes to mind, ask God again, *"Is there anything else?"*

When you ask, "Is there anything else?" and God doesn't show you any more, you know your list is complete. You now have a list of every sin God wants you to confess.

The third step is confession. ***When you feel your list is complete, pray carefully through the list, confessing and renouncing each sin.***

In I John 1:9, God assures us that if we *confess* our sins, He is faithful and just and will *forgive* us our sins and *cleanse* us from all unrighteousness. *When we come into agreement with God about our sin, He restores us. We are forgiven and cleansed.*

The blood of Jesus has already paid the price for every sin in your life. Before you even existed, God loved you so much He took the penalty for your sin upon Himself. As we come before Him in humility to confess our sin, God applies the "Atoning Sacrifice" of Jesus to our lives and restores us to full fellowship with Him.

When you have prayed over every item on the list, confessing every sin, there is one more step. ***Take your sheet of paper listing all the sins you have confessed, turn the paper sideways and write across the list in BOLD letters the promise of I John 1:9:*** *"If we confess our sins, He is faithful and just and will forgive us our sins and purify us from all unrighteousness."* **Thank God that every sin is now *confessed* and *forgiven!***

Now take that list, tear it up, and destroy it! Don't show your list to anyone. As you tear up your list, you will experience what the Israelites experienced when they watched that second goat led away into the wilderness! *You will be assured that God has dealt with your sins and that your defilement has been taken away!*

EXPERIENCING ATONEMENT
A Repentance Exercise

1. Find a time to be alone with God and ask Him to show you the sins He wants you to confess. Write down everything He shows you.
2. Pray through your list, confessing and renouncing each sin. Thank God that every sin is now *confessed* and *forgiven!*
3. Turn your sheet sideways and write across it in BOLD letters the words of I John 1:9. Tear up your list and destroy it! You are FORGIVEN!

"Search me, O God, and know my heart; test me and know my anxious thoughts. See if there is any offensive way in me, and lead me in the way everlasting."– Ps. 139:23-24

_____   _____

_____   _____

_____   _____

_____   _____

_____   _____

_____   _____

_____   _____

_____   _____

_____   _____

_____   _____

_____   _____

_____   _____

_____   _____

_____   _____

_____   _____

_____   _____

_____   _____

*"If we confess our sins, He is faithful and just
and will forgive us our sins and purify us from
all unrighteousness." - I John 1:9*

Appendix Three – Part Five
The Feast of Tabernacles
Celebrating God's GLORY!

*"The glory of the LORD filled the tabernacle. Moses could not enter...
because the cloud had settled upon it, and the glory of the LORD
filled the tabernacle." - Exodus 40:33-35*

*"And the Word became flesh and TABERNACLED among us,
and we beheld His GLORY." - John 1:14*

The climax of God's cycle of blessing is the Feast of Tabernacles. Tabernacles, or *sukkot*, is an appointed time to come boldly into His presence, knowing that every hindrance is removed. It's a time to experience God's glory and joyfully fellowship with Him!

What is the Feast of Tabernacles?
Leviticus 23:34-43 gives instructions for celebrating this feast. God instructs the people to go out into the countryside and cut down palm fronds, leafy branches and poplars. They were to bring these branches back to their homes and build *tabernacles*, or temporary shelters. In Hebrew, the word for a temporary shelter is *sukkah*. *Sukkot* (the plural of *Sukkah*) is the Hebrew name for this feast. ***They were to feast in these shelters for an entire week and rejoice before the LORD!***

God instructed them, "Live in tabernacles for seven days... so your descendants will know that I had Israelites live in tabernacles when I brought them out of Egypt."

When God's people came out of Egypt they lived in tabernacles (*sukkot*). God told them to build a tabernacle for Him also, so His glory could come down and dwell in their midst (Ex. 25:8). ***The Feast of Tabernacles celebrated God's glory living with His people as they dwelt in tabernacles!***

In the Bible, there are actually five tabernacles where God's glory is manifested. ***In a broad sense, this feast celebrates all five of these tabernacles.***

The First Tabernacle is the Tabernacle of Moses. Exodus 40:33-35 describes Moses setting up the Tabernacle. When he did, the Glory of the Lord filled the tabernacle and dwelt in the midst of His people. Because God's glory dwelt with them, they enjoyed perfect provision. Manna came from heaven every day for them to eat. Their shoes did not wear out. God met their every need.

They also had complete protection. Every enemy that came against them was defeated. They enjoyed total health. Not one among them was weak, sick, or infirm. God's glory brought God's blessing!

The Second Tabernacle is the Tabernacle of David. David set up a tent for the Ark of the Covenant, surrounded it with praise 24/7, and God's glory came down. In Psalm 63:2, David writes of this tabernacle, "I have seen you in the sanctuary and beheld your power and your glory!" God's blessing was poured out, and Israel enjoyed incredible prosperity and victory over every enemy.

The Third Tabernacle is JESUS. John 1:14 says, "And the Word became flesh and *tabernacled* [literal translation] among us and we beheld His glory." In Jesus, God dwelt among His people and manifested His glory, releasing life, healing, salvation, and deliverance!

A Fourth tabernacle is the Eternal Tabernacle. Rev. 21:3-4 says, "Now the Tabernacle of God is with men and He will live with them." The result of this is continual blessing. It says, "He will wipe away every tear from their eyes. There will be no more death or mourning or crying or pain." Isaiah 4:5 says that *over everything* God's glory will be a tabernacle.

The Fifth tabernacle is the Church. Acts 15:16-17 describes the church as the *restoration* of David's tabernacle. God intended the church to be the place where God's glory is enthroned on the praises of His people. When the church is fulfilling its call, the glory of God dwells in our midst and great blessing is released in the earth!

All five of these tabernacles have this in common: At the tabernacle, God's presence – His GLORY – dwelt among men! From the place of God's presence, God's life and blessing were released to His people.   ***That's what the Feast of Tabernacles celebrates!***

Experiencing His Glory

To understand Tabernacles, we need to understand God's glory. What do we mean when we talk about glory?

***Glory* is the tangible manifestation of God's presence.** God is always present everywhere, but there are certain times when He reveals His presence in a way that is discernable to our five senses. In Moses' Tabernacle, God's glory was manifested as a shining cloud. At Mt. Sinai, it was revealed in thunder and fire. Sometimes God's presence is evident through miracles and acts of power. Elijah sensed God's presence in a gentle whisper.

There are many ways God can manifest His presence. Most of us can remember times when we have experienced God's presence with us. If you ask people to share a testimony of God's work in their lives, they will almost always say things like this:

"I knew God was speaking to me..."

"I felt I was surrounded by His love."

"The room was filled with a strange light."

"I had a strange sensation... I felt heat all over my body, my hands were tingling... I didn't know what it was."

"I sensed God in a way I can't explain... I didn't see, anything but He was there, face to face."

"I didn't understand what was happening. I couldn't stop weeping, tears were rolling down my cheeks, God was there with me!"

These are all testimonies of people ***experiencing*** God's presence. At a given time and place, they heard God's voice, they saw a vision, they had a physical response to His presence.

Any time you sense God's presence in a tangible way, what you are experiencing is His GLORY. In His presence, everything changes! In God's presence, we find salvation, repentance, empowering, healing, provision, and fulfillment. Most of the significant experiences we have with God take place when His glory comes down.

God doesn't want His glory to be a rare occurrence. He wants us to seek His presence, to dwell in His presence, to live with a continual experience of His power and goodness!

Celebrating His Glory

The Feast of Tabernacles is a celebration of God's glory. It's a time to remember past experiences of His glory. It's a time to seek His face and experience His glory now. It's a time to call out to God for a fresh outpouring of His glory in the new year.

One week a year God asks His people to *tabernacle* with Him. God promised a special blessing for those who would do this.

Tabernacles is a time to enjoy the Lord. It is a time to celebrate God's goodness. Leviticus 23:40 says, "***Rejoice*** before the Lord your God for seven days." Deuteronomy 16:14-15 says, "***Be joyful*** at your feast for the Lord your God will bless you and ***your joy will be complete.***"

Part of celebrating Tabernacles is to bring an offering as an expression of thanks to God. Deut 16:16-17 says, "No man should appear before the LORD empty-handed: Each of you must bring a gift in proportion to the way the LORD your God has blessed you." When we express our thankfulness in giving, it opens our heart to receive even more.

Tabernacles is a time to celebrate the fact that God *tabernacles* with His people. He wants His glory to be a normal part of our experience. He tabernacled with Israel in the wilderness. He tabernacled on earth in Jesus and He continues to tabernacle with us today through His Spirit!

As you celebrate Tabernacles, call out to God for His glory to come and dwell with you. Here are some ways to celebrate Tabernacles:

- Set aside time to "tabernacle" with God
- Find times to meet with Him.
- Spend relaxed times in His Word.
- Get together with family and friends.
- Share testimonies of His goodness.
- Eat your favorite foods.

- Thank Him for His blessings.
- *And especially if you have children,* build a **Sukkah** (a tabernacle, or temporary shelter).

Nehemiah 8:15-17 says, "Go out into the hills and bring back branches from olive and wild olive trees, from myrtles, palms and shade trees, to make *sukkahs* ... So the people went out and brought back branches and built **sukkahs** on their roofs and in their court-yards... The whole company built *sukkahs*... and their joy was very great."

What is a *Sukkah*? A *sukkah* is any kind of temporary shelter: it can be a tent, a lean-to, etc. It can be made of branches, fabric, wood, or other material, but it must be ***temporary***. The *sukkah* is designed to picture Israel living in *temporary shelters* when they left Egypt. It also pictures God coming down and dwelling in a temporary shelter with them.

Originally, God told Israel to live in *sukkahs* the entire week of Tabernacles. Today, many simply spend some time each day in the *sukkah*, perhaps to eat a meal together as a family.

The celebration of Tabernacles offers a wonderful way to teach children what God has done. When our kids were young, there was nothing they liked more than to make a tent. They would make tents in the living room, draping sheets and blankets over the chairs. They would build "forts" outside with tree branches.

Can you imagine how excited your kids would be to learn that God has set aside a special time for your whole family to make a tent? God wants you to "make a tent" and use it to teach your children about how God rescued Israel, and how His glory came down and lived with them.

So why not build a *sukkah*? If you don't have room to build a full-size *sukkah*, you can build a model *sukkah*. If you don't have room for a "proper" outdoor *sukkah*, you can use sheets and chairs and build one in your living room. Have the whole family get in the *sukkah* and have a picnic together as you tell them the stories of

God's Tabernacles.

You can picnic in your *sukkah*; you can decorate your *sukkah*; you can sleep in your *sukkah*, or even party in your *sukkah*. But whatever you do in your *sukkah*, it should include three things:

- REMEMBER that God *TABERNACLES* with His people.

- ENJOY the *FUN* of celebration with God.

- ANTICIPATE God's glory. Ask God to *tabernacle* with you. *Expect* His presence to visit you as you seek Him!

Seeking Ritual or Reality?

Last year, during our Tabernacles celebration, I taught a course about the feasts of God. Eleanor, a friend of ours from Alaska, came down to attend the course. Eleanor is an Eskimo and has an unusual sensitivity to the Lord and His Spirit.

During the week, we invited Eleanor and some other friends to our home to sit with us in our *sukkah*. We had done this with other friends on previous nights, and it was always a joyful celebration. We would talk and laugh, enjoying the fun of being in a *sukkah* together.

With Eleanor it was different. She had just heard my teaching about Tabernacles and came with the *expectation* that the glory of God wanted to meet with her in the *sukkah*. As soon as she sat down in the *sukkah*, she closed her eyes and began to pray very intently for God's glory and presence to come.

We were amazed! Almost immediately the glory of God fell! The place was filled with His Presence in such great power that we could hardly stand up. It was wonderful!

I learned an important lesson from Eleanor. I had been going into the *sukkah* as a ritual. It was the "thing to do" to celebrate the feast. It was a fun ritual, but still a ritual. I had not come into the *sukkah* seeking or expecting God's Presence, and all I had experienced was a fun ritual. But when Eleanor came with an expectation of His Presence, that's exactly what she received!

As you celebrate these feasts, you can celebrate them as wonderful rituals, a way of remembering what God did in the past, and a way of identifying with the Jewish people today. It can be very meaningful. You can go away from them blessed and satisfied, and yet miss the greatest blessing. If we celebrate them only as a ritual, we miss the incredible fact that God truly *desires* to meet with us during these celebrations.

I would encourage you, as you celebrate Tabernacles, to seek and expect nothing less than the awesome Presence of God to meet with you!

Jesus' Promise for Tabernacles

Jesus gave us a very important promise at Tabernacles. In John chapter seven, we find the account of Jesus celebrating this feast. John 7:37-38 says, "On the last day of the feast, Jesus said in a loud voice, 'If anyone is thirsty, let him come to me and drink. Whoever believes in me, streams of living water will flow from his innermost being.'"

It is important here to understand the context of what Jesus was saying. One of the key elements of Tabernacles is *outpouring.*

Every year at Tabernacles, the High Priest performed a prophetic act. He would bring water from the pool of Siloam, carry it up to the temple, and pour it out beside the altar. This symbolized an appeal to God for the latter rain to fall on the land. It also symbolized an appeal to God for the outpouring of His Spirit, the "spiritual rain" spoken of in Joel chapter two: "I will pour out My Spirit on all people. Your sons and your daughters will prophesy, your old men will dream dreams, your young men will see visions."

This action of pouring out the water from Siloam was repeated every day of the feast. Finally, they come to the last day, the "great day," of the feast. This was the climax of the Feast of Tabernacles and the climax of the entire cycle of feasts.

As the Priest brought water from the pool of Siloam and carried it up to the temple, huge crowds would have accompanied him. The temple court would have been packed with people anxious to watch this important ceremony. As the priest stood beside the altar and prepared to pour out the water, a hush would have fallen over the crowd.

But as the priest began to pour out the water, Jesus stood and cried out in a loud voice, **"If any man is thirsty, let him come to Me and drink. He who believes in Me, from his innermost being**

shall flow RIVERS OF LIVING WATER!"

That's the climax, and the goal, of all of the feasts! As we walk with God through His yearly cycle, He wants to bring us to the place where we experience His **OVERFLOWING LIFE!**

That's why God gave His APPOINTED TIMES. As we draw close to Jesus, He wants to release His LIFE to US.

He wants to remind us of His great deeds of the past to build our FAITH.

He wants to remind us of His promises for the future to give us VISION.

He wants to accomplish spiritual transactions in us to break Satan's power.

He wants to link us into His cycle of life, to receive ever-increasing blessing.

It is not a SIN to miss your appointed times. God doesn't want them to be a legalistic thing. The New Testament instructs us not to let anyone judge us on how we celebrate them (Col. 2:16). It's not a matter of getting every detail of the celebration right. It's a matter of meeting with HIM.

God's appointed times enable our lives to resonate with His timing. They cut off the enemy's strategies against us and keep us from drifting from God. They cause us to be "in sync" with God's rhythm. They help us not to miss windows of opportunity. They allow God to bring us to a new level.

Let me encourage you this year to "enter in" to God's Cycle of Life!

Appendix Three – Part Six
Dates of the Feasts (2006-2020)
(The Appointed Times Begin at Sundown on These Dates)

	Passover	Pentecost	Trumpets	Atonement	Tabernacles
2006	Apr 12	Jun 1	Sep 22	Oct 1	Oct 6
2007	Apr 2	May 22	Sep 12	Sep 21	Sep 26
2008	Apr 19	Jun 8	Sep 29	Oct 8	Oct 13
2009	Apr 8	May 28	Sep 18	Sep 27	Oct 2
2010	Mar 29	May 18	Sep 8	Sep 17	Sep 22
2011	Apr 18	Jun 7	Sep 28	Oct 7	Oct 12
2012	Apr 6	May 26	Sep 16	Sep 25	Sep 30
2013	Mar 25	May 14	Sep 4	Sep 13	Sep 18
2014	Apr 14	Jun 3	Sep 24	Oct 3	Oct 8
2015	Apr 3	May 23	Sep 13	Sep 22	Sep 27
2016	Apr 22	Jun 11	Oct 2	Oct 11	Oct 16
2017	Apr 10	May 30	Sep 20	Sep 29	Oct 4
2018	Mar 30	May 19	Sep 9	Sep 18	Sep 23
2019	Apr 19	Jun 8	Sep 29	Oct 8	Oct 13
2020	Apr 8	May 28	Sep 18	Sep 27	Oct 2

PERSONAL NOTE
What about Christmas?

When I teach on the biblical holidays, I'm often asked, *"What do you do about Christmas?"* Some think that if we celebrate biblical feasts, we must *stop* celebrating all traditional ones.

My belief is that, as followers of Jesus, we are free to receive Christmas as a wonderful celebration of God's love. The Lord has never led me to teach *against* traditional holidays, but to present the *blessing* of the biblical ones. In our church we place great emphasis on celebrating the biblical feasts, but we also have a wonderful time at Christmas.

While Christmas was not part of God's original cycle of feasts, there is good biblical precedent for **adding** new holidays to celebrate the great works of God. Both *Purim* and *Hanukah* are holidays added to God's yearly cycle in remembrance of God's deliverance. If it is valid to institute a new feast to celebrate a great work of God, then Christmas certainly qualifies!

While there is good evidence that Jesus was not actually born in December, it's not wrong to celebrate Jesus' birth at Christmas. **It's always a good time to celebrate Jesus!** Christmas provides a wonderful opportunity to remember that "God so loved the world that He gave His Son!" (John 3:16)

While the traditional date of Christmas probably had pagan origins, I believe we are free to *redeem* that date, and use it to celebrate God's love for the world! In our family we celebrate both Christmas and *Hanukah... a double celebration!*

Many also ask me if it's okay to have a Christmas tree. My answer is that a tree can symbolize many things. Some point out that pagans cut down trees and use them to make idols (Jer 10:3-4).

But a tree can also have a godly symbolism. Trees are made by God and display the beauty of His creation. Jesus died on a "tree" to redeem us, and we are promised that one day we will eat from the tree of life!

A tree lit with tiny lights, and decorated with stars and angels can be a beautiful reminder of what the shepherds saw in the fields around Bethlehem when the angels announced the birth of Jesus!

Each believer must follow their own conscience, but personally, I have found Christmas to be a wonderful time to remember God's love in sending Jesus!

ENDNOTES

Chapter One

1 Acts 4:4 says the church numbered more than five thousand *males*. Counting adult males was a common way of numbering a community in those days. If the church numbered five thousand males, its total population was probably *well over* ten thousand!

2 Pliny to Trajan, (Epp. X.97).

3 Phillip Schaff, *History of the Christian Church*, Chapter I: The Spread of Christianity. *§ 4. Hindrances and Helps.* <http://www.ccel.org/s/schaff/history/2_ch01.htm> [12-20-2005].

4 Chrysostom, in *Nicene and Post-Nicene Fathers of the Christian Church*, Philip Schaff, ed, Chapter VI, *Chrysostom as Deacon, Priest and Preacher at Antioch, A.D. 381–398.* <http://www.ccel.org/ccel/schaff/npnf109.iii.vi.html> [12-20-2005].

5 "Some older writers… even represent the Christians as having at least equaled if not exceeded the number of the heathen worshippers in the empire." Phillip Schaff, *History of the Christian Church*, Chapter I: The Spread of Christianity. *§ 7. Extent of Christianity in the Roman Empire, NOTES.* <http://www.ccel.org/s/schaff/history/2_ch01.htm> [12-20-2005].

6 Phillip Schaff, *History of the Christian Church*, Chapter I: The Spread of Christianity. *§ 7. Extent of Christianity in the Roman Empire* <http://www.ccel.org/s/schaff/history/2_ch01.htm> [12-20-2005].

7 Ibid.

8 Clement of Alexandria, *Exhortation to the Heathen,* Chapter XII, Christian Classics Ethereal Library, <http://www.ccel.org/ccel/schaff/anf02.vi.ii.xii.html> [4-3-2006]

9 Debbie Roberts, *Rejoice: A Biblical Study of the Dance*, Little Rock, Ark: Revival P, 1982. p. 40.

10 Ibid.

11 Ibid.

12 Many don't realize that the New Testament lists a number of apostles in addition to the 12. In Acts 1:26 Matthias was designated as an apostle to replace Judas. Acts 14:14 lists both Paul and Barnabas as apostles. In Phil 2:25 Epaphroditus is called an apostle (*apostolos*) of the church. Romans 16:7 lists Andronicus and Junia as apostles. Gal 1:19 identifies James, the half-brother of Jesus, as an apostle. I Cor 4:6&9 identifies Apollos as an apostle. Comparing I Thess. 1:1 and 2:6, we see that Paul considered Sylvanus and Timothy to be apostles also.

13 Some modern translations, not willing to acknowledge the possibility of a woman apostle, change this name to Junius, but the earliest writers all identify Junia as a woman. For example, Chrysostom (4th century) comments on Romans 16:7, **"How great the wisdom of this woman must have been that she was even deemed worthy of the title of apostle!"** – Eldon Jay Epp, *Junia: The First*

Woman Apostle, Minneapolis: Fortress Press, 2005, p. 32. (Epp's book is an excellent study of Junia, and is highly recommended!)

[14] Eusebius, *Ecclesiastical History*, Popular Edition, Grand Rapids: Baker Book House, 1973, p 186-187.

[15] Augustine, *City of God*, Garden City: Image Books, 1958. Book 22, Chapter 18.

[16] Edward Gibbon, and D. M. Low, *The Decline and Fall of the Roman Empire*, 1st American ed., vol. 1, New York: Harcourt, Brace, 1960, 15. Vol 1, Chap 15.

[17] Origin, *"Homily on Numbers 23," par. 4, in Migne, "Patrologia Graeca," Vol. 12, cols. 749, 750.*

[18] The Constitutions of the Holy Apostles, *The Anti-Nicene Fathers*, Vol 7, p. 413.

[19] Socrates Scholasticus, *Ecclesiastical History, Book V, chapter XXII.*

[20] Clement of Rome, The First Epistle of Clement to the Corinthians, (1Clem 32:2) Translated by J.B. Lightfoot. <http://www.earlychristianwritings.com/text/1clement-lightfoot.html> [12-20-2005].

Chapter Two
[1] Steven Silbiger, *The Jewish Phenomenon: Seven Keys to the Enduring Wealth of a People,* Atlanta: Longstreet Press, 2000, p 4.

[2] Thomas Sowell, *Ethnic America, a History*, New York: Basic Books, 1981, p 98.

[3] Silbiger, p. 9.

[4] Silbiger, p. 2.

[5] <http://en.wikipedia.org/wiki/W._N._Ewer> [7-12-06]

Chapter Three
[1] Christopher S. Mackay. Notes for *Class 379, Later Roman Republic*, © 1999 Dept of History and Classics, University of Alberta, <www.ualberta.ca/~csmackay/class_379/constantine2.html> [06-05-2000].

[2] <http://www.roman-emperors.org/conniei.htm> [7-12-06]

[3] Tim Dowley, ed. *Eerdmans' Handbook to the History of Christianity*, 1st American ed., "Building for Worship", Henry R. Sefton, Grand Rapids: Eerdmans, 1977. p. 150.

[4] *Ecclesiastical History of Sozomon*, Book II, Chapter XXXII, <http://www.ccel.org/ccel/schaff/npnf202.iii.vii.xxxii.html> [12-15-2005].

[5] Tim Dowley, ed. *Eerdmans' Handbook to the History of Christianity*, p. 133.

[6] Ibid p. 144.

[7] "Rome, the Power and the Glory" narrated by peter coyote DVD, Aired on The Learning Channel, 2000, 312 minutes, Release Company: Questar, Inc. (09/21/1999), episode 6, "The Fall," UPC: 03393703082.

[8] Dudley, Dean. *History of the first Council of Nice*. 4th ed. Boston: D. Dudley & co., 1886. p. 112.

[9] Eusebius, *Life of Constantine, book 3,* Chapter XVII, *Constantine's Letter to the Churches Respecting the Council at Nicæa.* <http://www.ocf.org/OrthodoxPage/ reading/St.Pachomius/VitConst3_17.html> [1-27-2005].

[10] Lazare, Bernard. *Antisemitism its history and causes.* 1st Bison Book ed. Lincoln, NE: University of Nebraska P, 1995. ch 4.

[11] Council of Antioch (canon I, second part).

[12] Council of Laodicea (360) Canon 37).

[13] Council of Agde (506) (canon 40).

[14] Council of Toledo X (canon 1).

[15] Council of Nicea II (AD 787, canon VIII).

[16] Tim Dowley, ed. *Eerdmans' handbook to the history of Christianity,* 1st American ed., "Constantine and the Christian Empire", Richard A. Todd, Grand Rapids: Eerdmans, 1977. p. 130.

[17] Ibid. p. 131.

[18] Ibid.

[19] <http://en.wikipedia.org/wiki/Christmas> [7-12-06]

[20] Tim Dowley, ed. *Eerdmans' handbook to the history of Christianity,* p. 131.

[21] "Originally, the Persians, and later the Egyptians, exchanged colored eggs to celebrate the return of spring. ... Later the Greeks adopted the custom and used colored eggs during the spring festivals as sign of fertility" <http://www.hangtide.com/holidayhistory/Easter/> [12-20-2005].

[22] Tim Dowley, ed. *Eerdmans' handbook to the history of Christianity,* 1st American ed., "Popular Religion", Caroline T. Marshall, Grand Rapids: Eerdmans, 1977. p. 296.

[23] Tim Dowley, ed. *Eerdmans' handbook to the history of Christianity,* 1st American ed., "Constantine and the Christian Empire", Richard A. Todd, Grand Rapids: Eerdmans, 1977. p. 132.

[24] Ibid.

Chapter Four

[1] *Didache,* 7:1-4, *Apostolic Fathers* (trans. and ed., J. B. Lightfoot) <http://www.earlychristianwritings.com/text/didache-lightfoot.html> [12-20-2005].

[2] *Didache,* 8:1-2, *Apostolic Fathers* (trans. and ed., J. B. Lightfoot) <http://www.earlychristianwritings.com/text/didache-lightfoot.html> [12-20-2005].

[3] "When one passes from the Apostles to the Apostolic Fathers he feels as if he has fallen from a cliff at the edge of a veritable garden of Eden into a desert wilderness. Schaff and Berkhof confirm this observation." <http://www.vor.org/truth/rbst/hist-theology-004.html> [12-20-2005] and Philip Schaff, *History of the Christian Church, Volume II: Ante-Nicene Christianity.*

A.D. 100-325, § 161. The Apostolic Fathers.
<http://www.ccel.org/ccel/schaff/hcc2.v.xv.iii.html> [12-20-2005].

[4] "Origin," *Concise Columbia Encyclopedia.* © 1996 Franklin Electronic
Publishers, Inc., Burlington, NJ, Based on the Concise Columbia Encyclopedia 3rd
Edition © 1994, Columbia University Press.

[5] "Neoplatonism," *Concise Columbia Encyclopedia.*

[6] "Scholasticism," *Concise Columbia Encyclopedia.*

[7] "Chalcedon," Everett Falconer Harrison, *Bakers' Dictionary of Theology*, Grand
Rapids: Baker Book House, 1960.

[8] Ibid.

[9] Marvin R. Wilson, *Our Father Abraham: Jewish Roots of the Christian Faith*,
Grand Rapids, Mich: W.B. Eerdmans, 1989. p. 153.

[10] "Instances of Rabbinically learned women do occur. What their Biblical
knowledge and what their religious influence was, we learn not only from the
Rabbis, but from the New Testament. Their attendance at all public and domestic
festivals, and in the synagogues, and the circumstance that certain injunctions and
observances of Rabbinic origin devolved upon them also, prove that, though not
learned in the law, there must have been among them not a few who, like Lois and
Eunice, could train a child in the knowledge of the Scripture, or, like Priscilla, be
qualified to explain even to an Apollos the way of God more perfectly." Alfred
Edersheim, *Sketches of Jewish Social Life*, chapter 8, 1876
<http://www.kjvuser.com/sjsl/chap08.htm> [12-21-2005].

[11] Daniel C. Juster, and Patricia A. Juster, *One People Many Tribes: A Primer On
Church History From a Messianic Jewish Perspective*, 1st ed., Clarence, NY:
Kairos Pub., 1999. p. 42.

[12] Mike Dowgiewicz, and Sue Dowgiewicz, *Restoring the early church*,
Alpharetta, GA: Aslan Group Pub., 1996. p. 190-191.

[13] Ibid. p. 190-191.

[14] Ibid. p. 93.

[15] Ibid. p. 108.

Chapter Five
[1] Tim Dowley, ed. *Eerdmans' handbook to the history of Christianity*, 1st
American ed., "Columba", Robert G Clouse, Grand Rapids: Eerdmans, 1977. p.
194.

[2] *History Of The Scottish Nation*, Vol 2, Chapter 22 - Organization of Iona;
Ecclesiastical Government,
<http://www.electricscotland.com/HISTORY/wylie/vol2ch22.htm> [12-20-2005].

[3] Adamnan: *Life of St. Columba* chapter X,
<http://www.fordham.edu/halsall/basis/columba-e.html> [12-20-2005].

[4] Benjamin George Wilkinson, *Truth Triumphant*, chapter 8, Columba and the
Church in Scotland. <http://www.giveshare.org/churchhistory/truthtriumphant/
chapter8.html> [12-20-2005].

[5] Dr. John Hannah, unpublished class notes, Church History 401, Dallas Theological Seminary, 11-9-1973.

[6] Judith Collins, "Heritage of the Waldensians" <http://www.holytrinitynewrochelle.org/yourti16626.html> [12=20-2005].

[7] J. A. Wylie, *The History of Protestantism,*"The Vaudois (Waldenses) and Their Valleys," http://www.bereanbeacon.org/history/history/the_waldenses_and _valleys.htm8> [12-20-2005].

[8] Benjamin George Wilkinson, *Truth Triumphant*, chapter 16, The Church of the Waldenses, <http://www.giveshare.org/churchhistory/truthtriumphant/ chapter16.html> [12-20-2005].

[9] Dr. John Hannah, unpublished class notes, Church History 401, Dallas Theological Seminary, 12-5-1973. References to Waldensian practice of prophecy, tongues, and healing come from Rev Dr David Hilborn, <u>Charismatic Renewal in Britain: Roots, Influences and Later Developments</u>, section 1.4.2, found at <http://www.eauk.org/theology/key_papers/upload/CHARISMATIC%20RENE WAL%20IN%20BRITAIN%20Typescript.pdf> [9-1-2006] and A. J. Gordon, <u>The Ministry of Healing</u> (Harrisburg, Pa.: Christian Publications, Inc., 1961), p.61

[10] Tim Dowley, ed. *Eerdmans' handbook to the history of Christianity*, 1st American ed., "John Wyclif," Tim Dowley, Grand Rapids: Eerdmans, 1977. p. 296.

[11] Jerusalem Post Online Edition, *The Six Day War Special*, "Live from the Western Wall," *By Yossi Ronen* <http://info.jpost.com/C003/Supplements/ SixDayWar36/live_ww.html> [12-20-2005].

[12] "Liberation of the Temple Mount and Western Wall by Israel Defense Forces," Transcript of Live Broadcast on Voice of Israel Radio, June 7, 1967, <http://www.isracast.com/Transcripts/060605a_trans.htm> [12-20-2005].

[13] Jerusalem Post Online Edition, *The Six Day War Special*, "Live from the Western Wall," *By Yossi Ronen* <http://info.jpost.com/1998/Supplements/30years/ronen.html> [7-12-2006]

[14] Jerusalem Post <http://info.jpost.com/1998/Supplements/30years/june15.html> [7-12-2006].

Chapter Six
[1] Dan Gruber, *The Church and the Jews: The Biblical Relationship* Hagerstown, MD: Serenity Books, 1997, p. x.

[2] Ibid, p. ix.

Chapter Seven
[1] From the USA Weekend magazine, Apr 2. 1999, article entitled, "Remember the Sabbath?" Exerpted from the book, Remembering the Sacred Rhythm of Rest by Wayne Muller, Bantam Books: New York, 1999

[2] Origin, *"Homily on Numbers 23," par. 4, in Migne,* **"Patrologia Graeca,"** *Vol. 12, cols. 749, 750.*

[3] The Constitutions of the Holy Apostles, *The Anti-Nicene Fathers*, Vol 7, p. 413.

[4] From the USA Weekend magazine, Apr 2. 1999, article entitled, "Remember the Sabbath?" Exerpted from the book, Remembering the Sacred Rhythm of Rest by Wayne Muller, Bantam Books: New York, 1999.

[5] My own paraphrase. See <http://artists.sparrowrecords.com/pressroom/docs/ passion/Passion-Hymns-Bio.pdf.> and <http://www.smithcreekmusic.com/ Hymnology/Greek.Hymnody/Phos.hilaron.html> for other versions [6-18-2004].

Chapter Eight

[1] Chuck Pierce, unpublished prophetic newsletter, July, 2000, "Catching a New Wind for Your Future: Your BEST is Ahead!"

Chapter Eleven

[1] Jarl Fossum, *Understanding Jesus' Miracles.* <http://members.bib-arch.org/nph proxy.pl/000000A/http/www.basarchive.org/bswbSearch.asp=3fPubID=3dBSBR &Volume=3d10&Issue=3d2&ArticleID=3d9&UserID=3d0&> [June 12, 2006]

Appendix Two

[1] Tim Dowley, ed. *Eerdmans' handbook to the history of Christianity*, 1st American ed., "The Christian Church and the Jews," H.L. Ellison, Grand Rapids: Eerdmans, 1977. p. 50.

[2] Marvin R. Wilson, *Our Father Abraham: Jewish Roots of the Christian faith*, Grand Rapids, Mich: W.B. Eerdmans, 1989.

[3] PBS Online Report , *From Jesus to the Christ, part 4, The First Christians,* Eric Meyers, "Early Tensions Between Christians and Jews Exaggerated," web site copyright 1995-2005 wgbh educational foundation <http://www.pbs.org/wgbh/ pages/frontline/shows/religion/first/wrestling.html> [12-20-2005].

[4] Mark D. Nanos, *The Mystery of Romans: the Jewish Context of Paul's Letter*, Minneapolis: Fortress P, 1996.

[5] Ibid.

[6] Bargil Pixner, *Biblical Archaeology Review,* May/June 1990, "Church of the Apostles Found on Mt. Zion" p. 87.

[7] *Shepherd of Hermas* (49:29-31).

[8] *The Epistle of Ignatius to Polycarp* (4:2).

[9] PBS Online Report , *From Jesus to the Christ, part 4, The First Christians,* Wayne Meeks, "Separation from Judaism," web site copyright 1995-2005 WGBH educational foundation.
<http://www.pbs.org/wgbh/pages/frontline/shows/religion/ first/wrestling.html> [12-20-2005].

[10] Joseph A. Dunney, *Church History, St. Jerome*, Catholic Information Network, <http://www.cin.org/books/dunney4.html> [12-20-2005].

[11] Mark D. Nanos, *The Mystery of Romans: The Jewish Context of Paul's Letter*, Minneapolis: Fortress P, 1996.

[12] Origin, *"Homily on Numbers 23," par. 4, in Migne, "Patrologia Graeca,"* Vol. 12, cols. 749, 750.

[13] The Constitutions of the Holy Apostles, *The Anti-Nicene Fathers*, Vol 7, p. 413.

[14] Socrates Scholasticus, *Ecclesiastical History, Book V, chapter XXII.*

[15] Cassian, *Antiquities of the Christian Church*, Book 13, Chapter 9, Section 3).

[16] Ecclesiastical History of Sozomen, *The Nicene and Post Nicene Fathers*, Book 7, Chapter 19).

[17] Coleman, *Ancient Christianity Exemplified*, Chapter 26, Section 2, p. 526.

[18] Eusebius of Caesaria, *The Life of the Blessed Emperor Constantine*, Book 3, Chapters XVIII & XIX. Medieval Sourcebook, <http://www.fordham.edu/halsall/basis/vita-constantine.html> [12-23-2005].

[19] Council of Antioch (Canon I, second part).

[20] Council of Laodicea (Canon 37).

[21] Council of Laodicea (Canon 37).

[22] Council of Agde (Canon 40).

[23] Council of Nicea II (Canon VIII).

[24] John Kiesz, *Sabbath History Through the Ages*, <http://www.nisbett.com/sabbath/sabbath-history.htm> [8-29-2004]

[25] A. H. Newman, *A Manual of Church History, Volume 1*, p. 646, 1933 edition.

[26] Ambrose, *DeMoribus, Brachmanorium Opera Ominia*, 1132, found in *Migne, Patrologia Latina*, Vol.17, pp.1131, 1132.

[27] Arthur P. Stanley, *History of the Eastern Church*, p. 91. <http://www.nisbett.com/sabbath/sabbath_history.htm> [12-29-2005]

[28] Lyman Coleman, *Ancient Christianity exemplified in the private, domestic, social, and civil life of the primitive Christians*, Philadelphia: Lippincott, Grambo & co., 1853. p. 573.

[29] Coleman, *Ancient Christianity Exemplified*, p. 573.

[30] Schaff-Herzog, *The New Schafff-Herzog Encyclopaedia of Religious Knowledge*, "Nestorians." London: Funk and Wagnalls Company, 1908.

[31] John Kiesz, *Sabbath History Through the Ages*, <http://www.nisbett.com/sabbath/sabbath-history.htm> [8-29-2004]

[32] Dellon, *Account of the Inquisition at Goa*, 1684. translated from the French, Hull, England, 1812, pp. 56, 58, 64 quoted in "From Saturday to Sunday" <http://www.geocities.com/Heartland/Plains/8936/SAB-HIST.HTM> [12-29-05]

[33] Schaff-Herzog, *The New Schafff-Herzog Encyclopaedia of Religious Knowledge*, "Nestorians."

NOTE:

Additional copies of this book, and other
books by Robert Heidler can be ordered from
Glory of Zion International Ministries,
PO Box 1601, Denton TX 76202,
or online at www.glory-of-zion.org.
or by calling Glory of Zion toll free at
1-888-965-1099.

**Other books by Robert Heidler available
through Glory of Zion:**

Experiencing the Spirit (Regal)
Develop a living relationship with the Holy Spirit!

Morning and Evening Sacrifice (Glory of Zion)
A 31-day guide to establishing a daily watch with God

Restoring Your Shield of Faith (Regal)
With Dr. Chuck D. Pierce
Reach a new dimension of faith for daily victory!

Set Yourself Free: A Deliverance Manual!
(Glory of Zion)

Biography for Dr. Robert Heidler

Dr. Robert Heidler is an apostolic teacher with *Glory of Zion International Ministries*, Senior Pastor of *Glory of Zion Outreach Center*, and Dean of *The Issachar School*.

He holds a B.A. from the *University of South Florida*, a Th.M. from *Dallas Theological Seminary*, and a Doctor of Practical Ministry from *Wagner Leadership Institute*.

Robert has served as Curriculum Coordinator for the *International Educational Fellowship* and ministered extensively in Russia and Eastern Europe. He has been a visiting teacher at the *Messianic Jewish Bible Institutes,* teaching in Budapest, Hungary; Moscow, Russia; and Odessa, Ukraine. Robert and his wife, Linda, are also visiting teachers at the *Gateways Beyond* Messianic training center in Cyprus, *Wagner Leadership Institute*, *Colorado Springs*, and *Wagner Leadership Institute, Korea.* Robert serves on the boards of *Shekinah Messianic Ministries* and *Glory of Zion International Ministries*.

Robert's books include *Experiencing the Spirit* (Regal Books), *Restoring Your Shield of Faith* with Chuck Pierce (Regal Books), and *Set Yourself Free: A Deliverance Manual,* published by Glory of Zion.

Robert and his wife, Linda, have three grown children, and live in Denton, Texas.

You can contact Robert by email at Rheidler7@aol.com.